BLIZZARD

RACE TO THE POLE

BLIZZARD

RACE TO THE POLE

JASPER REES

This book is published to accompany the television
series *Blizzard* produced by Keo Films.

Published by BBC Books, BBC Worldwide Limited,
Woodlands, 80 Wood Lane, London W12 0TT

First published 2006
Text copyright © Keo Films and Jasper Rees 2006
The moral right of the author has been asserted.

ISBN-13: 978 0 563 49326 6
ISBN-10: 0 563 49326 7

Commissioning editors: Sally Potter and Martin Redfern
Project editor: Eleanor Maxfield Copy editor: Trish Burgess
Designer: Linda Blakemore Picture researcher: Cath Harries
Production controller: Peter Hunt

Printed and bound in Great Britain by Clays Ltd, St Ives plc
Colour separations by Dot Gradations

For more information about this and other BBC books,
please visit www.bbcshop.com

Contents

To my mother and father

Foreword

There have been many books and films about Captain Robert Falcon Scott. In recent decades not all of them have been complimentary. He has been portrayed as a bungler, an incompetent, and a man with no natural ability as a leader – unfairly, in my view.

As posterity has slung mud at his memory, so the reputation of Roald Amundsen, the Norwegian who beat Scott to the South Pole, has risen. To my mind, Amundsen was a coldly efficient polar explorer – intelligent, focussed, flexible. He also made bad mistakes. The scope of his journey was much narrower. He went south with the sole determination to reach the pole before his rival. Scott did not know that he was meant to be racing, but set out with a very careful, clever plan to reach the pole and bring back a great deal of scientific information. In the event he produced far more information about Antarctica in various research fields than all the other international expeditions in the first half of the twentieth century put together. That's an achievement in itself.

In my biography of Scott I attempted to wrestle him free from the clutches of revisionism. As a polar traveller myself, it seemed a good idea to measure his experiences of travel in extreme cold against my own. But I could make comparisons only up to a point. The equipment that Scott used was certainly the best available at that time for man-haul. It is still pretty good for heavy man-haul today. Dr Mike Stroud and I found that using ventile Lancashire cotton, which was available to Scott, was preferable to using Gore-Tex, which was not 100 per cent breathable. You will sweat doing heavy man-haul if you have a Gore-tex outer even in extreme cold. In other areas, huge strides have been made. We man-hauled far heavier sleds, but they were better designed. The technology that has changed most of all is navigation. I have spent over 35 years in the north and south poles on and off as a navigator. The effort of navigating outside the tent, of trying to get the altitude of the sun or some other heavenly body, involves very cold work. The time when you're meant to be resting and getting warm inside the tent is cut down hugely. With GPS (Global Positioning Systems), none of that is now necessary. Sat phones are also a great deal easier than High Frequency radio communications.

However, since 1911–12, few people have travelled in the polar regions with anything like the full array of handicaps endured by Scott and, to a lesser extent, by Amundsen. Now eight men have gone a step further and, as accurately as possible, have re-enacted Scott's man-haul journey, while a party of five men have undertaken to copy the journey with dogs made by Amundsen. *Blizzard*, the BBC's reconstruction of the race to the South Pole, is a fascinating attempt to make polar history live again, and to test the theories tossed about in so many books against the cold hard reality of practice.

It brings a fresh perspective to the question often asked of the explorers of the Heroic Age. For all our interest in them, do those men have any relevance today? Scott and his like are easy meat to the determinedly cynical because anybody who has striven for non-materialistic goals can always be laughed at so easily.

But on a very basic level, Scott was hugely instrumental in making millions of individual servicemen and women appreciate the value of bravery and steadfastness through two World Wars. More mundanely, both he and Amundsen encouraged people to enjoy the outdoor life. Those things may seem to have lost their value now. The popularity of *Blizzard*, suggests that perhaps, after all, they have not.

Sir Ranulph Fiennes

The Modern Race

Blizzard is not a carbon copy of the race that inspired it. With the participation of an eight-strong British team and a five-strong Norwegian team, the intention of the BBC television series, and of this book, is to illustrate what it was like to travel in Antarctica between October 1911 and March 1912. Perhaps it will also settle a few arguments that have echoed down the century.

All of the equipment, food, clothing and style of transport were as near identical as possible to those which were taken by Captain Robert Falcon Scott, Roald Amundsen and their men to the South Pole.

Of the inevitable discrepancies between the two expeditions of 1911–12 and their television re-enactment, the obvious one is in the calendar. As it's in the southern hemisphere, Antarctica's brief sledging season is spliced by Christmas Day. The race was re-run in the northern hemisphere, and took place between April and July 2005.

The Greenland ice cap is itself a largely accurate substitute for Antarctica, being cold, white and apparently endless. But it is not an exact likeness. There are no vast stretches of sea ice such as Scott and Amundsen had to traverse for the first 400 miles of their journey. Nor is there a mountain range quite so imposing as the Transantarctics, which separated the explorers of old from the Polar Plateau.

The other deviation was in the use of animals. It would cost millions to film in Antarctica, but even more than the prohibitive cost, the reason for not reconstructing the original journey over the original terrain was the ban on non-indigenous animals in Antarctica. And yet it was also impractical to follow Scott's lead and take ponies to Greenland, so the modern British team was given more dogs than Scott had, with the proviso that they shed them at roughly the same points in the journey as Scott lost his ponies and dogs.

Scott is thought to have died on the 150th day of his journey. Amundsen needed 99 days to travel over 700 nautical miles from his base at Framheim to the South Pole and back. Scott had 60 more miles to cover, but in order to make the reconstruction more symmetrical, both modern teams are required to travel the same distance as Amundsen did towards a putative 'pole' on the ice cap.

The modern teams had huge advantages over their pre-decessors. They travelled in the knowledge that, barring accident, they would not lose their life, or be allowed to succumb to frost-bite. But there was one disadvantage: Scott and Amundsen were not being filmed for a television documentary series. Both Bruce Parry and Rune Gjeldnes, the modern team leaders, complained in their diaries about losing time thanks to the demands of the film crew, though they both conceded that without the film crew they wouldn't be there. Those sections of their diaries that deal with these frustrations – the timing of the flights in and out, the dealings with the skeletal crew and safety guide – are often illuminating about the process of making a television programme, but that is not what this book is about. The important thing to make clear is that while the expeditions had to be organised in tandem with the series's producers, at no point did the modern explorers receive any material assistance from the safety guides and the camera crew travelling with them. The best they could hope for was the accurate time when their 1920s chronometers proved too unreliable for the purpose of navigation.

Other than that, they were on their own.

The Scott/Amunsden Race Timeline

1902

31 December
Scott, Shackleton and Wilson on the *Discovery* expedition reach
82 degrees 11 minutes, the furthest point south ever reached.

1907

Amundsen announces his plan to explore the polar sea in the north, and
begins raising money.

1909

9 January
Shackleton's *Nimrod* expedition sets a new record for furthest south, at
88 degrees, 23 minutes: 97 miles from the pole.
26 March
News of Shackleton's achievement reaches England.
1 September
American explorer Frederick Cook claims to have reached the North Pole.
3 September
American explorer Robert Peary claims to have reached the North Pole.
13 September
Scott announces a new expedition bound for Antarctica.

1910

March
Scott tries to meet Amundsen in Kristiania (present-day Oslo).

7 June
Amundsen sets sail from Kristiania on the *Fram*.
15 June
Scott leaves Cardiff on the *Terra Nova*.
9 September
In Madeira Amundsen announces to his crew his intention to go south instead of north.
12 October
Scott learns of Amundsen's plan when the *Terra Nova* docks in Melbourne.
29 October
Terra Nova sails south from Port Chambers, New Zealand.

1911
5 January
British party begins disembarking at Cape Evans.
15 January
Norwegian party begins disembarking at the Bay of Whales.
3 February
Terra Nova encounters *Fram* in the Bay of Whales.
23 March
Norwegians return from third depot-laying journey, having reached 82 degrees south.
21 April
Scott returns to Cape Evans from depot-laying journey, having reached 79 degrees, 28 minutes.
8–16 September
Amundsen's party of seven sets out for the South Pole, but is beaten back by the cold.
20 October
Amundsen's reduced party of five sets out again.
2 November
Scott's polar party leaves Cape Evans.
17-21 November
Amundsen's party finds, names and climbs the Axel Heiberg Glacier to reach the Polar Plateau.
4-8 December
Scott's polar party held up by storm at base of Beardmore Glacier.
10 December
Amundsen passes Shackleton's furthest south record, 92 miles from the pole.
11 December
Cecil Meares and the dogs leave Scott's polar party and turn for home.
15 December
Amundsen's party reaches the South Pole.

21 December
The first four of Scott's man-hauling party of 12 turn for home near top of Beardmore, 180 miles from the pole.

1912
2 January
Scott's party reaches the Polar Plateau.
4 January
Three more of Scott's man-hauling party turn for home, 90 miles from the pole leaving Henry 'Birdie' Bowers, 'Taff' Evans, Captain Laurence Oates, Dr Edward Wilson and Scott.
17 January
Bowers sees Amundsen's black flag near the pole.
26 January
Amundsen's party arrives back at Framheim (base camp).
30 January
Fram sails north with Norwegian party safely on board.
17 February
Evans dies at the foot of the Beardmore Glacier.
3 March
Apsley Cherry-Garrard arrives with dog teams at One Ton Depot to relieve Scott's polar party.
7 March
Fram docks in Hobart; Amundsen telegraphs home news of his triumph.
10 March
Cherry-Garrard leaves One Ton Depot.
17 March
Oates dies.
21 March
Scott, Wilson and Bowers make their last camp.
29 March
Presumed date of Scott's death.
Oct 29
Search party leaves Cape Evans.
12 November
Scott's tent discovered with three bodies inside.

1913
17 January
Terra Nova returns to Cape Evans to collect the southern party.
10 February
Terra Nova docks in Oamaru, New Zealand. News of Scott's death is telegraphed back to London.

Flag

THIS CROSS AND CAIRN ARE ERECTED OVER THE BODIES OF CAPT. SCOTT, C.V.O., R.N.; DR E.A. WILSON, M.M., M.A. CANTAB.; LT. H.R. BOWERS, ROYAL INDIAN MARINES. A SLIGHT TOKEN TO PERPETUATE THEIR GALLANT AND SUCCESSFUL ATTEMPT TO REACH THE POLE. THIS THEY DID ON THE 17TH JANUARY 1912 AFTER THE NORWEGIAN EXPEDITION HAD ALREADY DONE SO. INCLEMENT WEATHER AND LACK OF FUEL WAS THE CAUSE OF THEIR DEATH.

ALSO TO COMMEMORATE THEIR TWO GALLANT COMRADES, CAPT L.E.G. OATES OF THE INNISKILLING DRAGOONS, WHO WALKED TO HIS DEATH IN A BLIZZARD TO SAVE HIS COMRADES, ABOUT 18 MILES SOUTH OF THIS POSITION; ALSO OF SEAMAN EDGAR EVANS, WHO DIED AT THE FOOT OF THE BEARDMORE GLACIER.

THE LORD GAVE AND THE LORD TAKETH AWAY. BLESSED BE THE NAME OF THE LORD.

Relief Expedition (signed by all members of the party)

A black flag. There was a black flag planted squarely across their path. It fluttered in the hazy distance.

Of the five of them hauling breathlessly across that infinity of ice, it was the short, beaky navigator they named 'Birdie' who spotted it first. He was the only one not on skis, the only one who had to mind his every step as the treadmill edged them forward on their quest. But he looked up and there it was. At these frozen latitudes mirages can occur. As they neared, there was no wishing it away as a trick of the southern light. The object swimming into focus was made by man. 'The flag was of black bunting,' noted the doctor in his diary, 'tied with string to a fore-and-after which had evidently been taken off a finished-up sledge.'

Its colour mocked them. The great virtue of black in a prairie of whiteness is that it draws the eye. That was evidently the intention of those who left it. White, the only colour under their frost-nipped feet these past months, speaks of birth, newness, innocence, of virgin territory. And what of its opposite, its omega? It cannot have escaped the attention of the five men who found the flag flapping in the stiff breeze of the plateau that black is the shade of the end of things. If nothing else, it meant the end of hope.

It was with hope undimmed that they had left home 18 months earlier, officers and ratings, scientists and enthusiasts. They had taken leave of their wives and mothers, and they had pointed the ship's prow towards the other hemisphere. At every stop on the way down they set foot on soil of the Empire. They left the last outpost of civilization laden with dogs and horses brought from the north. And the ship, slung treacherously low in the water with the weight of livestock, equipment and supplies, somehow contrived not to drown them all as she breasted the angry ocean on her way down to a largely uncharted continent.

Their aim, once they had sliced through the belt of sea ice and made landfall, was to find their way to the very heart of this uninhabited landmass. They wanted to be the first men there. They would plant the flag in honour of king and country, and they would turn triumphantly for home, feeding off the depots of food they had so meticulously placed in their path on the way south.

And this they did, but only up to a point. That point was marked by a black flag in the middle of nowhere at the bottom of the world. Around it were tracks, and the frozen droppings of dogs. They had trudged through 76 days and 750 nautical miles to reach here, and at the moment of epiphany, the moment where epic struggle should have been converted into triumph, a flag silently, succinctly advised them that their effort had been in vain. There was no note attached, but words were scarcely needed to convey the shattering message.

The man they called the 'Owner' had feared the worst. The previous night he had written in his diary, 'It ought to be a certain thing now, and the only appalling possibility the sight of the Norwegian flag forestalling ours'.

But it was the black flag that dashed the cup from their lips. Their rival planted it there on the meridian he supposed the British party would be travelling along, to give them an early warning that they had been preceded. Three days later they did indeed find the pennant of a small, newly independent nation fluttering atop a pyramid-shaped tent. Inside it was a pile of discarded equipment, plus two letters, one of them addressed to the man who found it, kindly requesting him to ensure that the other letter be delivered safely into the hands of the King of Norway. A scientist on his expedition would later remark that, in that instant, the Owner was 'degraded from explorer to postman'.

In the event, the Owner would not need or, indeed, be able to deliver the letter. Elsewhere on this inhuman continent his five rivals were hastening home on skis, their supplies pulled by fit, well-fed dogs. They had reached their goal more than a month earlier. In another week they would arrive safely back at their base. Within ten weeks, the Owner and his four followers, debilitated by hunger and frostbite, weakened by the back-breaking task of hauling all they needed to sleep in and eat, defeated by distance, would be dead.

When their bodies were discovered six months later, the inquest began. It has never really ended.

* * * * * * * * * * *

The first man to stand in judgement over the mortal remains of Robert Falcon Scott – the Owner – was a naval surgeon called Edward Atkinson. When Scott failed to return to the base camp at Cape Evans by April 1912, when the Antarctic winter set in, he and his four companions were known to have perished. Atkinson took the helm of the *Terra Nova* expedition as the men, now under his command, hunkered down forlornly for the long night of the polar winter. They set out again on 29 October. On 12 November, just over a year since Scott's party headed off from Cape Evans for the pole, the search party found a tent out on the Great Ice Barrier. They were more than 150 miles from real safety, but only 11 miles short of the nearest depot. Inside were the frozen bodies of Scott, Dr Edward 'Uncle Bill' Wilson and Henry 'Birdie' Bowers. Scott's diary, kept up until he lost the strength to continue, would reveal all.

The tent was lowered over the dead, and they were interred under the weight of a huge snow cairn topped by a pair of skis in the shape of a cross. Then Atkinson retired to read about their journey to the pole, the discovery that Roald Amundsen's team of five men had beaten them by a whole month, about the turn for home and the long trudge off the Polar Plateau, down the treacherous 120 miles of the Beardmore Glacier, at the base of which they lost Petty Officer Edgar 'Taff' Evans. He read how they continued on to the Great Barrier, where Captain Laurence 'Titus' Oates made his famous exit. The three survivors struggled on until a storm descended, impeding their search for One Ton Camp, where food and fuel promised relief. As the storm raged on, cold and malnutrition forestalled any prospect of further progress. There might have been a faint hope of rescue, but Scott had given orders that prevented anyone proceeding beyond the depot.

Through ten days, perhaps more, the men lay in their reindeer-fur sleeping bags and awaited the inevitable. Wilson and Bowers were both ardent Christians and must have found comfort in their profound belief that they were passing to a better place. But Scott was more interested in arranging his own afterlife, and used the guttering candle of his remaining strength to write, to see his own story through to the very end.

'Every day we have been ready to start for our depot eleven miles away, but outside the door of our tent it remains a scene of whirling drift. I do not think we can hope for any better things now. We shall stick it out to the end, but we are getting weaker, of course, and the end cannot be far. It seems a pity, but I do not think I can write more. R. Scott.'

The words have a powerful impact, even at a distance of nearly a century. Imagine how Scott's bathetic valediction must have worked its spell on Atkinson, with the dead entombed in ice only yards away from where he read. His medical report on the cause of death concluded rousingly, 'I don't think men ever died a nobler death'.

Every Englishman present shared the feeling, but in the search party Atkinson drew around him to hear the sorry tale, there was also a Norwegian called Tryggve Gran. Gran was a young man Scott had taken on as ski instructor for his novice sledgers. When they dismantled the sledge that Scott and his men had hauled through nearly 1000 miles, they found 30 pounds' worth of geological specimens. Gran hazarded a sceptical note in the privacy of his diary: 'I think they might have saved themselves the weight.'

On the sledge they also found Amundsen's letter to King Haakon of Norway. Although they didn't yet know it, delivery was no longer necessary. Amundsen and his party had long since escaped the Antarctic continent and headed for Hobart. The world was informed of his pioneering journey to the pole when Scott, Wilson, Bowers and Oates were still struggling out on the Barrier.

* * * * * * * * * * * *

Outside his native Norway, posterity knows little of Amundsen, still less of his companions Olav Bjaaland, Sverre Hassel, Helmer Hanssen and Oscar Wisting. While five Britons walked straight on to a plinth in the national imagination, the five Norwegians who reached their goal turned round and hastened back to a century of obscurity. Amundsen's dogs had hauled him to the pole first, but the efficiency of his enterprise made his achievement somehow unmemorable. The dryness of his journal did not help: his practical account of skiing and sledging to 90 degrees south contrived to keep the spirit unfired. There was nothing Amundsen could do to prevent a juggernaut of Scott hagiographers from squashing his story into the margins of the popular myth. Scott's martyrdom was not only moving and extremely well written, it was also useful. When Britain went to war, it was Scott's inspiring example of noble self-sacrifice that was industrially deployed to send all those young men over the top in Flanders and into a hailstorm of German machine-gun fire. After the war, Captain Scott's reputation was cemented by art. It took Apsley Cherry-Garrard, the man who had waited for Scott's polar party at One Ton Camp, nearly a decade to write *The Worst Journey in the World* (1922), but it still goes unchallenged as the most remarkable book about British exploration ever written. After the next war came *Scott of the Antarctic* (1948), a film starring John Mills, memorable chiefly for the bleakly beautiful score by Ralph Vaughan Williams which went on to become the *Sinfonia Antarctica*. So Captain Scott remained on his plinth, a symbol of English stoicism who laid down his life at the start of a century in which his country laid down her empire.

It took many many years for Scott to be knocked off his perch, but when the attack on his reputation came, it was implacable. Roland Huntford's book *Scott and Amundsen* was published in 1979, the same year that Chapman Pincher exposed Anthony Blunt, the Keeper of the Queen's pictures, as the 'Fourth Man' in *The Climate of Treason*. There is an argument to be had about which book did more to dent the British establishment's sense of itself. Huntford's dual biography did its best to expose the imperial hero as a bungling amateur with severe and unattractive flaws in his personality, most damaging of which was his final desire to put his own glorification in death above the survival of his comrades. And in denigrating Scott, he raised Amundsen on to a pedestal as a bold man of action who could do almost no wrong.

Where Scott is concerned, the Huntford version became the orthodoxy, appropriate for a nation in decline and newly steeped in the ways of self-doubt. The explorer's name became a byword for incompetence, an emblem of British arrogance. Where Amundsen had sensibly relied on huskies to drag him to the pole, and enlisted a team of expert skiers and dog-handlers uniquely qualified for the task, Scott had ambled up to the start line with a muddled transport plan involving motorized sledges, ponies, dogs and man-hauling. His men did not know how to ski, and though he had taken the precaution of bringing a skiing instructor from Norway, he soon took against Gran and did little to ensure his explorers were drilled in this arcane art. The litany of criticisms is extensive: Scott was moody, distant, too dependent on ossified naval structures, while at the same time prone to last-minute improvisation. He issued confusing orders, was over-reliant on man-hauling, fostered the contempt of the more independent-minded members in his party, allowed his men to succumb to scurvy ... and so it goes on. Aside from biographies of dictators, never has a writer found less to venerate in his subject than Huntford did in Scott.

There is a great deal of evidence put forward by Huntford to underpin his argument. Scott appears to have suffered from depression, and certainly missed a trick in his wariness of dog-sledging. The thing that holds the book back from conclusiveness is less its righteous indignation than the frequency with which evidence for crucial claims is withheld. An obvious example comes when the book alights on the most iconic moment in the entire saga. After Oates crawled out of the tent to his death, Scott wrote in his diary that Oates 'took pride in thinking that his regiment would be pleased with the bold way in which he met his death'. Huntford is sceptical. 'Scott ascribes heroic thoughts,' he writes, 'leaving the unanswered question of how he knew.' Unfortunately, this is often the problem with Huntford too. He writes that Oates, contemplating death, 'has to face the hideous realisation that he had been betrayed by incompetent leadership'. Although Oates gave vent to intemperate thoughts earlier in the journey, there is no actual evidence that he was thinking this as he died. But Huntford's most damning accusation was in the vein of pure character assassination. With Oates close to death on the long march home, his feet frostbitten, 'he sat there in the tent, Scott staring at him, with the unspoken expectation of the supreme sacrifice'. George Bernard Shaw, who befriended Cherry-Garrard as he wrote his great tome and disliked

Scott, was the first one to make this suggestion. But Huntford does not quote Shaw. He does not quote anyone.

The book that rescued Amundsen from oblivion needed to be written. The book that asked questions of Scott's unblemished reputation also needed to be written. But the book that performed both these tasks so radically was inevitably going to excite some form of riposte, some form of counterbalance. It came 24 years later, when Ranulph Fiennes, the polar explorer, set out to debunk the debunker in his bestselling biography, *Captain Scott* (2003). Using his experience of polar travel, Fiennes sought to correct what he saw as the calumnies visited upon Scott by an author who, he pointed out, had never set foot on the southern continent.

'No previous Scott biographer,' Fiennes advised, 'has man-hauled a heavy sledgeload through the great crevasse fields of the Beardmore Glacier, explored icefields never seen by a man or walked a thousand miles on poisoned feet. To write about hell,' he concluded, 'it helps if you have been there.'

He dedicated his book 'to the families of the defamed dead'.

Based on his own experiences of Antarctica, Fiennes's book re-evaluates issues of leadership, navigation, health, transport and sundry other areas of decision-making thrown up initially by Huntford, and subsequently pounced on by others who have laboured in his slipstream. The result is a book that is not quite as finely written as Huntford's, but much more alive to the deadly reality of polar travel. Where the books are each other's equal is in their fixity of purpose. Nothing will persuade either author out of his entrenched position.

But it is not as if Scott and Amundsen have had merely each other to contend with, as they did in 1911. In the period between the books published by Huntford and Fiennes, the polar rivals have lost ground to a third explorer. One of Amundsen's posthumous problems has always been that in the brief period of Antarctic exploration known as the Heroic Age, Scott already had a nemesis in the form of Ernest Shackleton. And once Scott's value in the stock market of polar heroism plummeted, it was this rivalry that embedded itself more deeply in the popular imagination.

Scott first went south in 1902 on the *Discovery*, and set a new record for the most southerly latitude reached by man when he man-hauled to 82 degrees and 17 minutes. His companions on that trip were Wilson and Shackleton. The evidence for it is patchy, but somewhere out on the ice Scott and Shackleton seem to have had a falling out. Shackleton succumbed to scurvy on the long march back to base, and Scott invalided him home. Depending on who you read, the two men either did or didn't become confirmed enemies.

When Shackleton returned to Antarctica in 1907 it was at the head of his own expedition on the *Nimrod*. In a display of astonishing strength and courage, he and his party of three men made it across the Barrier to the foot of the Transantarctic Mountains, where they discovered and named the Beardmore Glacier, a vast 120-mile pathway up to the Polar Plateau. Navigating their way through the maze of crevasses strewn in their path, they managed to trudge to within a degree and a half of the pole – a tantalizing 97 miles – before turning back. They could certainly have reached 90 degrees south, but just as certainly they would have perished on the way home. 'I thought you'd prefer a live donkey,' Shackleton wrote to his wife, 'to a dead lion.'

Shackleton was knighted by Edward VII on his return from the south, and it was in his footsteps over the Barrier and up the glacier, neurotically attempting to keep up with his daily distances, that Scott travelled in 1911. But as far as posterity is concerned, Shackleton is now remembered not for that heroic march, but for an expedition that took place after Scott's death. The Imperial Transantarctic Expedition set out from England on the *Endurance* in August 1914, with the declaration of war ringing in the ears of all aboard, to make the first crossing of the Antarctic continent. As stories go, it is far greater than the sum of its parts, and those parts are great indeed. It is a story of survival and comradely fortitude in the face of extreme danger and lasting hardship, and perhaps the ultimate example of triumph snatched from the jaws of catastrophe. The expedition failed in its stated task, and yet despite the loss of his ship in the ice, Shackleton managed to shepherd all his men back to safety through a two-and-a-half-year odyssey.

Returning home to news of unparalleled slaughter in Flanders, Shackleton and his exploits seemed somehow redundant, even a little vulgar. Although four years dead, Scott was now the useful man of the hour, and so he remained. When Huntford's biography of Shackleton was published in 1985, an American reviewer wondered who would read a life of a man no one had ever heard of. But society changes, and in doing so it develops a need for different heroes. Shackleton's story gripped a generation somehow turned off by the old Edwardian virtues of sacrifice and hierarchy. Dramas were made, documentaries filmed, a travelling exhibition mounted, even a motivational business guide written, which posited Shackleton as the ideal model for commanders of the boardroom. Suddenly there was a debate about which Edwardian explorer you'd rather follow up a blind alley: the one who died (but could write his way to immortality), or the one who survived (but used ghost-writers)?

In the bitter controversy over Scott, accusations of lying have made their way into print. Lawyers have been mentioned in dispatches. In the end, the bitterness is testimony to the life that courses through the veins of this great story. The craggy explorer of the Heroic Age will go no more a-sledging in an uncharted wilderness of snow, but there is yet a sense in which he is still strapped into his harness and hauling across the sastrugi of the plateau. A century on from the decade in which men went south in search of knowledge and glory, victory and vindication, they have moved into the encrusted realm of legend; the stories of endeavour, comradeship and, in the case of the British party, death have acquired the status of Nordic myth, of a cryogenically frozen soap opera, its frost-nipped heroes the characters in a never-resolving narrative.

But for all the books, for all the scholarship, no one really knows what it was like for these men who did, after all, once live and breathe. Even Fiennes is separated from final insight of how it must have been for the men who went before him by the invention of the woollen fleece, the modern boot, the greater understanding of diet. And of course these days there are satellite telephones and GPS (Global Positioning Systems).

Questions about Scott's tactics remain unanswered. Was he

fatally handicapped by the lack of an instinctive feel for travel in cold climes, despite his experiences on the continent ten years earlier? How genuinely efficient is dog travel when the teams of huskies are required to haul their own food over hundreds of miles? Did Amundsen's experience of living among the Inuits, as he successfully attempted to become the first man to navigate his way through the Northwest Passage, give him an incalculable advantage when it came to surviving in the extreme cold? Or was the advantage simply that he was a Norwegian? Hindsight has prompted successive generations to ask a different, but key question: what, ultimately, is the point of man-hauling?

There is only one way to answer some, if not all, of these questions and to find out what those men might really have gone through between October 1911 and March 1912. And that, with the closest possible attention to historical accuracy, is to run the whole race again.

CHAPTER ONE

Selection

I DON'T HOLD THAT ANYONE BUT AN ENGLISHMAN
SHOULD GET TO THE SOUTH POLE.
Captain Scott

In March 1910 Captain Robert Falcon Scott, who had announced his plan to conquer the South Pole six months previously, went to Kristiania, as Oslo was then known. Among the calls he paid on the various Norwegians who might be helpful to his quest, he contacted the distinguished 37-year-old explorer Roald Amundsen, who was himself planning to lead the first expedition all the way to the North Pole. Amundsen's monumental plan was to sail as far north as possible, allow his ship to be trapped in the ice and spend the next four or five years drifting across the Arctic ice cap. Scott was all for suggesting that they launch a joint scientific venture in which their findings would be pooled for the greater furtherance of knowledge. But Amundsen would not meet Scott. For the duration of the Englishman's stay, he made himself scarce. Thus the two leaders of this great story never clapped eyes on each other.

For his costly expedition Amundsen had raised many of the necessary funds from the government and private business. A young nation was behind him, and expectant after his triumph in navigating the Northwest Passage. But there was a problem. The previous September, just before Scott announced his expedition, two Americans emerged from the frozen north each claiming to have reached the North Pole. To this day the argument thunders on over whether Frederick Cook or Robert Peary verifiably got there first. To Amundsen it didn't matter. It was no longer going to be him, so he turned the ship of his ambition through 180 degrees. He would try for the South Pole instead. But he couldn't tell anyone, least of all the south-bound Englishman who had come to extend an offer of cooperation.

* * * * * * * * * * * *

High above the North Atlantic, a small aeroplane crosses the stretch of water between Iceland and Greenland. Though small, the plane is not full. On one side of the aisle sit eight Englishmen. On the other are four Norwegians and an American. They talk among their own group: no conversation breaches the aisle.

Nearly a century later, they are acting out their own version of Anglo-Norwegian frostiness. The east coast of Greenland, spectacularly fringed with aquamarine bergs, nears through the window, but no one appears ready to play the unmanly tourist and whip out a camera. Before the spring is out they will have seen more than enough of Greenland.

The 13 men tip out of the plane and into the waiting lounge, where a shop sells classic polar pipes: the Scott, the Amundsen, the Shackleton and – a good one, this, for Antarctic anoraks – the Crean. It's not clear how many of the British party have heard of Tom Crean. He was a modest Irish sailor who happened to be the only man present on both great iconic quests of the Heroic Age: Scott's *Terra Nova* expedition, and Shackleton's on the *Endurance*. Crean had a remarkable capacity for work and cheerfulness in the face of extreme hardship. It can be legitimately argued that if Scott had taken him to the pole instead of Taff Evans, the polar party might have survived. The modern British team could certainly use someone of his dependability as they embark on a re-creation of that journey.

Do they make them like Crean any more? One of the issues the reconstruction that they are about to embark on is designed to look at concerns toughness. Both physically and mentally, the polar explorers of 100 years ago endured things that the mollycoddled modern male may find intolerable. A childhood spent in the warm embrace of central heating does not encourage a tolerance of extreme cold. The men attempting to suffer anew the conditions borne uncomplainingly by Scott and Amundsen and the stoics they travelled with are used to a much-improved diet, to proper medicine and, of course, to efficient kit. Are they really fit to lace Crean's boots? To fill his pipe? Ninety-nine days in Greenland will tell.

A helicopter on the runway sputters into life, and the parties are ferried in groups across the 17 miles of the sound to Tassilaq, the largest settlement on Greenland's eastern seaboard. The tiny Hotel Nansen, named after Norway's pioneering explorer Fridtjof Nansen (1861–1930), whose great deeds were all accomplished at these northerly latitudes, will be their home for the next fortnight. In these confined quarters, in this town of 3000 mainly Inuit inhabitants hemmed in by mountain and fjord, with only one dining room between them, the British team and the Norwegian team will exchange scarcely a word.

They have come here to rerun the journeys made by their iconic compatriots. The plan is to do it as accurately as possible, to put themselves through an experience as close as can be arranged to that undergone by their predecessors. Accuracy, of course, is more easily achieved in some areas than others. It is a huge logistical operation to track down manufacturers who can produce supplies identical to those mentioned in the diaries, letters and memoirs of the original participants, and, indeed, depicted in the photographs. But as near as makes no difference, the British and Norwegian teams will keep warm in clothes of the same design, sleep in the same sort of sleeping bags and tents, pull the same sledges and clip themselves into the same skis. They will navigate with the same equipment. They will have to stomach the same food. In some cases, the sources remain unchanged. The Norwegians' hickory-and-ash skis come from Amundsen's own supplier, while the British team's oatmeal biscuits come, as they did in 1911, from Huntley & Palmer, and are made to the original recipe.

But there will be undeniable differences between now and then. The journey will not be over identical terrain. In 1911 Scott installed himself, as he had in 1902 on the *Discovery*, at the eastern end of what was then known as the Great Ice Barrier, a vast sheet of ice covering a bay at the edge of the Antarctic continent, which is roughly the size of France. Conscious that he was the interloper, Amundsen sensibly headed for the western end of the Barrier, 400 miles away. He intuited, from the evidence of previous expeditions, that a place known as the Bay of Whales would be a better landing place anyway, and so it would prove.

It wasn't called the Barrier for nothing. In terms of miles, half of both journeys were taken up in crossing it before they made land. Thereafter their path to the pole was blocked by another rampart – a huge range of peaks known as the Transantarctic Mountains running diagonally along the edge of the Barrier. Both expeditions had to make their way up glaciers that sluiced down through the gaps. Having negotiated the crevasses strewn in their path, they emerged on to the high Polar Plateau, 10,000 feet above sea level, and headed south.

Dogs are integral to the story of the conquest of the South Pole. Both Amundsen and, to a lesser extent, Scott used huskies. However, since 1994 it has been impossible to take dogs to Antarctica. Huskies may be inclined to clear up after themselves by eating their own excrement – Amundsen let them eat human excrement too – but that was not enough to prevent a ban from Antarctica on all but indigenous species – principally seals, penguins and skuas. (Man, of course, is still allowed to take his eco-friendly Hercules planes, snowcats and helicopters.) So the experiment had to be transplanted to the only other vast, ice-covered and largely uninhabited landmass that could offer similar conditions.

Greenland had its own role to play in the original quest for the pole. Through a trusted agent Amundsen placed an order for 100 of the finest Greenlandic huskies to take with him on the long journey to the southern hemisphere. Knowing that Scott might also be on the lookout for dogs, he took care to ensure that the best came his way, and that no more dogs were available from Greenland that year. (He needn't have bothered: Scott got his dogs from Siberia.) Despite its tiny population, Greenland remains one of the hubs of traditional dog-driving. Almost every house in Tassilaq has a husky chained up outside it, hunched without a care in the deep snow. They are never allowed indoors. With their thick, insulating fur, they might as well have been built for Antarctica.

For the reconstruction of the original race, both teams will make for a putative 'pole'. The journey is constructed in such a way that the modern explorers, starting from different points, will cover similar terrain and similar distances to their predecessors. In the interests of symmetry, the task set before the Scott team has been reduced to the more manageable dimensions of the journey completed by Amundsen. From Framheim, the hut in which Amundsen based himself, to the pole was a journey of 700 nautical miles. Scott was a whole degree of latitude (60 nautical miles) further north, so he had 120 more miles to cover. This disparity has been ironed out so that both teams will travel over Amundsen's distances. A time limit has also been stipulated in accordance with the precedent set by Amundsen. Scott calculated before he left that he would need 144 days to march to the pole and back, but the two modern teams will be limited to the time set by the successful Norwegian quest. They have 99 days to reach the pole, turn round and head for home.

In many ways Greenland is a perfect stand-in for the only uninhabited continent. The Greenland ice cap, which covers the vast majority of the landmass, rises to the same altitude as the Antarctic Plateau – well over 10,000 feet. On the coasts there are glaciers slotted with crevasses. And even in summer it gets very cold. The only major difference is that there is no equivalent to the Great Barrier, or the Ross Ice Shelf as it has subsequently been renamed. Sea ice does form off the coast, but not in the acreages required to make a meaningful symmetry with the expanse of ice over which Scott and Amundsen travelled.

The other discrepancy is psychological. Before departure Scott warned the public, 'We may get through, we may not. We may lose our lives. We may be wiped out.' To make a faultless copy of Scott's journey, five men would have to perish out in the frozen wastes. There is still a debate about precisely how Scott and his four companions died, but to make significant discoveries in this area is not part of the experiment. No life will be endangered. No one will suffer from frostbite (or not much), or go blind from the glare of the snow and then be treated with cocaine drops, as Dr Wilson treated himself from his medicine bag. And for the seriously stricken there is the promise of a Twin Otter aircraft to remove them to civilization.

Just because they are not going to die, or even be driven ever homewards by the fear of death, the experiment will still offer as compelling an insight as any book into what it was like to be with Scott and Amundsen at the defining moments of their lives. The aim of the re-enactment is to shine an unprecedented light into that small but perennially fascinating point in history when two expeditions set out more or less simultaneously for a distant, featureless spot on an uninhabited continent that just happened to be the bottom of the earth.

****

The first task is to select leaders. If anything has changed out of all recognition since 1911 – even more than the quality of clothing, the understanding of diet and health, and the ease of navigation with global positioning systems – it is the style of leadership. 'The past is a foreign country,' read the opening words of L.P. Hartley's novel, *The Go-Between* (1953), 'They do things differently there.' They certainly did in Edwardian England. Captain Scott was an officer marinaded since youth in the nineteenth-century traditions of a navy that had not seen meaningful combat in more than 50 years. His expedition, composed of officers, scientists and ratings, reproduced in a microcosm the class system of the day. It was subject to the growing social fluidity brought about by the rise of the mercantile class and the retreat of the aristocracy from the epicentre of British life. Scott, the emerging middle-class meritocrat eager to get on in a post-Victorian climate of opportunity for all (or all except the working classes), assumed command over not only cap-doffing men such as Tom Crean and Taff Evans but also old money in the form of the cavalry officer Captain Oates and the landowner Apsley Cherry-Garrard.

Nowadays Scott is criticized by those with a retrospective distaste for the hierarchy of empire for leading *de haut en bas*. In fact, Scott was far less of an autocrat than Amundsen. The Norwegian's ruthlessness might never have been apparent to posterity, but for the presence on his expedition of a gnarled polar veteran by the name of Hjalmar Johansen. Amundsen was prevailed upon to take him by Nansen. Nansen is not unlike Shackleton, in that his fame depends less on his outright successes, such as making the first crossing of Greenland in 1888, than on a tale of remarkable survival: in his case, his failed attempt to reach the North Pole in 1895, and his death-defying journey back to civilization. His companion on that epic trek was Johansen, but that was a decade and a half in the past. By the time he applied to join Amundsen's five-year drift over the Arctic, Johansen was irascible and opinionated. His marriage had ended, he was always on the scrounge for money and he was an intermittent alcoholic. On the other hand, he was the only one in the party whose experience of the ice was equivalent to the leader's.

At the first sign of incipient mutiny, Amundsen was ruthless. It came after he made a near-disastrous mistake, when in his haste to ensure that he had the best head start possible over Scott, he set off for the pole far too early in the season. After a few days' toiling through the bitter winds of the polar spring, with temperatures dropping down to minus 56 degrees Celsius, he was forced to admit his own fallibility and turn back. Five dogs froze to death. Johansen had advised against a precipitate start, and now reminded Amundsen of it, for which honesty he was summarily demoted from the Polar party. Amundsen never forgave him, just as Shackleton, in his own great feat of survival after he lost his ship *Endurance*, peevishly refused to forgive the brilliant carpenter Henry 'Chippy' McNish for a moment of insurrection.

In the twenty-first century it would be difficult to reproduce the hierarchy that held Scott's expedition in place. It would also be impossible to lead an expedition in the style of Amundsen, a style calling for absolute subservience to his vision. The contract he drew up for those he took with him made this clear: 'I affirm on my honour,' it stipulated, 'that I will obey the leader of the expedition in everything at any time.'

* * * * * * * * * * * *

Clearly, there are no carbon copies of Scott and Amundsen, but are there men of comparable calibre and experience?

For the Norwegian team, the main requirement was a man with vast experience of the polar regions. By the time he went south in 1911, Amundsen was a veteran of cold climes. As well as having discovered the Northwest Passage, by the time he headed for the South Pole he had already overwintered off the coast of Antarctica and lived with the Inuit people in northern Canada, studying their skills in dog-sledging and survival in extreme cold with great curiosity and open-mindedness. If he has a counterpart in modern Norway, it is a polar traveller (these days they don't call themselves explorers) by the name of Rune Gjeldnes.

Rune, 33, is a former Navy Seal. Quiet, unassuming, exuding an understated authority, he doesn't look like one of the hardiest men on the planet, but he undoubtedly is. Like Amundsen's navigation of the Northwest Passage, he has one great record under his belt. In 2000 he and a fellow Seal, Torry Larsen, became the first men to walk unsupported across the frozen ice of the entire Arctic Ocean from Siberia to Canada. They did it in 109 days. 'Crossing the Arctic Ocean is like eating an elephant,' he wrote in his account of the journey. 'You do it one bite at a time.'

This has been Rune's philosophy throughout his career. Like Amundsen, he spent his formative years on skis in the great Norwegian outdoors. Unlike Amundsen, he didn't lie to his parents about what he was up to. 'They knew, but they couldn't do anything about it,' he says. 'From thirteen until I went into the navy I was doing almost all the trips by myself, especially the more extreme ones. It was hard in the beginning, but after a while my parents gave up. I've been training since I was a little boy. But again the most important thing is the mental strength and that is very hard to explain. If you break a sledge or a ski or a leg you will fail. It's about preparation and learning from experience and taking one step at a time. A lot of people take a huge step and then they fail. But from when I was 13, I was stretching a little bit every time. How can I cope with these conditions? I can't explain. It's just so natural for me. When I'm coming out into nature, I'm home.'

Intriguingly, Rune is the youngest of four, just as Amundsen was. The youngest are often the most stubbornly motivated. It was at the age of 13 that Rune set his sights on joining the most elite military unit in the Norwegian armed forces. 'In that unit I learnt a lot about planning and preparation, with a high success factor, because we were not allowed to fail. We had a very good physical training, which also meant a mental training. We were limit-breaking all the time.'

By the time he joined the Navy Seals, he had made another vow to himself to travel the 1800-mile length of Greenland on skis. In order to test the water, he and Larsen walked across Greenland, a mere 540 miles, 'just to get some training'. It took 35 days. They did the lengthways trip in 1996 in 88 days. Then he made his first attempt on the North Pole with the British Polar traveller David Hempelman-Adams. On the second attempt they succeeded. Then, with Larsen, came the crossing of the Arctic Ocean. 'Sixteen expeditions have tried but every one has failed,' he says. 'I am proud of [achieving it] because so many people have tried to do it and everyone has failed. I am very confident that no one will do it again.'

The result of these peregrinations in the far north is that Rune has already spent 500 days out in the polar regions. Even a round trip of 1500 miles is for him another training run for his next expedition – to walk solo across 2800 miles of Antarctica itself. 'I do really feel that I should try one big expedition by myself.' And there is the key. In re-creating Amundsen's journey across terrain he has covered before, the real test for Rune will not be the conditions: it will be using the unfamiliar equipment and leading a group of men. He is used to the dynamic of a two-man team. Even in the middle of nowhere on the Greenland ice cap, a tent with four other people, and 48 dogs tethered outside, is a heaving metropolis to a man like Rune.

As for his adversary, finding an exact copy in terms of experience is difficult. Scott came at the tail end of a naval tradition in which the mightiest mobile force in the world branched out during peacetime into terrestrial exploration. As is explained in Fergus Fleming's bestselling book *Barrow's Boys* (1998), it began in the aftermath of the Napoleonic Wars (1800–15), when Britain had no one left to fight. The Admiralty sent its men – William Parry, James Ross, John Franklin – to the hottest and coldest places on the planet, with the task of filling in the blank spaces on the map. When Scott went south in 1902, he went in the wake of James Clark Ross, who sailed there 61 years earlier. On that expedition Scott spent the first summer season trekking across the Great Barrier first discovered by Ross with Edward Wilson and Ernest Shackleton, pulling up alongside the Transantarctic Mountains at a new furthest south record of 82 degrees 11 minutes. The next summer he navigated a way up on to the Polar Plateau with, among others, Taff Evans for company.

These days naval officers don't spend a great deal of time on land, but marines do. In the form of Bruce Parry, 36, Scott has a rough modern equivalent. Very rough, he would contend. 'I don't want anyone to compare me with Scott,' he says, 'because I would come out very poorly.'

If anything, he has a greater experience of travelling in harsh conditions than Scott. As a troop commando in the Royal Marines, he did exercises in Norway and was posted to Iraq. Like Gjeldnes, he gave the forces six years of his life, then left to organize and lead his own expeditions in a variety of continents and climates. Like Scott, who in his early forties remained the fittest and toughest man in his entire party, Bruce is confident in his own fitness. He was the youngest ever officer to be made responsible for all physical aspects of Royal Marines Commando Training. There is a (possibly feigned) amateurishness that is uniquely characteristic of the British in his claim that these days he's not very fit.

'I do five runs a year. I haven't done a push-up or a sit-up in ten years. Really, I don't train at all. I used to be very, very fit. It's quite worrying. But the thing that the Marines give you is I know how hard I can push myself. I'm not in any shape at all. But I know that I keep going.' In other words, he already has in common with Scott the vague credo that everything will be all right on the night. But there is a more intriguing parallel. By the time Scott left on the *Terra Nova* in the summer of 1910, he was already a figure of some stature on the national scene thanks to his earlier exploits in Antarctica. True, some of the gloss had been removed from his fame by the success and subsequent knighting of Ernest Shackleton, his sledging partner on the *Discovery*. It meant that Scott was not the most famous explorer in Britain. And nor, thanks to survival specialist Ray Mears, is Bruce the most famous outward-bound presenter on British television. He first appeared on the BBC in *Cannibals and Crampons*, in which he and cavalry officer Mark Anstice spent three months trekking across the jungles of Papua New Guinea. Their video footage tracked an alarming loss of weight. Bruce's reward, apart from awards, was to present *Tribe*, a popular anthropological series on indigenous peoples. So he has in common with Scott an ability to communicate with a large audience (although, of course, the full weight of Scott's charisma as a writer emerged only after his death).

The differences between Scott and Bruce are legion, but the most pressing one for Bruce is his intolerance of the cold. 'I've always had an urge to go to the jungle. The first thing I did the day I left the marines was I went off to the jungle. I hate the cold, my fingers go blue in London, I've got really bad circulation, I'm a small chap, I'm not experienced at all in Polar exploration. So taking this on was a risk.'

* * * * * * * * * * * *

How do you choose a team to travel in such footsteps? By design, obviously, but also by accident.

When they made their selections in 1910 there was a fundamental difference in approach between the two leaders that is not entirely explained by the fact that only one of them knew they were in a race.

Amundsen, who went south solely in order to reach the pole first, opted for expertise. He knew long in advance that if he was going to have any chance of reaching the pole, it was going to be huskies that would get him there. With dogs pulling the sledges, and sometimes the men driving them also, the need for numbers was reduced. In the early months of 1911, once the *Fram* had delivered its cargo of men, dogs and supplies to the Bay of Whales, there were only eight men who stepped ashore and made their winter quarters in Framheim. In Helmer Hanssen, whom he had taken with him through the Northwest Passage, and Sverre Hassel, Amundsen had two world-class dog-drivers, and a very good one in Johansen. In Olav Bjaaland he had a champion skier. During the long winter of preparation at Framheim, the men would also prove resourceful in other ways, but it was for these skills that they were hired.

The five-strong Norwegian party of 2005 is similarly composed. The ski expert is Inge Solheim, 32, an all-round action man who, after a stint in the Norwegian army, has settled down to a life of polar guiding and extreme sports. Harald Kippenes, 31, is another hardened graduate of the Navy Seals, with whom he took part in operations in Afghanistan and the Balkans. He has done things such as cycling from Norway to China, skiing down the sixth-highest mountain in the world and taking the SAS on winter training. Ketil Reitan, 44, is a professional dog-driver who has participated in the four-longest dog races in the world, ranging between 600 and 1200 miles. He has run in the prestigious Alaskan race the Iditarod four times, and crossed 1200 miles of northern Alaska on a sledge he built himself, relying on the land for food and fuel. Just to round off his prodigious experience, he spent six years of his life in an Inuit village. His fellow dog-driver on the trip is an American, John Huston, 28, who works at a wilderness expedition school in northern Minnesota, where he manages and trains a 50-dog kennel of huskies. He is also a more than proficient cross-country skier who has raced in several 30-mile marathons.

'Historically we can't lose,' says Rune. 'I think we have a good team. We have a lot of different experience. Inge was the man who asked me to join. I didn't really know him before. Harald I know from our navy unit, and if you have been through that course, you know what a person is. We knew that we needed some really good dog-sledgers. We had a lot of alternatives but some of the people I met were too old, which could be a problem in leadership. I chose Ketil and John. John was really, really eager and motivated to join. He was really hungry. That is a good thing on this trek.'

In short, in terms of age, demeanour and expertise, these five men are as close a replica of Amundsen's polar party as it is possible to get in 2005. The fact that, Rune and Harald aside, they mostly didn't know one another before only adds to the link with the past.

To assemble a British team with some semblance of historical accuracy was more complicated. Scott took many more men south. A lot of them were scientists who stood slightly apart from the polar expedition. Their principal task was to make geological and meteorological observations. But the Scott plan was based on the pyramid theory in which the many contribute to the final success of the few. Thus it was that 16 men set out from the base camp hut at Cape Evans, a round dozen of them marched all the way up the Beardmore Glacier and on to the plateau, only for two groups to be successively turned back once they had served their purpose as pack mules for the polar party.

The only figure of a scientific bent whom Scott took with him in the final polar party was Wilson. In footballing parlance, he was the first name on his team sheet. After the *Discovery* expedition they were campaign veterans sharing a bond forged by grim ex-perience of the ice. Scott also retained the services of Taff Evans from the *Discovery*. The leader had huge faith in Evans's pure brawn, and knew from experience that he could survive in the extreme cold of the plateau. In the event, Evans tested Scott's faith by getting disgracefully drunk first in Cardiff, from where the *Terra Nova* sailed, then on the South Island of New Zealand. The second time Scott actually dismissed Evans, only to forgive the contrite petty officer when he begged and pleaded to be let back on board as the ship prepared to head out into the Southern Ocean.

Men like Evans were vital to Scott's plan because manpower was the only resource on which he could unquestioningly pin his hopes. When the final push came, there would be nothing but human muscle to drag the sledges, not only in the climactic sprint for the pole, but also on the interminable haul for home. That is why he also took the petty officers Tom Crean and Bill Lashly, two more dependable survivors from the *Discovery*.

Scott began by giving himself other options. When the *Terra Nova* reached New Zealand in October 1910 after a five-month journey, she took delivery of 19 Manchurian ponies and 33 huskies. They were purchased in Siberia by a man called Cecil Meares, who was hired by Scott as an expert in dog-driving. That he was not also a horse expert, yet was charged with buying the ponies, has always attracted the attention of Scott's critics. Oates, the upper-class cavalry officer with the Inniskilling Dragoons, invited to run the stable and nurse the horses across the Barrier, was dismayed when he first saw them.

It was a remarkable piece of wishful thinking on Scott's part to believe that he could ferry so many dogs and horses across 2000 miles of some of the wildest seas on the planet. The ocean did not disappoint, and the ship very nearly flooded, but somehow the dogs and the horses survived. That Scott needed both means of transport is proof enough that he didn't entirely trust either. Although Nansen had urged him to use dogs, his own memory of them was that they proved a failure on the *Discovery* expedition ten years earlier. As for horses, they had served Shackleton well – or the white ones had (the dark ones died), so he made sure Meares bought white ones too. To cover his bets, he also took along three motorized sledges, one of which was claimed by the sea when the ice on to which it was lowered from the ship cracked and gave way.

Four different transport systems required an array of specialists. So the party included a motor mechanic by the name of Bernard Day, and the dog-driver Meares. Then there was Oates, who knew enough about horses to realise that the specimens brought down from Siberia by Meares were not the ones he'd have picked.

The party, in short, was not quite a ragbag of talents, but it lacked the manifest specialism of Amundsen's team, in which everyone was more or less the best in the world at what they did. Scott's selection policy was not remotely as specific. Birdie Bowers, a young officer of the Royal Indian Marines, was taken on a recommendation before Scott had even met him. Cherry-Garrard had nothing to offer but youthful enthusiasm and a private income, which meant that he could not only turn down the offer of a salary, but could also contribute £1000 to the cost of the expedition. The selection of these men was fortuitous. While they both proved stout and reliable foot-sloggers, Bowers showed his true genius when taking charge of all the stores, while Scott did not live to see Cherry-Garrard's true contribution.

To simplify the equation, the reconstruction will remove two of Scott's sources of hauling power: the horses and the motorized sledges (which proved to be virtually useless anyway). Scott's party set out for the pole with 23 dogs and eight ponies. The modern equivalent will take 24 dogs so a dog expert is needed. These are less common in the UK than in Norway, but they find one in Nick Akers, a former police officer, who has been a full-time dog trainer and racer for only the last few of the 20 years he has worked with Greenland dogs.

For the rest of the eight-man team, Bruce turns first, like Scott, to people he knows he could trust. His companion on the trek through Papua New Guinea was Mark Anstice, who coincidentally hails from the same regiment as Oates. Of the entire team that was eventually selected, Mark has the clearest idea of why he accepted the challenge and what it will entail. 'Curiosity. I'm curious to know whether I can hack it. I've done endurance things before, but nothing quite like this, where there has been no mental stimulation other than from your teammates. It's all very well walking for days and days wasting away, but if you've got something to occupy your mind during the day, like a new bit of terrain or animals, it's rather different and makes it much easier. I've never done anything like this. Which is just tramping, feet hurting, you're on day 30, there's another 66 of the buggers to go, they are all very long, snow treacling by and there's absolutely nothing to look at except the bloke in front who you are probably beginning to detest. That is going to be the hard bit. The mental side of it. This is ticking a couple of boxes which I've wanted to tick. One is Greenland and the other is dogs. I'm fascinated by the history. I really do hope that this will go some way towards further vindicating Scott. It always irritated me that people called Scott a fool when they just didn't know what the hell they were talking about.'

Bruce also summons Dave, recently retired from the Marines after more than 20 years. He was one of the first soldiers into liberated Kabul, but he also has extensive experience of operations in extreme cold. In 2003 he climbed the north face of Everest, but more relevantly he has experience of re-creating famous climbs using period equipment.

After personal contacts, Bruce goes for experience and knowledge. Amundsen was wary of hiring medical expertise. Once two of his men had taken a crash course in dentistry, he was more than happy to trust to luck and textbooks. Scott, on the other hand, relied on Wilson's medical qualifications. Bruce ends up selecting two doctors. One of them, Rory O'Connor, 37, has previously spent a winter and two summers as the medical officer on a British Antarctica Survey station, so is particularly knowledgeable in the field of cold-weather injuries and ailments. His expedition CV also includes cycling from Lhasa to Kathmandu and crossing both the Greenlandic and Norwegian ice caps. His fellow doctor is Chris van Tulleken, 26, who picked up valuable trudging experience when he raced in a team of two over 360 miles and 18 days to the magnetic North Pole.

The final two members of the group are chosen in the dilettante style of Scott's team selection. Both are invited along on the recommendation of Chris. Rupert Elderkin, a 29-year-old lawyer, has confined his expeditioning to climbing mountains. Arthur Jeffes, 27, is a music producer with little or no experience of cold-weather conditions. But he can claim to add a strand of authenticity to the enterprise, as he is the great-grandson of Scott's widow Kathleen, who remarried after her husband's death.

If the British team selection looks eccentric, it is in the spirit of the original. 'I was looking for team players,' says Bruce. 'I had to remember the ethos of what went before, so I didn't want polar explorers. I wanted people who had done a fair bit, but I didn't want there to be a big disparity between the levels of experience. And I didn't want any massive egos. I didn't want anyone who was so knowledgeable that they would upset the balance. I just wanted people who would get on. People were saying to me, "Oh, so are you going to have some mad selection test?" and I was like, "No, that proves nothing to me." The most important thing to me is that after ninety days people can still pull it out of the bag and keep going. You can't test that by running someone up and down a field. Everyone here pretty much to a tee is a personal recommendation and the sort that can still hack it when the chips are down. And from a CV there is no way of knowing that.'

Five men against eight; 48 dogs against 24; 1400 miles, and 99 days in which to do it. This sounds challenging enough, without the hassle of doing it all with antiquarian equipment. And indigestible food.

CHAPTER TWO

Preparation

ONE OF THE BIG DIFFERENCES BETWEEN AMUNDSEN AND US IS THAT
WE HAVE TEN DAYS TO DO ALL THE PREPARATION AND GET KNOWN TO
EACH OTHER. IF YOU DO YOUR PREPARATION WELL YOU WILL ALWAYS
HAVE LUCK. AMUNDSEN'S SOUTH POLE PLAN WAS GENIUS. IT WAS VERY
WELL PLANNED AND PREPARED, NOT JUST BY HIM BUT BY HIS MEN.
Rune Gjeldnes

Amundsen may have successfully avoided Scott in Norway, but he
could not avoid Scott in Antarctica. On 4 February 1911 the *Terra
Nova,* having deposited the main shore party and all its stores at
Cape Evans at the other end of the Great Barrier, steamed into the
Bay of Whales, discovered and named by Shackleton three years
earlier. The Norwegians had had no contact with the outside world
since their spectacular U-turn in the waters near Madeira in
September of the previous year, so they knew nothing of public
reaction. The watch on the *Fram* who spotted the British ship, was
wise, therefore, to be circumspect. One of his fellow sailors wrote,
'If they are planning something bad (we are constantly asking
ourselves in what light the Englishmen would view our competition)
the dogs will manage to make them turn back.'

In anticipation of one sort of exchange or another, the watch armed himself with a gun and a phrase book. Neither proved necessary.

On board the *Terra Nova* was a group of men dubbed the 'western party', so named because they were to explore the land fringeing the western perimeter of the Great Barrier. But Victor Campbell, the party leader, and his men found that they had been preceded. It was a personal blow for Campbell, who now felt obliged to give up the plans that had brought him to the bottom of the world and find some other coastline to map (thus condemning half a dozen men to a hellish survival drama to outdo them all, but that is another story). More pertinently, it was a reverse for the expedition as a whole. They had known since the previous October that Amundsen was planning to land somewhere on the Antarctic continent, but never suspected that he would be here, if not quite on their own doorstep, then near enough that he would certainly have to use the same route up the Beardmore Glacier (they turned out to be wrong about that). The party had always assumed – or, more accurately, massaged the hope – that Amundsen would approach the continent from the South American side.

Courtesies were extended by both sides. Harry Pennell, the captain of the *Terra Nova*, offered to carry letters to New Zealand. Campbell spoke some Norwegian. Amundsen spoke some English. The English party was invited to dine at Framheim. They were impressed, even taken aback, by the vast number of dogs the *Fram* had managed to ferry south – more than a hundred of them – and by their prodigious speed over the ice in the 3 nautical miles separating the base and the ship. The snugness of Framheim, the size of its library and the sight of a makeshift sauna, were also noted. Amundsen was just as nosy when the hospitality was returned. Lunching along with two of his men on the *Terra Nova*, he was quietly relieved to note that there was no radio mast with which the ship might relay news of success faster than he would ever be able to. He also enquired after the motorized sledges. When Campbell replied that one of them was already on terra firma, he anxiously assumed that it had already powered its way across the Great Barrier and had reached the Transantarctic Mountains. He need not have worried. Campbell did not convey that the terra firma he referred to was under the sea ice against which the *Terra Nova* had moored.

There was only one thing Amundsen knew he could do to enhance the possibility of success. Prepare. He brought with him a lifetime's experience of survival in and travel through snow, ice and cold, and that vast store of knowledge was now practically applied to ensure that the finest, minutest detail was attended to. By the time the sun rose on Framheim the following August, the Norwegians had been preparing all winter. They had already spent the autumn running a huge amount of supplies out to a series of three depots as far as 82 degrees south. Wintering down for the four months of the polar night in the hut and a network of snow caves they built around it, they stitched and sewed, planed and chiselled, tinkered and fastened, so that when the time came to leave, they were in a state of extreme readiness.

The preparations fell into two main categories: to make sure that their equipment was robust enough to withstand the test ahead, and to ensure that it weighed as little as possible. Bjaaland, a brilliant carpenter, reduced the weight of the sledges themselves by 33 pounds, while the cooking equipment was miraculously reduced from 66 pounds to 11. He also made new sledges with bespoke runners for the plateau, and an extra pair of hickory skis for each man. Meanwhile, in another cave Johansen filled and stowed small bags of dried milk to stash in the gaps between the round tins of pemmican. Ski boots, which had proved ineffectual on the spring depot-laying journey, were modified and improved to allow greater durability and insulation. Amundsen even contrived to dye the tent so that it wouldn't, like everything else in their world for the next few months, be white.

* * * * * * * * * * * *

Some things do not change. The modern Norwegian team get involved in the planning stage as early and as thoroughly as they can, and set to work on their equipment the minute it arrives in Greenland. They do not have an entire winter to make themselves ready, but for most of the next two weeks the Norwegian team adheres to its chosen tasks. Rune Gjeldnes, Inge Solheim and Harald Kippenes work on the sledges, which have turned up in poor condition, retying the lashings and removing metal bolts that reduce the flexibility of the wood (this despite the fact that there is clear evidence of Amundsen using bolts in his sledges).

Harald, in particular, is a modern Bjaaland. 'I'm quite amazed how focused I am,' he says. 'I haven't been thinking about anything else. It's all about how the binding is attached to the ski. If everything is good enough, will it last for three months? Can we do some adjustments here or there? What about the anoraks? Are the neck straps good enough? Will the sleeping bags be comfortable enough? We are getting into such minor details that there is not much else on our minds at this point.'

'We all are proud individuals,' explains Inge. 'We couldn't afford the reputational risk of doing this halfway. So we wanted to get involved in the production of the clothes, the skis, the food, so we know that we won't get any surprises on the ice. There can't be any compromises on quality. We would look stupid if our skis fall apart. We are trying to make it as good as the original. They spent years of planning and preparation. They were sitting in their cabin in Framheim making changes. "Is it making blisters between our legs? We have to change it." Nothing was left to chance. We are just limiting the number of X-factors. I learnt the seven Ps from a Royal Marine friend of mine when I was just five or six years old. Proper planning and preparation prevents piss-poor per-formance.'

Meanwhile, Ketil Reitan and John Huston get to know the 48 dogs they will take out on the Greenland ice cap. Again, Hassel and Hanssen had much longer to make friends with the huskies who would pull them to the pole. There being so many of them, their care was divided up between everyone at Framheim. Over the winter, each man took charge of 15 dogs, which were housed in tents to give them some protection against temperatures lower than anything they would have known in Greenland. Ketil and John learn their dogs' names – phonetically in some cases – and give them name tags. Twice a day they feed them. But the main task is to take them out running on the frozen bay and familiarize themselves with the canine personalities that will haul them through the 1390 nautical miles of the coming journey. Which dogs are the leaders? Which ones are content to pull from the back? Which dogs are inclined to fight each other? At the same time, the huskies learn to work to the sound of new voices. On his second ride out, Ketil has already taught a team to move left and right using Greenlandic commands he has learnt that morning.

The plan is to tally as faithfully as possible to the style of Amundsen's dog journey, but compromises on detail are necessary. As with Amundsen's party, the 48 dogs will pull four sledges in four teams of 12. Each sledge will be manned by a driver, while one of the party will ski ahead, as huskies are much happier following a trail than breaking new ground.

At the top of the Axel Heiberg Glacier, Amundsen and his men slaughtered 24 animals and fed them to the rest. The dogs were their own food. At a similar point in the journey, the reconstruction will remove a comparable number of dogs. It's for this reason that Ketil and John experiment with the two basic styles of dog-sledging: the 'fan hitch', in which up to a dozen dogs are tethered by an individual trace to the sledge, and 'nome style', in which they are secured to a central line. Both dog-drivers are conscious of the historical precedent, but not certain they will adhere to it.

'Amundsen used the fan hitch the whole way,' says Ketil. 'He had brought his dogs from West Greenland and those dogs were used to fan hitch. They had never been run nome-style before. It takes some time to get dogs adapted to nome style when they are used to fan hitch. When they run their dogs in Greenland every dog on the team has the same length on the line. In East Greenland they always have a staggered fan hitch where [the length is] different. So the East Greenland style of mushing is more similar to the nome style. We started from the same point of view. An advantage for us is when we drop dogs we want to be able to drop the poorest dogs. I don't think that would be possible if we were running the dogs in fan hitch. It would be a lot harder for us to avoid dog fights.

But when we run them in nome style we have a much bigger opportunity to mix the team the way we want it.'

They have already decided, however, to turn to individual lines on one section of the journey. 'The one advantage of fan hitch,' explains John, 'is in glacier conditions where there are crevasses everywhere. In nome style you could potentially – since the dogs are following each other and the sled can be difficult to stop – have a whole team cascade into a deep crevasse. And Amundsen did have dogs fall into crevasses, but because each dog had a single tug line going back to the sledge they were independent of each other. So they were able to pull them out. Others could scuttle away from the crevasse.'

For all this talk, when the five Norwegians together take a team of eight dogs out for the first time, they flirt with disaster. Rune takes up the story.

'We have been out on our first training trip. A very short one. The dogs didn't pull very well. Maybe they were a bit confused. We had an accident which could have been much worse. The sledge tipped over very close to the river. The sledge went into the river together with Harald. He got hit by the snow anchor and has some big bruises on his elbow and back. He was just very lucky. We did it the way we shouldn't have and I'm definitely not going to do that again. We need to get the routines going and today we didn't. It was just a mess. But we are not very experienced with the dogs. We should learn a lot about what happened but not think about it too much. My experience is that when an accident happens, another one is very close. Harald will be up again and fit to fight again. He is a strong guy. I think he became a bit scared. He could have got really hurt. But life must go on and in two days we are on the ice.'

* * * * * * * * * * * *

Meanwhile, over in the modern British camp there are two genuine ex-marines, but the party overall seems less familiar with the seven Ps. Take skiing. One day they attach bindings to the long hickory skis, then take them outside to test them. It is apparent that not many of the eight men have much experience of what the Norwegians call Telemark skiing. They may have skied in the Alps, but Telemark or free-heel skiing across flat ground and sometimes uphill seems altogether new to those who haven't been in the Marines. When they've finished, they leave their wooden skis outside to ruin under a rivulet of melting ice.

Then comes the day when they take a sledge out on to a frozen lake in Tassilaq and, for the first time, tie themselves into their harnesses. This is one of the famous images of Scott's expedition as captured by the expedition photographer Herbert Ponting in a specially stage-managed photo shoot: the human cart-horses trudging across the snow, putting on a pretence of struggle when the real struggle lies ahead. So it is for the modern team. They load three men on to the sledge and begin to haul. Now, for the first time, they have a true sense of what lies ahead.

Bruce Parry, far more than Scott ever did, becomes aware in this period of preparation that the dogs will be crucial. All eyes are on Nick Akers, the dog man. 'Without him we would not stand a chance of winning,' says Bruce. 'I think that's dawned on everyone.' In terms of the re-creation, Nick comes direct from central casting. When Scott went south, he took with him a dog handler of a decidedly eccentric hue. Cecil Meares was a moustachioed veteran of both the Boer War and, bizarrely, the Russo–Japanese war. His years as a sledge-bound fur trader in Siberia had given him serviceable Russian, which was useful when it came to buying the dogs and horses. 'Meares is the wanderer of us all,' wrote Frank Debenham, one of the expedition's three geologists, 'and with all the faults and virtues of such men. China, Siberia, India, anywhere " 'ot and unwholesome" is his hunting ground and he has already tired of this place.'

If anyone doesn't quite fit into the fabric of the modern British team, it is their dog man. 'He loves dogs more than us, and we know that we're second in the team to the dogs for good old Nick,' says Bruce. 'But he cares so much. He's actually the most competitive of all of us by a factor of about 300 per cent. And that's good. I need to temper it a little bit occasionally. Sometimes over-competitiveness can upset ... and maybe push people more than they necessarily need to be pushed.'

The reason Nick cares is that this is his most public chance to put himself in the shop window as a dog-driver. His stated ambition is to achieve a double first in the Iditarod in Alaska: to compete with pure-bred Greenland dogs, and ones born and raised in Britain. He is conscious that in the Norwegian team there are more dogs and more handlers with more dog experience. 'My motivation,' he admits, 'is to try and beat the other guys.' Other team members soon pick up on this. 'The race element isn't important to me in the slightest,' says Rupert Elderkin. 'Nick is very keen on the winning part. He's in charge of the dogs as well, so he can make us win.'

But as a member of the modern British team, Nick has his hands tied behind his back. In order to be as faithful as possible to the original template, he will have to lose his dogs after 40 days on the ice. Scott's plan, as elaborated to the rest of his party at the beginning of the winter, was to proceed south, pulling supplies with a combination of horse, dog, man and, as far as they could manage, machine. The dogs would stop at a certain point, while the horses would be driven till they could go no further, killed and either fed to the dogs or depoted for future human consumption. In the event, Scott took the dogs on for longer than he anticipated. There was a large dog-shaped gap in his knowledge of ice travel and it was filled in only when he saw what they could do on the Great Barrier. Meares eventually turned for home at the foot of the Beardmore Glacier, with only a quarter of the whole journey completed, and that is what will happen in the reconstruction.

Unlike the two Norwegian dog-drivers, Nick has no one to help him get used to the dogs. Even Meares took a pair of 18-year-old Russians with him to help look after the horses and dogs on the way from Siberia to Antarctica. Anton Omolchenko was the groom who would assist Oates in the stable; Meares's fellow dog-driver was Demetri Gerof. No doubt taking the lead from their English companions, they have come to be known to polar historians by their first names.

Nick is also more concerned about animal health than Meares could ever reasonably hope to be. 'Scott should have kept the dogs for as long as possible,' he says. 'I think that was possibly a mistake he made. But having said that, 40 days out on the ice is quite a long time with the dogs. For me it's about meeting their welfare needs. I will compromise their level of performance to meet their welfare needs because that's the kind of person I am.' This partly explains why in the preparation stage, Bruce can't get any straight answers from his dog man. 'I'm saying to Nick, "How fast can we go a day?" And he's saying, "I don't know." I say, "You need to tell me because I need to know how much food to start out with and I can only figure that out when you've told me the average daily speeds, because then I'll know whether or not we'll make that depot."'

Perhaps Bruce is trying to do things the Scott way. It is one of the criticisms levelled at Scott that his entire expedition was run on an improvisational basis, with decisions made at the last minute. And sometimes they were the wrong decisions. One of the worst of them brought disaster.

After the base was established at Cape Evans that autumn, Scott led a caravan of horses and ponies out on to the Great Barrier to lay depots of food and fuel. By the end of journey, he had already lost four of the eight ponies used to drag the sledges, and two dogs had tumbled down a crevasse. As they returned to the coast, the party was caught in increasingly bad weather so, needing shelter for themselves and the surviving ponies, they headed for Hut Point, where Scott's old quarters from the *Discovery* expedition still stood. It could be reached only by crossing seasonal sea ice, but at this point the ice was being broken up by a combination of warm temperatures and high seas.

Nonetheless, under strict orders from their leader, Bowers, Crean and Cherry-Garrard each led a pony on to the ice. Later, as they rested in their tent, they found the surface breaking up under their feet. Killer whales patrolled the lanes between the ice floes, their heads popping up menacingly through the surface of the water to look for potential prey. In the heart-stopping saga that followed, two more ponies were lost and one saved. Scott was relieved to have lost none of his men. (Aside from penguins and seals, killer whales were the party's most attentive neighbours. Ponting's film has powerful footage of these whales hunting in packs, though, sadly, none of the separate incidents in which he found himself hauling his camera and tripod across breaking ice floes, being chased by hungry killers who must have mistaken him for a seal.)

Eventually the party found its way to Hut Point but, until the sea ice froze, Cape Evans was inaccessible. A mounting number of men were confined to the old *Discovery* hut for weeks on end as the winter closed in. By mid-March there were 16 there, and they could sleep only in shifts. After three weeks' confinement, they hastened back to their main hut at the earliest opportunity, and settled down for a winter of – by Norwegian standards – desultory preparation. Taff Evans and Crean spent much of the winter working on the reindeer skin overshoe known as finnesko. Gran, whose skiing had impressed Scott in Norway, was available to give skiing lessons, but only Sub-Lieutenant Teddy Evans, the youthful second-in-command whose ambition was to be in the polar party, was truly determined to master the art: he challenged Gran to races, and even led a spring journey out to the nearby depots to clear them of drift. On the way back he insisted on testing his adeptness by doing the final 30-plus miles in 24 hours.

Meanwhile, back at the hut, Scott fostered a collegiate atmosphere. From his pool of scientists he insisted on regular evening lectures. Oates gave one on equestrian management. Cherry-Garrard produced the second (and last) edition of *The South Polar Times*, ten years on from its predecessor. If nothing else, this was a much more learned assembly than Amundsen's. But like the dramatics occasionally laid on to while away the evenings, it was also much more amateur.

* * * * * * * * * * *

It is curious that while you can reconstruct the physical circumstances of a historical feat of endurance, other elements must be left to take care of themselves. Is it possible, for example, to re-create a mood, an atmosphere? There is no doubt that both polar expeditions drew some of their character and shape from the nationality of the participants. One thing that two weeks' preparation in a hotel in Greenland proves is that nothing much changes in the personality of nations.

Amundsen's team talked at table when they needed to. 'Silence is not depressing,' wrote the leader of the quiet that sometimes visited the Framheim dining table. At table in Tassilaq the five-strong Norwegian team are similarly inclined: they keep themselves to themselves, and generally behave in the muted fashion of their predecessors. Even the presence of an American on the team does little to alter the silent dynamic, although after a few days John, who is the youngest in the party, does start to emerge from his shell. The seriousness of Rune's team can be easily explained. 'It's very important for us to win,' says Inge. 'It's like if you lost to Norway in cricket it would be embarrassing, wouldn't it?' Thus Amundsen in 1911: 'Our plan is one, one, and again one alone – to reach the pole. For that goal I have decided to throw everything else aside.'

Across the dining hall in their own corridor, the eight men of the British team are as loud as expected. They bond through banter. Nick has a wry turn of phrase, while Chris van Tulleken emerges as the group jester. Each member of the team has a subtly different reason for accepting the challenge of re-enacting Scott's journey, but it is the doctor who gives a sense of the light-hearted mood of the enterprise. 'There was almost no reason not to do this,' says Chris. 'Firstly, it's just going to be quite a laugh. When you first meet Bruce you realize he's quite keen on having a bit of fun and he's going to pick some good people. And, indeed, I've been allowed to bring along a few of my mates. It's a jolly in that sense.'

This is surely how some of Scott's mostly young party saw it. In addition to their eagerness for advancement in the armed forces or the sciences, they were fired by a vague wanderlust and thirst for adventure. In the specific case of the land-owning Cherry-Garrard, who contributed £1000 of his private income to the expedition coffers, he was above all looking for something to fill the vast emptiness of his work-free time.

However, it was not always easy to conjure up a jocular atmosphere when Scott was deep in one of his periodic depressions, to which he was already predisposed. His expedition members had received their first indication of his propensity to gloom when the *Terra Nova*, on its long journey to the southern hemisphere, docked at Melbourne in mid-October 1910. A telegram awaited Scott: 'Beg leave to inform you *Fram* proceeding Antarctic. Amundsen.' The last he had heard of Amundsen he was heading for five years' drift over the Arctic Ocean, and now apparently he was heading for the same small pinprick of snow at the bottom of the world. He was sufficiently bemused by the news to summon Gran, Amundsen's compatriot, for elucidation. Gran, who was only 21, was unable to shed further light.

Once they had landed at Cape Evans and built the hut that would be their home for the next two years, the *Terra Nova* brought worse tidings back from the other end of the Great Barrier. The news of Amundsen's presence in Antarctica percolated through to Scott as he was returning from the depot-laying journey. Cherry-Garrard witnessed his initial reaction. 'For many hours, Scott could think of nothing else nor talk of anything else. Evidently a great shock for him – he thinks it very unsporting since our plans for landing a party there were known.'

'Captain Scott took it very bravely,' wrote Teddy Evans, 'better than any of us, I think, for he had done already such wonderful work down here. It was he who initiated and founded Antarctic sledge travelling, it was he who had blazed the trail, as it were, and we were very, very sorry for him.'

Scott's written response was more measured: 'There is no doubt that Amundsen's plan is a very serious menace to ours. He has a shorter distance to the pole by 60 miles – I never thought he could have got so many dogs safely to the ice. His plan for running them seems excellent. But above and beyond all he can start his journey early in the season – an impossible condition with ponies.'

He was starting to think in terms of a race, but it was a race he had not prepared for. Some of his men privately acknowledged that they could not win. 'If it comes to a race,' wrote the independent-minded Oates, 'Amundsen will have a great chance to get there as he is a man who has been at this kind of game all his life and he has a hard crowd behind him, while we are very young.' Later, in the days before departure, Scott wrote to his wife Kathleen: 'I decided at a very early date to act exactly as I should have done had he not existed.

Any attempt to race must have wrecked my plan, beside which it doesn't appear the sort of thing one is out for.' At least to his wife, he appeared to be privately conceding defeat on the start line.

No one in the British team of 2005 is more keenly aware that Scott laboured under a huge disadvantage than the great-grandson of his widow. 'It would be nice if we won, but you win a race in the preparation,' says Arthur Jeffes. 'When I told my grandfather he said, "Scott didn't prepare for a race. When Scott left Britain, Amundsen was still preparing to go to the North Pole." We've got Scott's equipment. We are not prepared for a race.'

Except that they are. It is Chris who puts his finger on precisely how this may not be a race in the conventional sense, but it remains very much a race, only one in which the opponents are supplied by history. 'It's hard to know what the motivation on a day-to-day basis will be,' he says. 'You can walk at a certain speed for a certain number of hours and then you have to put up your tent. The idea of walking faster every step with the Norwegians biting at your heels, that doesn't motivate me hugely. It's a completely handicapped race, so none of us is going to feel too bad if we lose. I'm much more interested to see if we can do the mileage that Scott did. Racing yourself against history in that way is really interesting. Can we get back to our putative One Ton Camp? How thin are we getting? Are we still able to do the mileages? How are we all getting along? Are we able to keep up our spirits and write diaries and do the navigation?'

By the same token, Rune's team have their own target. They are determined to beat Bruce's team – 'We might not be allowed to go back to Norway if we don't win,' says Ketil – but they know the race is tilted in their favour and that it has already been won once. As they are travelling over precisely the same distance as that covered by Amundsen to get from Framheim to the pole, they want to do it faster than Amundsen did.

Racing against history, the modern teams would appear to hold all the advantages. They travel in the knowledge that this is only a reconstruction. They will be allowed to wear modern lenses in their goggles in order to protect their eyes against the glare of the sun on the snow. They know far more about the impact of diet on stamina, health and fitness. They know, above all, that they are not going to die.

Amundsen had to worry less about diet than Scott. He was not man-hauling, so the rate of depletion on the body was not going to affect his team as much as it would the British. In the form of the dogs, he also had a supply of fresh meat, which he suspected – though the best preventative measure had yet to be established – would ward off the predations of scurvy. Scott left it till he was already in Antarctica to work out what would supply the best calorific intake. The opportunity for experiment in this area came when Wilson led a party of three to a penguin rookery 67 sledging miles away at Cape Crozier on the other side of Mount Erebus, a huge volcano dominating Ross Island at the edge of the Great Barrier near Cape Evans. Wilson, a keen zoologist as well as a qualified doctor (and water-colourist), was eager to get to the rookery when the penguins were still incubating their eggs because there was an untested theory that the embryo of an emperor penguin might supply evidence of the missing genetic link between birds and dinosaurs. Indeed, it was the promise of pursuing this scientific holy grail that had lured Wilson south for the second time. But there were drawbacks. The emperors laid their eggs in the dead of winter. And Cape Crozier was, according to Cherry-Garrard, 'the windiest place in the world'.

Cherry-Garrard was fond of the deadpan superlative, which is why he called his book *The Worst Journey in the World*. The title nominally refers to the entire *Terra Nova* expedition, but the pages within leave the reader in no doubt that the worst part of the worst journey was the one the author took with Wilson and Bowers to that rookery in the depth of the polar night. 'Antarctic exploration is seldom as bad as you imagine, seldom as bad as it sounds. But this journey had beggared our language: no words could express its horror.' Scott was reluctant for them to go, but made a virtue of their absence by putting each of the three men on a slightly varying diet. The aim was to test the efficacy of different rations in extreme sledging conditions. From the conclusions, Scott would work out the contents of the so-called Summit Rations he would take with him up on to the Polar Plateau. And the conclusion was to make the food as fatty as possible. Cherry-Garrard had been on the fattiest ration and, for all the appalling privations caused by marrow-chilling cold, lost the least weight over the five weeks out on the march.

The modern British team in Greenland have taken a leaf out of his book by putting on a lot of weight. The tallest members – Jeffes, Elderkin and van Tulleken – have all developed substantial pot bellies and, in one or two cases, breasts. Even Bruce has bulked up from his regular 9 stone to 11.

But there are disadvantages for the twenty-first century polar traveller returning to the Heroic Age. Almost all the equipment secured for the re-enactment is a modern replica, or as close a copy as can be conjured up nearly a hundred years on, and neither of the modern teams has the same affinity with it as their predecessors. The Norwegians may have vastly more experience of the cold, but they have never travelled in sealskin anoraks before. No one under-stands the need to get clothing right more than Geoff Somers. Before the ban on non-indigenous species in Antarctica, he was part of an international team that in 1989–90 drove three dozen-strong teams of dogs for 220 days across nearly 4000 miles from the north end of the Antarctica peninsula through to McMurdo Sound. Somers is a safety adviser on the re-enactment.

'Although what they are wearing is alien to us now in the modern age,' he says, 'it is still good if it's used in the right way. Any clothing that you wear, any system that you have, will work provided you understand the properties of it. Some people doing mammoth journeys a hundred years ago fell by the wayside and died, but a lot also did these journeys without injury. During Scott's trip they got superficial frost injuries, but none of them lost any limbs. So Scott, Amundsen, all these guys had either furs or they had cotton and wool. They are not intrinsically bad. But to those that haven't used them they could be problematical. They can all be used to do the job, but it's going to be a big learning curve. On the kit side there is almost no comparison. The Norwegian team have far superior gear. They have three alternative sets of clothing.

The British team have one. They will be able to mix and match to the conditions that are out there. Norwegians are born with skis on their feet. They have been brought up to understand snow, the properties of snow and the properties of kit. The Norwegians have a colossal advantage.'

Bruce Parry's Diary

Mark Anstice – Second in command. Brilliant and a good mate. Can't say how happy I am (and grateful) to have Mark on board. He's a mellow, funny, industrious guy who's done wonders in the prep for the trip. He's the unofficial master of all the kit and nothing has been modified or built without his expert eye and hand. I've left him to it and as a result have rarely visited the workshop to avoid the temptation of sticking my oar in. I hope this hasn't been confused with laziness.

Dave Pearce – Bootneck PTI [physical training instructor] from my own troop 12 years ago. Recently left corps. I was worried at first cos I didn't want any 'too' military types, but he has proved to be an absolute legend. V experienced (climbed Everest etc) and a v good social pawn for me. Understands my philosophy of leadership v well. My buddy pair.

Chris van Tulleken – An instant like and I offered him the gig within minutes of meeting. The only person chosen by CV alone. V intelligent, funny (dry and silly) and up for it. An immense character for this trip and will be a friend for the future.

Rory O'Connor – Doctor and expeditioner. V placid and mellow and strong. Will be our rock I'm sure. Fits in v well despite being less overt. Experience (not as outdoor leader, but as participant) BAS [British Antarctic Survey], Greenland and Norway (with a mutual friend who vouched for him too). V likeable and reliable. Top asset and our only knowledge of the ice plateau.

Nick Akers – Dogs, dogs, dogs. Wasn't sure about Nick at first and I reckon he wasn't sure about us either. Just lives (totally) for his Greenlanders and his sport. By far the most competitive and outside me had most to lose in this race. Desperate to win and show his skills. Not sure of his initial motives, maybe some publicity/sponsorship for the future, but either way has totally bought into our team and must be hard for him at times in the new social setting. (Openly admits to preferring dogs to human company.) He's least socially adept and can seem caustic at times but each team member is bigger than our over-reactions. Nick has now become probably, outside Mark, my biggest help and worker in the team. Our success directly relates to him and I have *every* faith in him. As a leader I have occasional worries with him as he's outspoken, direct and opinionated, but I think he's happy so far with my style. I cut him loads of slack and he is outwardly grateful. A good relationship so far.

Rupert Elderkin – Another Everest type. Super clever, big and strong. V likeable though his humour is just not. Many mannerisms, including physical gesticulations which are v his but cannot detract from his v likeable demeanour. An incredibly analytical mind which has been (and will continue to be) put to v good use. A good team member and a physical bonus. Friend of Chris VT.

Arthur Jeffes – Our Arthur. Lovely guy and another friend of Chris VT, who got him and Rupert on the team without me even meeting them (time was tight by the end). Arthur is the least experienced in this field but doesn't seem daunted at all and I only hope that is a good sign (and not foolhardiness). As a relation of Kathleen Scott he has an encyclopedic knowledge of 1911–12. Arthur is another v fine chap who I sometimes worry about cos he could challenge my authority from inexperience and fatigue. I hope not.

CHAPTER THREE

Departure

I WAS THINKING YESTERDAY WHAT MY TEN-YEAR-OLD SELF
WOULD HAVE MADE OF ME BEING ASKED TO GO ON A TRIP LIKE
THIS AND THINKING HE'D BE PRETTY ECSTATIC REALLY. AT THE
END OF THE FIRST DAY I'M RATHER FEELING MY TEN-YEAR-OLD
SELF IS PROBABLY A BIT OF A DIMWIT.
Chris van Tulleken

Amundsen set out again on 20 October, six weeks after his first
abortive attempt to forge a southerly path. In the second week of
September, he had asked his men to endure the bone-numbing cold
of the Antarctic spring out on the ice shelf. They made it as far as
their first depot, at 80 degrees south, then turned for home. The
retreat proved nearly fatal for a couple of the stragglers. Once they
had all limped back to Framheim, frostbitten and humbled, an air
of recrimination simmered in the hut. Privately, Bjaaland referred to
the debacle as a 'fiasco', but only one man went public. The old
polar hand Johansen openly criticized Amundsen for his reck-
lessness. The leader took swift action to lance the boil, while at the
same time weeding out the under-performers. Johansen, Kristian
Prestrud and Jorgen Stubberud were instructed to abandon all hope
of reaching the pole, and travel instead to the nearby King Edward

VII Land, the unexplored western edge of the Great Barrier. This was to have been the goal of Victor Campbell's party until they encountered the *Fram* the previous February.

Amundsen glossed over the unpleasantness within his team in his written account: 'Circumstances had arisen which made me consider it necessary to divide the party in two.' But Johansen's humiliation, and Amundsen's refusal to talk to him now or acknowledge his contribution once back in Norway, might well have contributed to Johansen's subsequent suicide. 'Desolation hovers in the air,' Johansen wrote, 'and nevertheless we are forced to live cheek by jowl, day and night.'

The leader was unrepentant about both his disastrous early start, and the decisive action he took in its aftermath. 'To sit still without doing anything would never occur to me, criticise me who will ... Our little journey has not caused us any loss. It was a good trial run. Besides we got everything up to 80 degrees.' From all but Johansen he now made sure to extract an oath of loyalty.

It wasn't just the burning urge to reach the pole that had hastened Amundsen into action. Both the Norwegian and British expeditions navigated with the help of the *Nautical Almanac*, as would their successors nearly a hundred years later. Without it, there is no way of plotting a position against the sun. A new edition is published every year, but in an extraordinary oversight the 1912 edition had been left behind, while the only copy for 1911 was all but burnt to a crisp when it caught fire next to an oil lamp. The combustion spontaneously put itself out just as the indispensable pages – September to December – were about to be consumed by the flames. There is no accounting for luck, but here is evidence that Amundsen had it in spades. A similar double gaffe committed on Scott's expedition would, without question, have provoked an orgy of recrimination among his detractors. Roland Huntford merely refers to Amundsen's misadventures with the *Nautical Almanac* as 'a ludicrous mistake'. The upshot of the ludicrous mistake was that the Norwegians now had to be back by the end of the year. If they were still out on 1 January, they would have to rely on finding their own tracks to navigate their way back.

It was a more compact unit of five that eventually set out again after a further week's delay caused by unfavourable weather. That first day out would also suggest that someone was watching over the Norwegians. There were four sledges and 52 dogs. With Hanssen on the front sledge to steer by compass, the huskies bounded on to the ice shelf into a headwind. It was bitterly cold, with poor visibility, and they lost the route lined by flags (laid out the previous autumn) that would guide them to their first depot. At one point they unwittingly sledged into an area of critical danger. The front of the rear sledge, on which Amundsen and Wisting were both perched, tipped momentarily upwards, the rear end jerked downwards, and below them the two men saw a bridge of snow tumble away to reveal a yawning cavity. Fortunately, their momentum took them over. 'Did you see that?' Amundsen said to his sledge-partner. 'That would have liked both us, the sledge and the dogs.' It was their first crevasse. It would not be their last. 'A few more inches to one side,' he wrote later, 'and we should have taken no part in the polar journey.'

It could be argued that Amundsen was even lucky with his bad weather. The flags proved more reliable when, on the fourth day, they navigated their way through a dense fog towards their depot at 80 degrees south, 600 nautical miles from the pole. A blizzard now struck at the precise moment when he was perfectly happy to rest and fatten up his dogs on depoted seal meat before they pressed on, pulling greater weights. They now had the luxury of reducing their dog power. To keep the speed from wearing out the husky teams too early, some dogs had been lashed on to the top of the sledges. An unlucky quartet who would not pull their weight were released. That left 48 dogs, a dozen to each sledge, precisely the same configuration as the modern Norwegian team's on Day 1 of their polar re-enactment.

* * * * * * * * * * * *

By the time they camp out on the night before they start for the pole, the modern Norwegians have established a domestic routine very similar to Amundsen's. Their spacious five-man tent, with its built-in groundsheet, is held up by one central pole and held down by a combination of wide wooden pegs fashioned by Inge Solheim and further weighted down by spadefuls of snow piled around the outer rim. The tent is a deep red, providing relief from the monotony of white that will be the only colour to assault their vision for the next 99 days. The only problem with it is that they can't tighten the pegs. When they do the tent rips. For a team with a tendency to get grouchy at the slightest failing in their equipment, this is an unwanted annoyance.

There is a cloudless sky on the morning of departure. 'Today's big question,' says the trail-breaker Inge, 'is will the dogs follow the ski tracks?' The plan is to establish a formation. Ketil Reitan, the more experienced of the dog-drivers, will be on the front sledge, with John Huston placed between Rune Gjeldnes and, in the rear, Harald Kippenes, neither of whom has any experience of dog-driving. Harald has built large storage boxes that sit at the back of each sled. On each of them is written the name of one of Amundsen's companions.

They immediately have problems with fights. Huskies fight anyway, but after a period of enforced idleness, they are on edge. Ketil, who has seen it all before, seems unfazed. 'When we get them tired, then they won't fight so much. They have been sitting around for a week and they are really crazy. When they get used to us, they will be easier to handle.' Fights have to be broken up, sometimes ruthlessly. John is bitten while trying to intervene. 'It's a tall order trying to run with 48 dogs when you've only been with them for three days,' he explains. The Norwegians make it their task to let the dogs know that they have new masters now. Not all their efforts in this direction are broadcastable.

The first day is a slog. Every one of their 7 nautical miles has to be fought for. By the end of the second day, they have completed 11 miles in six hours, including a break of 90 minutes halfway through. Rune ends the day in a much happier frame of mind. 'Hopefully we can continue in this way,' he says. 'We haven't had much trouble compared to yesterday.'

* * * * * * * * * * * *

The departure of Amundsen's team was filmed by Prestrud, while Scott's phalanx of sledges was captured by Ponting as they headed out into the white. It was, as Oates predicted it would be in a letter to his mother, 'a bit of a circus getting off'. Their departure from what passed for civilization at these latitudes was a piecemeal affair spanning many days. The motorized sledges were the first to head out, on 24 October, only four days after Amundsen had started. The four-man motor party was led by Teddy Evans. Each of the two motors pulled sledges carrying a ton and a half of supplies. At the other end of the schedule, Meares was instructed to tarry at Hut Point with the dog teams long after the main party had left a week later. Initially, the dogs were expected to be quicker over the Great Barrier surface than the ponies, so there was no sense in them coming out too early and wastefully consuming food. Scott knew dogs could go fast over a short distance, but had no great faith in their ability to endure over hundreds of miles. He would change his mind.

On the last afternoon in October, two of the weaker ponies were sent on their way several hours ahead of the rest. In the early hours of 1 November Scott led out the main party of eight ponies and sledges, but not before he had harnessed his own pony on to Bowers's sledge. Oates, whose job it was to look after them, never had a high opinion of the nags Meares had brought down from Siberia. He took charge of the worst of them, Christopher, who 'as usual behaved like a demon,' wrote the geologist Griffith Taylor. They left behind the Union Jack, presented to Scott by Queen Alexandra. It was only because there was a telephone line along the 15 miles between Cape Evans and Hut Point that they were able to summon the Norwegian, Gran, to bring it out the next day. So for at least the early furlongs of its journey the flag that would fly at the South Pole travelled at a fair old lick: 5 miles an hour. It would never get up to such heady speeds again.

It was not an auspicious overture to the coming drama. If there was a further air of amorphousness in what should have been a momentous event, it was caused partly by the nature of the terrain. Although they left Cape Evans, the first night's stop brought them to Hut Point. It was only once they'd left Hut Point and rounded the pair of islands, rimmed by crevasses, that blocked the path south that they could truly be on their way.

Shackleton had brought a motor car south on the *Nimrod* three years earlier. Try as he might, the mechanic Bernard Day could not get it to work on anything other than smooth sea ice. Day had little more success with the motor sledges. On the fourth day the pony party discovered for themselves the evidence that one tier of Scott's complicated transport system had already collapsed. A mere 14 miles from Hut Point they came upon a motorized sledge 'drifted up with snow', according to Cherry-Garrard, 'and looking like a mournful wreck'. The second one turned up a day later. It was the remotest scrap-metal yard on the planet. 'It is a disappointment,' wrote Scott. 'I had hoped better of the machines once they got away on the Barrier surface.' Oates grumbled that the three motors had cost £1000 each, while dogs came at a rather more reasonable 32 shillings. The motors represented a significant proportion of the overall cost of the entire expedition. They had proved, on the whole, an expensive and wasteful speculation. Evans, who had had to live with them and then abandon them, gave the motors a more generous obituary. They 'advanced the necessaries for the southern journey 51 miles over rough, slippery and crevassed ice and gave the ponies the chance to march light as far as Corner Camp.' Better than nothing, in other words.

When the temperamental engines broke down for the final time it was a relief for the men charged with perpetually nursing them into life in the extreme cold. Day and Lashly seemed to spend their every free minute in futile spurts of finger-chilling maintenance operations. 'I can't say I'm sorry,' wrote Lashly, 'because I am not, and the others are, I think, of the same opinion as myself.' How much of a relief it was can be gauged from the eagerness with which they stepped into their man-hauling traces and, as instructed by Scott, began pulling as much as possible of the weight that had been previously borne by the motors. 'We shall not be much more tired,' Lashly continued, 'than we had been at night when we had finished.'

When, in the following March Cherry-Garrard and the Russian

dog handler Demetri Gerof went out on to the Barrier in the hope of meeting the returning polar party at One Ton Camp, they passed the drifted-up corpse of one spent sledge, and what they thought was the flag marker for the other. Entombed in the snow, they must have looked like malign omens.

Evans's orders were to journey as far as 80 degrees 32 minutes south. On the way they stopped every 3 miles to build cairns for the benefit of those following. They reached their destination on 15 November. It took Scott six days to catch up with them. To fill the time, and no doubt to keep warm, they built a 15-foot cairn they called Mount Hooper, after the expedition steward, who was one of their party. More distinguished members of the expedition would have less perishable features of the Antarctic landscape named after them.

Scott's plan had been meticulously worked on. Every calculation was predicated on the need to put the appropriate amount of supplies in place to get 12 men all the way up the Beardmore Glacier, before two parties of four successively turned for home, leaving the final four to march all the way to the South Pole and then back to Cape Evans on stomachs as full as the depot system would allow. Scott had four means of lugging supplies – motors, dogs, ponies and men – but he worked on the assumption that the lion's share of the work would be done by the ponies over the 370 nautical miles to the base of the Beardmore Glacier, whereafter all the hauling would fall to themselves. The first part of the journey was to see the main party advance 10 nautical miles a day from Hut Point. The ponies were to pull light loads as far as One Ton Camp, where they would pick up further stores and take them as far as the Gateway, as the mouth of the Beardmore had been named by Shackleton. Despite the heavier loads, they were to increase their daily average to 13 miles.

On the march south, Scott's idea was to stagger the daily departure of three parties – two of them with three ponies, one with four – so that they would arrive at the same point at the end of each march. Oates was in the fastest and therefore last group, which didn't stop for lunch because his pony Christopher could not be persuaded to stand still.

It was cold enough at night that when they reached Hut Point on the first day, they were forced to bring three of the ponies into the hut to shelter them against the cold. Scott resolved to travel by night and sleep during the day, when it was warmer. It goes without saying that it was light throughout the 'night'. The nights were decidedly on the nippy side but, when the sun appeared from behind the blanket of cloud, it was comparatively warm during the day. For the veterans of the winter journey to Cape Crozier it must have seemed like a holiday. 'One had forgotten that a tent could be warm and a sleeping bag dry,' marvelled Cherry-Garrard.

The good weather did not last. On 6 November they wandered into a gale that rapidly escalated to force 8. The entire caravan was tent-bound. Progress was impossible – or so it seemed until Meares materialized through the blizzard with the dogs.

* * * * * * * * * * * *

Given the absence of horses from the re-enactment, Bruce Parry's team are acquainted with the realities of dog travel rather earlier than Scott was. For Scott the dogs came as a pleasant surprise. For his successor they are an unpleasant one. 'The dogs are a problem,' he says at the end of a sobering first day. 'They are at once our biggest asset and our greatest hindrance. Until we learn how to use them properly we are going to go round and round in circles.'

The day starts badly anyway. It is their first, uncomfortable night in the tents. Rory O'Connor sums up the jolting initiation of a night on the ice in an old-fashioned tent with old-fashioned sleeping bags. 'Long, uncomfortable, full of reindeer hair, snoring, dogs howling, rolling over, drips on your head. Apart from that it was absolutely fine. Looking forward to another 98 of them.' Dave Pearce, the old man of the expedition, complains of a bad back, with pain radiating down his leg, which sounds uncannily like the sciatica that tends to strike at precisely his age. In which case, he has picked the wrong expedition to emulate. It was Shackleton on the *Endurance*, also in his early forties, who had that particular cross to bear.

For Nick Akers the night is more uncomfortable than most. He has contrived to rip his reindeer-fur sleeping bag, with the result that he is extremely cold and almost entirely unrested before what he knows will be, for him, the biggest and most testing day of the expedition. Responsible for asserting his control over 24 dogs he has only just met, he has to rely for assistance on seven men who, at the start of a projected 40 days in their company, know absolutely nothing about dog-sledging, nor about chaining out the animals at the end of the day to keep them apart, nor even about feeding them. Opportunities to learn about the huskies were hampered by the warm weather in the fortnight of preparation in Tassilaq. Aside from a run or two on the slushy sea ice of the fjord, the team has zero experience of running with dogs. It is the very deepest of deep ends into which they have been collectively plunged.

The first thing to go wrong is the alarm clock. Bruce has brought along a vintage model from 1911. With a certain inevitability, it freezes overnight and fails to go off at the appointed hour of five o'clock. The team rises nearly two hours late, no doubt hoping that none of the other retro-gear on which they must exclusively rely for the next 99 days will prove to be quite so shoddy.

Dave, mounted on skis, heads out on his own, his task being to navigate across an entirely featureless waste of snow. Behind him the departure of the modern British team skirts along the edge of pure farce. Almost everything that can go wrong does go wrong.

The three sledges are heavy. The snow surface is treacly. The dogs, eight of them to a sledge, are cantankerous, possibly disorientated by their crowded flight up on to the ice cap, and therefore unwilling to obey orders from so many new masters who don't yet know any of their names and whose nervousness they can doubtless smell on the cold breeze. There are fights galore as alpha males square up to one another, barking and biting madly. When he intervenes in one ruckus, Bruce sustains a bite to his finger.

In one sledge team a bitch has come into season, wreaking havoc among all her male neighbours. This is an untimely extra dose of bad luck. Nick moves her round to the back of the sledge, but the dogs simply chase round to the rear, as if to bite the sledge's tail. He tries harnessing her to the front of the line in order to encourage her suitors to chase. 'But she's only a youngster and can't cope with it,' he explains. 'She just lies down all the time and everything bunches up.' She also, for the record, contentedly invites her companions to have their way with her. The first day of the re-creation of Scott's journey turns into a canine gang-bang. Bruce rues the impossibility of deploying the solution used by Amundsen. 'When he had a bitch on heat,' he says, 'he shot it.' (There is sober documentary evidence for this in Bjaaland's diary: ''The Sheep'' took the opportunity to serve ''Lussi'',' Bjaaland wrote on the Barrier, 'who in consequence got a lead bullet in the forehead and was put on the depot.' They also drowned all female puppies born on the long sea voyage.) The fate of the modern team's female is less dire. She is handed over to Dave to lead out in front.

Bruce's hope is to cover 7 miles a day. 'If we get behind our minimum daily rates I've calculated that we then start running out of food. And we don't want to run out of food out here. That wouldn't be clever.' At the start of the day it looks like they will be lucky to travel 7 yards. After several hours of demoralizing negotiations with two dozen huskies, Nick sums up the progress thus far. 'We've moved 0.6 of a mile from camp.'

When they are asked to run, the dogs veer off in all directions, like lawless iron filings. A lead dog on a sledge manned by Arthur Jeffes and Rupert Elderkin chews through the main line and escapes, releasing other dogs in the process. They have to be rounded up and re-attached to a new line from a limited supply of spares. The dog does this four times. 'If he bites through the line again,' Nick tells Bruce, 'shoot him.' He is only half joking. On the sledge manned by Chris van Tulleken and Mark Anstice the dogs fall behind and are unable to smell the sledges in front. The result is a disrupted rhythm. 'We'd go 10 yards,' says Chris, 'then we'd stop, have a massive bun fight, chew through the lines, have to re-sew all the lines and then kick off again. It's just exhausting.' When the dogs do move, they go at such a pace that the dog-drivers break into a sweat to keep up. The sweat then freezes in the 20-minute stops to sort out the lines. So do hands. Progress is further impeded by snow adhering to the base of the wooden sledge runners like mud caked on to the soles of football boots, thus creating friction that stalls any momentum in the runners' glide motion. Bruce spends much of the first day running up and down the line geeing on a disillusioned team.

Eventually, they start to move with some consistency, and the whole team is impressed. 'The part when the dogs were pulling was amazing,' says Rupert. 'If Arthur and I tried to give a shove, the sledge barely moved, but the dogs were tripping along and we had to ski quite hard to keep up with them.' In the end it is a triumph that they manage just under 4 nautical miles. But the leader needs to draw on his deep reserves of ingrained optimism to find something positive to say about such a gruelling initiation.

'It's been a real baptism by fire,' says Bruce. 'We've done 5 miles out of the 1200 or so we've got to do. There's no one here who isn't going to fall asleep. We're all really dehydrated and unfit frankly, as we've been getting fat for the past couple of months. Everyone was panting and shedding clothes, even though it's minus 12. Even though the race started this morning, it's as if we haven't learnt a thing. We are learning everything for the first time today. But people are just getting stuck in. Everyone is doing their utmost, despite the fact that it's very tough conditions. I'm going to go to sleep happy because I know that I've picked a good team that's willing to dig when the going gets tough. And it was tough today. I just hope it gets better. Nick is feeling it a little bit because he is very proud and he loves his dog work and wants to win this race, and especially in the dog phase wants to push it on. We don't understand like he does. Although we're learning as fast as we can, he's feeling a lot of the pressure now. He's biting his lip quite a lot with a few of us, which is good because nobody knows and you can't expect us to know.'

But there are other problems for Bruce's team. They have not slept in their tents before, so they have no established tent routine and have to learn how to do basic daily tasks from scratch. Earlier in the day someone contrived to pour kerosene into their water pot. All day they have to drink kerosene-flavoured water. Once they have made it into their tents, set up their Nansen cookers and prepared their first meal, there is another bitter shock lying in ambush.

It's called pemmican and it's verging on inedible. The polar scholar will find almost no evidence of disgruntlement with the basic polar foodstuff, a dry compound of meat and fat, in any of the diaries or letters written by the explorers of 1911. Only once does Oates, days from the South Pole, think that his pemmican may have 'disagreed' with him. In the depot-laying trips, and during the winter, both expeditions had grown used to a limited diet. But the diet back home was not what it is for their modern successors. Year-round fruit, exotic vegetables, global cuisine on the doorstep: these were not things that explorers missed in 1911.

The modern world has played a further nasty trick on the men retracing the old journeys. Thanks to strict rules designed to keep BSE at bay, Greenland will not allow the historically accurate beef pemmican through customs, so a pork-based pemmican is delivered as an alternative. Pemmican is already a fatty foodstuff, and the substitution of pork does not make it any leaner.

Back in the Heroic Age the British men brewing up their pemmican in the tent called it 'hoosh'. They found all sorts of ways of varying it, none more satisfying than the period at the bottom of the Beardmore Glacier, when they feasted on pemmican laced with the meat of the slaughtered ponies. But there were other ways to tart up the daily ration. On the depot-laying journey of the previous autumn, Cherry-Garrard found himself in Scott's tent for the first time. He was 'struck … forcibly' by the standard of the cuisine. 'We were of course on just the same ration as the tent from which I had come. I was hungry and said so. "Bad cooking," said Wilson shortly; and so it was. For in two or three days the sharpest edge was off my hunger. Wilson and Scott had learned many a cooking tip in the past, and, instead of the same old meal day by day, the weekly ration was so manoeuvred by a clever cook that we seldom had quite the same meal. Sometimes pemmican plain, or thicker pemmican with some arrowroot mixed in with it; at others we surrendered a biscuit and a half apiece and had a dry hoosh, i.e. biscuit fried in pemmican with a little water added, and a good big cup of cocoa to follow. Dry hooshes also saved oil … Then much could be done with the dessert-spoonful of raisins which was our daily whack. They were good soaked in the tea, but best perhaps in with the biscuits and pemmican as a dry hoosh. "You are going far to earn my undying gratitude, Cherry," was a satisfied remark of Scott one evening when, having saved, unbeknownst to my companions, some of their daily ration of cocoa, arrowroot, sugar and raisins, I made a "chocolate hoosh". But I am afraid he had indigestion the next morning.'

They were undoubtedly easier to please back then. The one who is most disappointed by the pemmican is Chris. More than anyone on the modern British team, as a doctor with an academic eye on the historical aspect of the experiment, he is intrigued by the prospect of accelerating physical depletion over a long journey. He is particularly interested in studying the team's calorific equation, in which the consumption of calories is measured against the loss of body fat. In preparation, he has put on a huge amount of weight. 'When we stop using the dogs and start man-hauling, potentially we'll be using a huge number of calories,' he says before departure. 'But we're probably not even eating enough calories anyway – even when we have the dogs. It's probably best not to dwell on it too much. I'm now the third heaviest of the group at 14.3 stone. I'm usually 11.8 stone. With a deficit on average every day of at least 3000 calories, that's potentially 14–18 ounces of fat a day that we could be using up. Your body will get more efficient when you start using different metabolic sources. But potentially you will be burning several ounces of fat a day. So if it's for a hundred days, that could be quite a lot of weight. As you work harder without the dogs towards the end, the problem is that you're colder, you'll be thin and therefore less able to insulate yourself.'

Before he leaves he is sanguine about the prospects of surviving on an unpalatable diet. 'The food is pretty awful,' he says in Tassilaq. 'One of the only benefits of starving will be that the food will become edible. The pemmican is essentially a block of 50 per cent lard with salami and dried fruit and honey mashed into it. It makes it like a very, very fatty sweet pepperami. It's also very salty, so you need to drink more water. Drinking water is difficult with the apparatus we've got. We don't have thermoses during the day.

It's difficult to melt.' At this point he still had access to hotel food and water. Actually having to eat the pemmican for real comes as a visceral shock. 'I was rather hoping that at the end of a day with very little food or water I'd be looking forward to my pemmican a little bit more than I am. Going back to the tent now and eating a bowl full of fat with bits of dried fruit and salami in it and a few of those biscuits and a cup of kerosene water full of dog hair, dog shit and reindeer fur is pretty uninspiring.'

Pemmican comes in the form of a rectangular block that looks not unlike a bar of scented soap. Once it is melted in the cooker and diluted/enlivened/masked by whatever ingredient the chef chooses from a limited larder, the lucky diner spoons it into his own mess tin and starts to eat. The only available supplements to pemmican are oatmeal biscuits, raisins, chocolate, curry powder, tea, coffee, butter and sugar. The first night they have it unadulterated. 'The first spoonful was palatable,' says Dave. 'Four or five spoonfuls later it was lying so heavy in your stomach and it felt so alien in your body that none of us could finish.' 'Absolutely revolting,' concludes Nick.

＊＊＊＊＊＊＊＊＊＊＊＊

Amundsen was even more ascetic in the food he took with him on the sledges: there was pemmican, biscuits, chocolate and powdered milk. 'I have never considered it necessary to take a whole grocer's shop with me when sledging; the food should be simple and nourishing, and that is enough – a rich and varied menu is for people who have no work to do.' He was particularly fond of the biscuits. A bespoke offering from a Norwegian factory, they consisted of oatmeal, dried milk and sugar: 'they were extremely nourishing and pleasant to the taste.' The chocolate also came in handy. 'The Thermos flask is a splendid invention,' he enthused during one of the autumn depot journeys. 'We fill it every morning with boiling chocolate and drink it piping hot at noon. Not bad for the middle of the Barrier.'

As for the pemmican, this is one area where there ought to be absolute parity between the two modern teams because over in the Norwegian tent they are also fighting to keep down their rations.

The telling difference is that they have already accepted the inevitability of their diet for the next 99 days, and are even prepared to extol its beneficial properties.

'The biggest surprise is the pemmican,' says a startled Rune. 'It tastes shit. I was looking forward to tasting it, but this mix is not possible to describe. We will have to eat it when we get more hungry. You have two choices. You can eat it or not eat it. The pemmican is our main nutrition and if we don't eat that, we'll be quite slim. We need to get used to it. But there is a lot of energy in it. You have to be really careful in the first days not to eat too much of this because I don't think our stomachs will take it. With some biscuits it tastes a lot better.'

'I think it'll taste good in three months' time,' says Harald. 'Right now it goes down the throat and works its way back up. You really have to force it down in the stomach. The excitement about that is you never know when it will suddenly come up again.'

'I don't mind it. I have an iron stomach,' says John, before conceding, 'I may eat my words.'

But Ketil has also brought along some seal meat, which he boils in the tent. Amundsen ate seal meat twice a day over the winter in Framheim, and before the winter he deposited a load in his first depot. 'When we have our lunch,' Ketil says, 'we can just have a piece of cold meat and that's very nutritious.'

Two weeks into the trip they will each have settled into a culinary routine. John and Harald take their pemmican in the form of soup. John glugs his in one evening session. It induces a gag reflex every time, but he manages to keep it down. Harald seasons his with a lot of salt and pepper and saves some of it to eat cold. Inge can only eat his cold off a stick on the grounds that the unbearable flavour is less pronounced when it's not hot. Rune refuses to consume his whole ration, preferring to eat into his reserves of body fat than endure the pemmican's punitive taste. And Ketil prefers to eat the dog pemmican.

What would they not give for a slice of rubbery seal meat in the British team's tents? The jokes fly; the mood encouraged by Bruce who is relentlessly upbeat. But only now have they been granted a glimpse of what lies ahead, and the prospect is forbidding. After 3.9 hard-won miles, there are still 686 to go. The Norwegians are already ahead.

Bruce Parry's Diary

DAY 1

The race started at 8 a.m. and we set the alarm for 5 a.m. to get ourselves ready for a push-off on the second of race start time. As usual, though, we disregarded that plan and a lie-in was the order of the day as Rory's alarm froze at ten past midnight. No one fretted too much, as we finally got under way at 9.30.

Didn't get far, though, as we spent all morning trying to stop the dogs fighting, breaking loose and generally f**king about. The milometer on A sledge was trashed by marauding dogs before we even started. Mark's D team broke free while I was holding them and the six dogs took me on a cartoon drag through the snow. Great fun, but very frustrating. Nothing went right and we basically got nowhere.

Morale was up, but realization had firmly set in that this was going to be no picnic.

Arthur found some Werther's Originals – f**king Werther's Originals – that's taking period mayhem too far. F**king tasted great though.

Bitch on heat causing us lots of problems. Tried her in the front, rear and everywhere, but the others just wouldn't concentrate on pulling (accidental pun). In the end we took her away from the group and I led her up front like a drag hunt for the team. It worked and is our preferred method to date. (Dave doing compass and me with bitch – but now Dave doing both.)

DAY 2

Good start. Alarm worked. Off by 8 a.m. Great. Rory on his own doing a good job and other teams with various harness and biting problems following in our wake.

Cold – headwind – felt jackets.

Dogs slow in p.m. and snow conditions worsen. Face masks come out. Dogs are f**ked.

DAY 3

Nightmare begins. Very deep snow today and a cold wind. Going very tough and dogs and sledges alike are hating the snow build-up. It's like dragging the sledge through porridge. Every few metres, the dogs stop and it takes an age to get them going again.

The wind picks up. Arrive last to see the sledges prepping for camp. Dave had made the call to make camp cos the wind was getting worse and worse (gusting 60–65 knots). Happy that this call was made in my absence as it was the right call, but at back of my mind would have liked Dave to have approached me on my arrival to have let me know in person. Not worried, though – too much to do to sort out camp.

Difficult having the storm of the year to deal with when you're still getting to grips with 90-year-old shit gear. Tents go up after a fashion and dogs are dug in as usual. All hands retire to tents, but the spindrift is coming in everywhere. This is where the nightmare began. The valances just cannot be pinned down on the windblown snow. This means that the spindrift just blows straight inside. The routine begins of people going outside to try to weigh down the valances with boxes, poles, whatever. Trouble is that the wind is so strong that whatever is used as a weight just blows off after a time. This goes on into the night and my last turn comes at about 2 a.m., when the weather is at its worst. I wake with Nick saying that he is under a snowdrift and sure enough so am I (about 1.5 ft high, my head inside the tent). I dress to go outside with my Mongolian hat and open my hold-all to find it full of snow too. Bugger. Outside is mental. Can hardly stand upright and definitely not look into wind. Sledge is about 8 ft away and barely visible, but on coming back to tent cannot see it at all. Had to look for blue dog traces and follow them. Ten difficult steps back to tent. V exciting but quite dangerous. Do a good job of digging in boxed-up valances and it seems to work. Come back in and take photo of myself with icicles from eyelashes, etc. Get into bag covered in ice and all my outside gear. V cold but manage to melt all the ice and wake up soaking.

Our vent is blocked with ice and impossible to clear without venturing outside to find a bamboo pole. Heated spoons and leather thongs are used to no avail. Try cooking but vent on cooker is playing up and tent is full of noxious fumes and potentially lethal. End up having to open door, which of course brings in snow and cold. Bummer!

Nick valiantly ventures outside to check on dogs to ensure they're not stuck in with their chains. He crawls on hands and knees to drag out each one. V commendable and showing great affection for those hardy beasts of burden. He finds all but four which are invisible. We can only hope they're okay. I fear that if we lose any dogs Nick will not stay with us. He's really not enjoying the experience at all and has alluded to it being the worst thing he's ever done on more than one occasion. Is deeply unhappy, I believe, despite his happy exuberance.

The tent seems to be better after the last securing of the valances. No more snow entering the tent but all is soaked and frozen inside. A couple of rips will need sewing up, but tent has done well. All agree that last night was in essence a survival night and that if we'd had a real problem, we would have ultimately been on our own. Sobering thought for some, especially Nick, who had somehow believed that we as a group had 100 per cent safety back-up at all times. I'm surprised at this because it was always made quite clear that we are still taking risks in being here despite our back-up. Nick seems to have overlooked this and shows some worry. Whatever.

DAY 4
All day in bed.

CHAPTER FOUR

Hound and Horse

THE GREATEST DIFFERENCE BETWEEN SCOTT'S AND MY EQUIPMENT LAY
UNDOUBTEDLY IN OUR CHOICE OF DRAUGHT ANIMALS. WE HAD HEARD
THAT SCOTT ... HAD COME TO THE CONCLUSION THAT MANCHURIAN
PONIES WERE SUPERIOR TO DOGS ON THE BARRIER. AMONG THOSE
WHO WERE ACQUAINTED WITH THE ESKIMO DOG, I DO NOT SUPPOSE I
WAS THE ONLY ONE WHO WAS STARTLED ON FIRST HEARING THIS.'
Roald Amundsen

Neither sailor nor scientist nor landed gent, Cecil Meares was
the odd man out on the *Terra Nova* expedition. He came on the
recommendation of Ponting, whose photographs of him at Cape
Evans hint at the maverick flavour of his character. There is anec-
dotal corroboration of this. When Cherry-Garrard once told him
out on the ice that his nose was frostbitten, the veteran of many a
Siberian dog journey 'left it, saying that he had got tired of it,
and it would thaw out by and by'. On one of the various ships he
boarded between Vladivostock and New Zealand with Scott's consignment of 33 dogs and 19 ponies, he excited complaints from
other passengers for wearing pyjamas on deck. The source for this
is Scott's brother-in-law, Wilfred Bruce, who had been dispatched to
help him shepherd the pack animals south. The two did not get on.

'Not a bit my style,' said Bruce. Perhaps this coloured Scott's view of the man, his abilities and, ultimately, those of his dogs.

Scott arrived in Antarctica with the belief, formed on the *Discovery* expedition, that huskies thrived only over short distances. He had yet to find out just how well adapted they were to the longer haul. When he first witnessed them in action as the *Terra Nova* was unloaded and supplies were lugged across the sea ice to Cape Evans, he saw nothing to change his mind. 'They only take very light loads still and get back from each journey pretty dead beat. In their present state they don't inspire confidence.' Scott may have been overlooking the gruelling effects of the sea journey south, which the often-soaked dogs spent on deck. He also believed that Meares underfed them upon arrival in Antarctica. The depot-laying journey that autumn gave him further cause for misgiving. Meares was all for hopping on to the sledge in the Russian style, rather than running alongside. Scott believed the dogs did not need to pull the extra weight of their driver. 'Meares, I think, rather imagined himself racing to the pole and back on a dog sledge. This journey has opened his eyes a good deal.'

But there was also a moral, even prissy ingredient to Scott's suspicion. He abhorred cruelty to animals – it could even be described as his Achilles heel – so must have reacted badly when a pack of Meares's huskies attacked a stricken pony on the depot-laying journey. Plus he deplored the huskies' habit of eating their own excrement. (At Framheim, Amundsen took advantage of this penchant of theirs to keep the camp clean, encouraging them to scoff their owners' stools, too.)

Nor did Meares personally impress Scott later on the same journey, when most of his dog team tumbled down a crevasse. All but two were hauled up on the ropes still clipped to their harnesses, but the remaining pair had landed on a ledge 60 feet below. Scott ordered Meares to go down on a rope and retrieve them. He refused. The leader went down instead. 'Up to this day,' wrote Cherry, 'Scott had been talking to Meares of how dogs would go to the pole. After this, I never heard him say that.'

Instead, the dogs were to work on the Great Barrier. At the

staggered start of the polar journey, Meares's instructions were to leave last and catch up with the main pony party at the Lower Barrier Depot at 80 degrees 32 minutes, where Teddy Evans's motor party would soon be kicking their heels for six days. Meares timed his start inopportunely, and caught up with a tent-bound Scott still scarcely out of the blocks, the horses blinded by the horizontal gusts of the blizzard. It was 7 November. They would need another two weeks to reach the rendezvous. Even in a white-out, navigation for dogs was no problem. Encased in thick fur, sweating through their tongues only, their eyes untroubled by the blown snow thanks to a nictitating inner lid (a clear inner eyelid which can be drawn across the eyeball as protection), the dogs simply followed the smell of the horses. 'It is satisfactory,' Scott noted, 'to find the dogs can be driven to face such a wind as we have had. It shows that they ought to be able to help us a good deal.' It would have been useful to come to this realization earlier.

From this point Scott's thinking changed. He had, absurdly, flirted with the idea of lashing dogs to the sledges as far as the Beardmore Glacier, then using them to pull the sledges up the 120 miles of ice. He grudgingly allowed that they could assist on the Barrier journey, but as soon as he saw their potential in the harsh conditions, Meares and Gerof would now come further than planned and help pull the pony food. Eventually, the dogs went 145 miles further and two weeks longer than originally anticipated. This entailed a redistribution of the supplies already earmarked for the complicated journey ahead. If Meares went beyond the base of the glacier, as now mooted, he, Gerof and the dogs would need to eat into some of the depoted food on the way back. That food had to come from somewhere, and it came from the rations of the 12 men due to sledge up the glacier and on to the plateau.

Scott had other plans for Meares too. He had originally supposed that Meares would return to Cape Evans by 10 December, and he had asked him to bring out further supplies as far as One Ton Camp to make up a shortfall in stocks. Once Meares stayed out for longer, he would not get back until 5 January 1912, and yet Scott's final set of orders asked more of him than the ones they had superseded. He sent back an order with the final returning party that Meares or Atkinson should come another degree of latitude south, beyond the Lower Barrier Depot at Mount Hooper, to meet Scott's polar conquerors as they made their way back home. This order was issued despite the fact Scott had already conceded that keeping the dogs for more than a month longer on the Great Barrier might render them useless for further sledging.

In the end, Meares made no more journeys. The *Terra Nova* reappeared from New Zealand in McMurdo Sound on 4 February, and within the groaning postbag was a letter informing him of the death of his father. He left for home.

But then nothing in a polar expedition goes precisely to plan. Scott kept his dog-driver on for longer than he originally expected. The man now following in his footsteps loses his dog-driver rather earlier than expected.

* * * * * * * * * * * *

'Huskies are pack animals,' says John Huston. 'Historically they were raised in Inuit villages in a pack, and they have two feet in the wild and two feet in domestic life as working animals. A lot of people see dogs as pets in everyday life. Huskies are more like horses, with a friendly personality that can make them seem pet-like, but they enjoy living in a pack and they fight to figure out the hierarchy.'

The lore of husky-driving cannot be learnt overnight. The Norwegian team has the rough equivalent of the expertise available to Amundsen. Helmer Hanssen, who was Amundsen's dog-driver on the famous exploration of the Northwest Passage, always commanded the lead sledge, just as Ketil Reitan does over the hundreds of miles of the Greenland ice cap. Hanssen saw his leader 'as a kind of father', and was in the front line when it came to showing his loyalty. Sverre Hassel, the other husky expert on Amundsen's team, was initially hired to look after the dogs in Denmark, where they were cared for after arriving from Greenland. He had no plans to sail with the *Fram*, but Amundsen persuaded him aboard. When he much later revealed his scheme to switch the expedition from North Pole to South, Hassel was one of the first men he cannily took into his confidence, and he duly consented to stay on. There would be no pole without the best men available to drive the dogs.

The hierarchy put in place by Amundsen in Antarctica, with one overlord and a team of men dancing unquestioningly to his tune, was not dissimilar from the social structure of a well-trained pack of huskies. 'Dogs are most comfortable when they know who the top dog is,' says John, 'If the top dog is well known, there is no need to fight. And ideally that top dog is metaphorically the musher. The musher is always in control. When the musher does not have enough control or the dogs haven't figured how comfortable they are with their structure, there can be problems.' At Framheim all but Johansen knew who the top dog was.

The less authority the musher – John uses the American term – has over his dog team, the greater the likelihood of fighting. 'The musher's job is to have a comfortable structure for the dogs as far as knowing when to wait and when to go and how to calm dogs down and who to place next to each other. Even if that is very strict, the dogs will appreciate it and perform better and they are happier. Most of the dogs fight just out of stress. They don't see the big picture. If something is feeling funny or they're tired of waiting in one spot, which is very difficult to do for dogs used to moving, then they will maybe take it out on their neighbour because that's the closest thing around. It's not necessarily aggression all the time. It's just stress. Dog fights often look extremely vicious, but aren't necessarily harmful. Dogs are physical animals who communicate physically.'

By Day 2, the Norwegian team have started to establish authority over their 48 dogs. One of the ways they do this is historically accurate: they use force, though nothing like as vigor-ously as their predecessors. Amundsen and his men first had to deploy it in the most trying phase of the depot journey. 'The poor dogs had to be whipped on,' wrote Johansen one day. The next day 'they don't take any notice of thrashing any more, just lie down in their tracks, and it is a terrible performance to get them going again.' They beat the dogs so vigorously in the autumn that over the winter they were obliged to fashion new whips with stronger shafts.

The problem was not the whipping action itself. The handle broke when they gave a dog what they called a 'confirmation': that is, a stronger reminder than a mere crack of the whip in their ears. 'It consists in taking the first opportunity when the sledge stops,' explained Amundsen, 'of going in among the dogs, taking out the defiant one, and laying into him with the handle. These confirmations, if they occur frequently, may use up a lot of handles.'

Amundsen knew that posterity would take a dim view of this unadulterated violence, and was ready with his excuses. 'One does not have to be more brutal than other people; one can suffer because one has to do so, but if one does not use the means he has to get the dogs forward, when it is difficult, he may just as well give up completely.' Only Hanssen was sparing with the lash ('he had his dogs well in hand, and they knew their master'). The dogs were more obedient by the time the main quest for the pole began. On the first day they could 'sit on the sledges and flourish our whips with a jaunty air'. After three weeks the dogs pulled 'with the greatest ease … we never had to move a foot; all we had to do was let ourselves be towed'.

Scott's men refused to carry pony whips altogether. If need be, they would use the reins. Bruce Parry's team send home their big leather whips, less out of a concern for animal welfare than simply to save weight on the sledges. 'The dogs respond to the noise of a whip,' explains Mark Anstice, 'but we couldn't use them properly and we didn't want to hit the dogs.' Later they regret ditching them 'as this is what they've been trained on. They don't respond to "good doggy". Their ancestry is wolves and they're not to be messed with. They don't respect us if we pussyfoot around them.'

With a show of force, the fighting among Amundsen team's dogs decreased, and the mileage increased. They did nearly 10 miles on Day 2. On Day 6 they did 13; on Day 9, more than 20. Unfortunately, their distances between these days were non-existent. Amundsen may have forged a path forwards in some extremely testing weather, but even he had to sit in his tent and twiddle his thumbs when conditions forced his hand. For the modern Norwegian team, the weather strikes early. Antarctica has its own violent katabatic winds. Greenland has a local variant, known as a *piteraq*. Descending when air falls from the inland ice and chases down the fjords and valleys towards the sea, it can show up at any time and will easily blow humans off their feet. Greenlanders, all of whom live on the coast, hasten indoors at the first hint of it to avoid not only the wind itself, but the assorted flying debris, which may include driven snow, sand, rocks and ice particles the size of golf balls.

The Norwegians are confined to their tents for Days 3 and 4, and again on Day 8. Three days lost to bad weather so early in the expedition ought to be deeply frustrating for Rune Gjeldnes. 'Delay is my biggest concern,' he admits, 'because then my schedule will not hold at all.' But he seems mostly positive. For all his vast Arctic experience, he has something new to think about: these have been his first few days in command of a dog sledge, and it is going well. 'It is hard being a musher. I'd never driven dogs, but I have a very good dog team, which is really nice – no big fights, happy dogs.'

In these days Ketil manages to drive the dogs for the first time without the help of Inge skiing out a furrow in front. 'If we can do that, we will pick up speed because the dogs can move faster,' says Rune. 'If Ketil can continue working with his dogs, I will be really lucky. We're going to take good care of those dogs because they are our engine. I'm starting to really like them all, or most of them. Some of them are not so good to handle.' He has a special word for John Huston, the second dog-handler and the youngest member of the team. 'Everyone sees what they have to do and no one has to be told what to do which is good. But John has amazed me most. He is an outstanding man, and always smiling and in a good mood all the time.'

Their growing affinity with the dogs is almost a carbon copy of Amundsen's. 'Drove off 9 a.m.,' wrote Bjaaland as they headed out from the first depot on 26 October 1911. 'Dogs as if possessed, careered off like madmen. Going good and terrain flat and fine. Distance 15.6 miles from 9 a.m. to 1.30 p.m.'

But the dogs could not always be counted on. On 1 November they ran into dense fog and a huge field of crevasses created by disturbance to the Barrier from a glacier flowing off land nearly

100 nautical miles to the east. Noting that the crevasses seemed for the most part to be both narrow and running perpendicular to their route, the Norwegians persevered. Not all the crevasses were so narrow, however. 'The ugliest formations we have found here are huge holes that could take *Fram*, and a lot more besides,' wrote Amundsen. 'These holes are covered by a thin wind crust, and the little hole that is visible doesn't seem so difficult. But if one gets on to such a delightful spot, one is irrevocably lost. We passed one of these holes in the "pea souper" today. Luckily HH [Helmer Hansen] saw it in time. There is not much that escapes his eye.

'We are all clear. What risk we run in our march over such unpleasant stretches. We go with our lives in our hands each day. But it is pleasant to hear nobody wants to turn back.'

Amundsen here made light of the near-catastrophe in which Hanssen, with the lead sledge, came close to a fatal summons from the deep. As his skis became entangled in the dog lines, he fell on to a snow bridge. Enough of the bridge fell away to afford him an unrivalled view of the darkening infinity below. But it held so long as the pressure was distributed around his prone form. Wisting dragged him to safety, while Amundsen attempted to impose peace on Hanssen's huskies, whose ensuing fight dragged the sledge and a quarter of their supplies perilously close to the lip of the crevasse. It became a joke among them that Hanssen rather enjoyed his brushes with the deep.

The fog persisted, but they slogged on unshaken. Making 15 nautical miles a day, every four days they knocked another degree of latitude off the distance separating them from 90 degrees south. They would soon start increasing their daily mileages.

(Much later on the journey Bowers would echo Amundsen's grim account of yawning holes in the terrain when he came upon 'vast crevasses into which we could have dropped the *Terra Nova* easily'.)

* * * * * * * * * * * *

After their disastrous first day on the ice, the modern British team might hope for an improved performance. If nothing else, they now know what havoc the dogs are capable of causing. But they are unprepared for the havoc caused by a *piteraq*. Scott encountered two fierce storms: one as he drew up in front of the Beardmore Glacier, the other as he, Wilson and Bowers lay stranded 11 miles short of One Ton Camp on the return journey. Bruce's team have never seen anything like it. Spindrift flies around the inside of one tent, and Bruce wakes up with a sleeping bag full of snow. In the other tent they note that the air within judders so dramatically that Arthur Jeffes can blow a smoke ring and make it move with the tent. They are confined to their tents on Days 3 and 4.

In these early struggles, Bruce seems to have one short, demoralizing sequence of film running through the private cinema inside his head: Ponting's footage of Scott departing at greater speed, and in better weather. 'It's just tough going,' he says. 'The dogs are very frustrating. They are weaker, they are very immature and, according to Nick, they are not used to the loads. We've reduced our loads. We've done everything we can and it's just part of the story. There's not much more that we can do.'

On Day 5, things improve ever so slightly – less in terms of distance than in the evidence that the dogs may now be starting to cooperate. A thick topsoil of treacly snow continues to limit progress to a heartbreakingly slow slog. When they do start to accelerate, a fresh layer of snow slows them down again. But the team manages 3.4 miles. It may not be much, but they would be buoyed to know that it's 3.4 miles more than the Norwegians have done.

Unfortunately, there is a price to pay. The team has yet to establish a means of controlling the 1911-style sledges, which have no built-in brake. The only feasible way of halting a runaway dog team is to deploy the snow anchor. A vicious-looking implement with several big hooks, it is thrown by the driver out to the rear of the sledge. Nick Akers advises the team to 'make sure they are planted properly and that you don't get in the way of them because it's almost a lethal weapon'. Nonetheless, Mark Anstice nearly lacerates a main artery on his snow anchor, Dave cuts himself, and then Nick has a more serious accident.

'The dogs were heading off first thing in the morning with a big loaded sledge,' he explains, 'and the guys who were looking after it couldn't get on it so as it came past I jumped on to add some weight and slow it down. The sledge was going down quite a dip into the ice, and as it bottomed out, the top of the snow anchor where the handle is came up under my ribs really hard. It was quite a big impact and I thought, this is going to hurt, and as the day has gone on, it's just got worse and worse.' He spends the rest of the day simply walking alongside the sledge. In the evening he is inspected by the team doctors Rory O'Connor and Chris van Tulleken. They diagnose suspected broken ribs, which he may just have been able to carry on with, but it is the possibility of a ruptured spleen that seals his early departure.

Thus Nick's journey is over almost before it has begun. In 1911 he'd have been on the first sledge home. In 2005 he's on a Twin Otter aircraft. He looks downcast as he emerges from the tent after an uncomfortable night on painkillers. From the plane he waves disconsolately at his companions through the window. Three days previously, however, he has all but admitted that he may have bitten off more than he can chew. Ripping his reindeer sleeping bag before departure condemned him to a freezing first night on the ice. He reacts worse than most to the prospect of eating pemmican for up to 99 days. And then the dogs run riot. He is used to running his own dogs at up to 25 miles an hour. The disappointment must weigh heavily.

'Even though we've been joking and are mentally up for it,' he says by the end of the Day 1, 'throughout today you always have these thoughts. You think about your family because you miss them a lot and you think, what am I doing here? The food that we have available is just awful. I had some pemmican last night and thought I was going to vomit it back up in the tent. It was just revolting. It was so awful that I haven't been able to eat anything today apart from three squares of chocolate. Hopefully things will improve in the next few days. My own fitness is awful, too. Even though I tried to be quite fit before I came, I'm just struggling. I was wondering today whether I'd be able to do a day of this, let alone a full trip.'

Even though he protests that he is 'gutted about going', it

doesn't take a psychologist to work out that there is a silver lining to his injury. No more cold nights, no more pemmican, no more unruly dogs. And when he gets back to Tassilaq his ribs are found to be intact, his spleen unpunctured. He has a clean bill of health. Back on the ice, Bruce seems to intuit that Nick will not return, nor perhaps be so welcome if he does. 'Unfortunately,' he says, 'that's the last we are going to see of Nick on this expedition. Whatever happens, he won't be able to come back.'

The leader is now presented with a dilemma. He is on Day 5 of a 690-mile trip to the pole, after which he has to turn round and come back again as far as he can. He has the dogs for 40 days in total, the same length of time as Scott kept Meares's dogs. But his Meares has been invalided home, leaving no one on his team with any experience in handling husky teams, beyond four trying days in which they have covered the miserly distance of 10.9 miles. Deprived of the expertise of his dog-driver, Bruce briefly wonders whether it might be worth ditching all 24 dogs when the Twin Otter flies in, even though he is meant to be shadowing the *Terra Nova* story. 'We should stay as we are with three teams of eight or get rid of some dogs,' he muses. 'It's just a nightmare that here it's very deep snow and they can't hack it all day. Everyone in their little moment will admit that they are finding it harder than they thought it would be. You can see they are just literally on their knees at the end of the day.' But, as ever, when there is a slough of despond to plunge into, Bruce's optimism carries the day. 'There is no doubt that the dogs are better than they were. We'd be foolish to lose them because, when the weather gets good, the dogs will come into their own. We've just got to persevere at the moment.'

* * * * * * * * * * * *

For Scott the problem turned out to be the horses, not the dogs. It was quite an army that mustered in the lee of Mount Hooper on 21 November. Cherry-Garrard counted: 'Sixteen men, five tents, ten ponies, twenty-three dogs and thirteen sledges.' There were a lot of stomachs to feed. The ponies were under the overall charge of the cavalry officer Oates, who had initially expressed approval of the specimens Meares had delivered to New Zealand. 'Dear Mother,' he wrote, 'The ponies themselves are first class.' He would soon modify his opinion, at least for Scott's consumption. Or perhaps he didn't wish to saddle his doting widowed mother with information that might alarm her. Scott remained optimistic. 'I withhold my opinion of the dogs,' he wrote on the autumn depot journey, 'in much doubt as to whether they are going to be a real success – but the ponies are going to be a real good ... They work with such extraordinary steadiness, stepping out briskly and cheerfully.'

By the end of the autumn depot journey, six of the eight ponies he took with him were dead, though it would have been the same if Oates had had his way. Oates had pragmatically advocated a controlled killing spree in which horse meat would be depoted out on the Barrier to be fed to the dogs on the polar journey. If Scott abhorred the sight of dogs contentedly guzzling their excrement, he squirmed even more at the sight of the horses suffering. 'I have had more than enough of this cruelty to animals,' he said when urged by Oates to drag the ponies another 30 miles further south, 'and I'm not going to defy my feelings for the sake of a few days' march.' Oates told him he'd rue the day, but Scott had taken his stance 'as a Christian gentleman'. (Ponting's stock of film includes a wonderful bit of hypocrisy in this vein: it shows killer whales closing in on a seal pup, only to be scared off by the firing of a protective harpoon. Whales could not kill seals, it seems, but Scott's men could slaughter them by the dozen for meat and blubber fuel.)

So the depot horses were spared Oates's *coup de grâce*. Then they died anyway, none in a convenient place for storing meat. Some met their end having staggered much of the way back from One Ton Camp. Others got most of the way home, only to star in the dreadful saga of the melting sea ice. They were pickaxed to death and their bodies left for the killer whales. Later on, Scott might indeed have regretted ignoring Oates's advice. If One Ton Camp had been half a degree further south, Scott, Bowers and Wilson would not have been stranded 11 miles short of it.

Scott's Christian values were never intended to survive the winter. On the polar journey the plan was to take the ponies south and, successively killing them once they could go no further, depot them for canine and human consumption. However dreadfully they turned out to suffer, Scott planned to rely on horse power because Shackleton had taken four ponies as far as the Beardmore Glacier on the *Nimrod* expedition. And if it worked once ...

Each of the ponies was led by a man condemned to proceed without skis, however yielding the snow, because the swooshing noise unnerved their charges. If human legs plunged knee-deep into the snow, it was worse for the horses. Scott had foreseen this and brought with him a consignment of equestrian snowshoes they called *hesterko* after the wooden horsehoes known in Norwegian as *hestertruger*. Oates, for whatever reason, left all but one pair behind at Cape Evans on the autumn depot-laying journey. The one pair he did bring out smartly improved the performance of the old crock on whom they were fitted. They tried to use them now, but the ponies turned out not to like them. Not long before they shot it, Wilson's pony was finally persuaded to wear the shoes, and they realized what they had been missing: 'There is no doubt that these snowshoes are *the* thing for ponies,' wrote Scott.

Scott's departure a week later than Amundsen was entirely due to the ponies' intolerance of extreme cold. On the polar journey, one sluggish pony party was swiftly dubbed the Baltic Fleet, after an ill-fated Russian navy squadron of recent memory, sunk by the Japanese. But the more able ponies were just as afflicted by the cold. Their winter coats notwithstanding, they simply weren't built for the temperatures they encountered. At every stop the men had to spend valuable time building snow walls to protect them from the worst effect of the wind.

Oates described the ponies as 'awful cripples', but admitted they had done better than he dared hope after the depot journey. They managed a dozen miles a day. 'Scott told me today he was very pleased with the way the ponies were going and was kind enough to say he owed me a lot for the trouble I had taken.' As the horses, each one at its own pace, slowly succumbed to exposure and exhaustion, icicles forming on their noses and blankets of frozen sweat gripping their flanks, the dogs were quite happy burrowing in their snowholes. Too late, Scott's eyes were starting to open. One night in the tent he talked about his previous experience with dogs on the *Discovery* expedition, which had so turned him against them. 'He thought they did everything wrong with their dogs,' noted Cherry-Garrard in his diary, adding, '[He] evidently thinks Amundsen with his dogs may be doing much better.'

The first pony was shot on 24 November, the same day as Hooper the steward and Day the mechanic became the first pair to turn for home with two underperforming dogs and a small sledge to pull. 'Two-men parties on the Barrier are not much fun,' noted Cherry-Garrard in sympathy. They bore home the news that Scott was changing his plans. 'Ponies doing fairly well,' he wrote to George Simpson, the meteorologist back at Cape Evans. 'I hope we shall get through to the Glacier without difficulty but to make sure I am carrying the dog teams further than I intended at first – the teams may be late returning, unfit for further work or non-existent … In case [they] are unable to [bring further stores to One Ton Camp] it will be necessary to organize a man-hauling party to undertake it.'

The first horse they killed, Jehu, turned out to have a surprising residue of flesh on him. Meares informed Scott that he had supplied 'four good feeds for the dogs'. He added that one more pony would see him through to the Glacier. There was more pony meat than the dogs could ever eat. After each kill, while the horse-drawn sledges marched out of camp, Meares and Gerof were to stay behind and bury the carcass under snow out of the light of the sun. It was a fitting end for the ponies: selected by Meares in Siberia, they were now interred by him in Antarctica. Not all the meat survived, however.

The killing continued sporadically, with the leader's Christian sensibilities wavering around the dial. 'Scott feels this kind of thing a lot,' wrote Cherry-Garrard, but not according to Scott's own diary. 'We hope Jehu will last three days; he will then be finished in any case and fed to the dogs. It is amusing to see Meares looking eagerly for the chance of a feed for his animals; he has been expecting it daily.' Bowers's conscience was certainly clear. 'A year's care and good feeding, three weeks' work with good treatment, a reasonable load and a good ration, and then a painless end. If anybody can call that cruel I cannot either understand it or agree with them.' Ever the sunniest of optimists, he did lament the death of his own pony, Victor, who was killed because the dogs were hungry. He 'did a splendid march and kept ahead all day, and as usual marched in camp first, pulling over 450 pounds easily. It seemed an awful pity to have to shoot a great strong animal ... Good old Victor! He has always had a biscuit out of my ration, and he ate his last before the bullet sent him to his rest ... I feel sorry for a beast that has been my constant companion and care for so long. He has done his share in our undertaking anyhow, and may I do my share as well when I get into harness myself.'

They all felt like that about their horses. There is little evidence that the dogs either aroused affection or even misbehaved, as they do with Bruce's team and as they sometimes did with Amundsen. But one particular horse was a constant, energy-sapping thorn in their side. Christopher, in the care of Oates, was cantankerous to the last. 'He was the only pony who did not die instantaneously,' recalled Cherry-Garrard. 'Just as Oates fired, he moved, and charged into the camp with the bullet in his head. He was caught with difficulty ... led back and finished. We were well rid of him: while he was strong he fought, and once the Barrier had tamed him, as we were not able to do, he never pulled a fair load.'

The remaining five ponies were shot at the base of the Beardmore Glacier on 9 December at a place they mournfully named Shambles Camp. Scott thanked Oates for getting them to pull at least some of the supplies as far as the glacier. Wilson thanked a higher authority. 'Thank God the horses are done with, and we begin the heavier work ourselves.'

* * * * * * * * * * * *

Suddenly shorn of their dog expertise, it is at this point that Bruce's team could do with some advice from the opposition. What makes a good dog team? How do you distribute the different personalities along the line? Who goes at the front, the back? Bruce's novice handlers need answers to these questions, and fast.

'These dogs are athletes,' says John. 'It's amazing the drive they have to work. We'll be very tired by the end of the day, and they'll be wagging their tails because they love what they do. The most important dogs in any team are the lead dogs. If your lead dogs aren't good, your team won't go anywhere. They must have a natural ability, a confidence in being up at the front, and enjoy being chased. But some dogs don't think so much. They just get in the harness and pull, pull, pull. Dogs like that are more often at the back. There is less decision-making. The dogs in the rear of a team will pull most of the weight, especially of a heavy sled. Their hips will sustain more of the downward force of the tug line as they are closer to the sledge and at an angle. So you can put strong dogs at the back. Sometimes it's good to mix up where you put dogs in the team based on how they get along with each other and to give them a different point of view. Some dogs will love being a rear dog their whole life. That's what they want to do. Anything else is too different. Also some dogs are fiercely loyal to who they run with and have a strong bond, while some dogs don't care so much who they run with but it's important to keep dogs who are aggressive toward each other separated in the team.'

It's this final point that the British team will have worked out for themselves. Bruce's line on the dogs stays, as it were, consistently inconsistent throughout 40 days in their company. They are 'our greatest asset' and 'our greatest hindrance'. They are 'frustrating' and 'rewarding', 'great friends' and 'terrible nuisances'. 'We have a love-hate relationship with the dogs,' he says at one point. 'When they're good they're very good but when they're bad they drive you to despair. They just get themselves into tangles, they're fighting, they won't pull, they won't go left, they won't go right.' But when it's going well 'you forgive them everything'. There are local variations to his attitude, depending on how well they are pulling. On Day 22 he says, 'One thing is for sure: they have helped us a massive amount'. But apparently it's not for sure because: on another day he says, 'The dogs haven't been as efficient as I thought.'

But Bruce's knowledge of the dogs, like Scott's, is at one remove. Although he helps feed them, he spends less time on the sledges than anyone apart from Dave Pearce. It's Chris van Tulleken and Mark Anstice on one sledge, Rupert Elderkin and Arthur Jeffes on another, and Rory O'Connor on the third, who become intimately acquainted with their caprices.

Curiously, on the day after Nick's departure, the daily distances improve: 7.5 nautical miles, 7.2, 9.6. Initially when they try leaping on the moving sledge, it grinds to a halt if the going is too treacly. But once they start to move, they all ride Russian-style, as Meares had hoped to all the way to the pole. 'My dog team is not really a team,' says Mark on Day 12. 'They are becoming a team. I've just been running all day, pushing the sledge, yelling at them every three seconds. At the end of each day I've been absolutely shattered. But today I've been sitting on top and it's been great. I got thrown off within about 30 feet. The sledge did the first of three overturns. But it was brilliant. It was good fun. Like a rollercoaster ride.'

From Day 13 they do clear 10 and then 11 miles three days running, but Mark's capacity for being baffled by their quirks is undiminished. 'I think I'm beginning to get the measure of the dogs. I don't understand what makes them just stop mid-afternoon. I know it's not because they're physically shattered because four of them will be pulling the sledge and four will be arsing around, not pulling their weight. So I know they're capable of it. I think it's just because they are just not used to working this hard or being out here in the middle of nowhere. They just seem to hit this mental wall mid-afternoon. My lead dog – I love him to bits, but he's hopeless. There is a fight for ascendancy going on between him and another dog. They were chewing chunks off each other today. Blood all over the snow. I tried mixing them up but then this other dog, the aggressor, just intimidates the other dogs further back in the chain. No one was running, so I had to put him back where he was.' The learning curve is not so much steep as vertical.

The one thing they know for certain is that they have to keep the bitch on heat well out of sight of her suitors. On Day 14, after those three days of solid mileage comparable to any of Scott's days on the

Barrier, Rupert is taken off the sledge and comes out in front with Bruce and Dave. He keeps the errant female on a short lead and she trots along cooperatively. 'I think she's spotted her boyfriend,' he says at one point. 'What?' says Dave. 'All fourteen of them?'

(Amundsen continued to shoot his bitches. At the depot at 83 degrees south, three admirers of one pined so much that they deserted and, Amundsen guessed, scampered back northwards to the cairn on which her corpse was thrown. The last received the bullet on 7 November. 'She was Hassel's pride and the ornament of his team; but there was no help for it.')

Then there are the problems arising from what happens when the going is simply too good. The navigator will set out on skis long before the dogs set out, and within a mile he has been caught up. Hence Scott's staggered start to the marches on the Barrier. Wary of the snow anchor, they work on various techniques for braking the sledge. Digging feet into the snow proves ineffectual if eight dogs have gathered any sort of head of steam. They experiment with putting ropes around the runners. 'I need to know I can stop the sledge,' says Rory, who describes one day's sledging as 'a bucking bronco ride. It took all our efforts just to hold on for dear life, let alone think about where we're going.' Later he has to concede that snow anchors exist for a reason: no other method works. 'Today has been all about using snow anchors, trying not to spike yourself. It's a definite art.'

However well they may go, the dogs suffer from overheating, which they remedy by rolling around in the snow. There are also injuries from fighting. 'One big fight today,' says Rory chirpily one day. 'Unfortunately, the lead dog had his ear chewed by one of the back dogs.' Bleeding paws are less easily dealt with. One of Mark's dogs has a split pad half an inch deep which becomes badly infected. 'I don't know how many litres they have but I expect him to drop dead any minute. They are amazing creatures.' The doctors, doubling as vets, put the dog on antibiotics.

Human injury is also a risk. 'With the dogs you get speed,' says O'Connor, 'and anything with speed can be dangerous.' One day he is careering along and only just avoids an accident when his sledge nearly collides with Mark's, which has come to a halt. 'I suddenly realized that if I didn't do something right away, I was going to plough dogs and all into the back of him. So I leapt off and I was holding on to the ropes on the side of the sledge, putting both feet into the ground trying to get some friction going. It wasn't working. My own rope breaks. The last thing is the snow anchor. We've had all kinds of trouble with these snow anchors and I'm always very wary of them, especially at speed. I came back along the ropes, got the anchor, and tried to place it in the ground. I think I caught one of my legs on the rope as I did that, and next thing I know I'm looking up at the sky and flat on my back. I think the anchor has hit my left leg and the sledge is about 6 or 7 feet ahead. The dogs had all pulled backwards and the sledge has slid alongside. I felt very fortunate when I was able to stand up. It was such an impact on my leg it felt like I'd done something quite serious.'

Elsewhere on the ice, the Norwegians with their dozen dogs per sledge and their two expert dog-drivers are racking up daily distances closer to the 20-mile mark, far more than Amundsen allowed himself at the same stage of the journey. The British team know nothing of this. As the dogs approach their big test, and they continue to deliver reasonable distances, Rory occasionally succumbs to a feeling of well-being.

'It's a shame that Nick is not here to enjoy it. He had the worst part of the dogs and now he'd be overjoyed with what they are achieving. Psychologically, we now think we are doing the distances that will count. Your mind is constantly on the dogs. What are they doing? Is anybody biting the line? Who is not pulling? You don't have time for any other kind of thought at all. We get back to the tent in the evening brain dead. But today was completely different. It reminds me of a print at home on my wall of [the polar explorer] Wally Herbert in Greenland. The picture shows the dogs fanned out in front and this beautiful landscape ahead with a dark, watery sky. It has always mesmerized me. Never for one moment did I think years later that I'd be here. It's a dream come true.'

Rune Gjeldnes's Diary

Finally, we got started, although much delayed. Set off at 11 a.m. Had 45, 50, 100 stops, arguing, trying, failing. Changed the order of the sledges. A minor chaos, but I guess you can't expect more. John got bitten by a dog. The tent got torn again in the evening. Need more routine. DEEP SNOW. Pemmican.

DAY 3

Up late last night. Harald was working hard at the navigation. We managed to correct a few errors, which were rather big. The sun reading was completely wrong. Not sure where the error lies, but most likely it's the watches. 50 sec increase per day is a lot. I can see the difficulty with motivation for the navigator when you know the answer is going to be wrong anyway. We came to the conclusion that our course is not so terribly wrong, though. A bit too far eastwards. The weather came before we'd managed to take the tent down, which was just as well. A quick, small storm coming on. Not a good idea to set off then, with our level of experience. So this became our first resting day. Oh yes, it's very windy! It looks as though everyone is having a nice time even though we're all very eager to get a move on. But we did a good summing up after having built a big snow wall behind the tent. The snow will firm up and the going will be better for us, or rather, for the dogs, plus two hard days and one resting day will do them good.

Otherwise the team is working well together. Proud of John who really is a tower of strength and shows a lot of initiative without ever taking over. The man is clearly a good diplomat. Anyway, everyone is doing what they should, but we could become more efficient. Don't want to stress people too much in the beginning. Get the routine, then push it, more efficiency.

Have been out with Harald and John. Done the sun readings and meridian passage, and the wind's blowing a gale outside. It looks like the dogs aren't very happy in the hard wind. Tried making a few small snow walls. Maybe it'll help. Otherwise …

DAY 4

So the small storm grew into something quite different. Got our first *piteraq*.

Had to repair the snow wall a couple of times. And dig out the tent every hour during the evening. Four men outside, one man inside. Hard work for us all. We had to buy and make wind-resistant mittens ourselves. If we hadn't done that, the journey would have been over. This has been survival, and made everyone understand that it's up to them to do their best for us. What we've been most worried about has been the tent. Is it going to hold? Amazingly, it has so far. Everyone is packed and dressed in case anything should happen. The sleeping bags are the most important things to take away with us in case anything does happen. Two men on guard all night. I'm one of them. The rest have been lying on top of their sleeping bags, freezing. Can see in everyone's eyes that they know this is for real. The worst winds came around 2–3 a.m. Out in shifts to dig the tent out, but the accumulation of snow ceased eventually. In the morning it felt important to have a man on watch. Have been lying dozing all day. The wind (GMT 0200) has receded a bit. We've all been sitting chatting about this and that. Now we're clearing the tent of ice and snow. Hopefully we'll all be able to sleep in our sleeping bags tonight. Hopefully we'll get to feed the dogs, those poor bastards. Tough animals. But we should be proud of our team. Everyone is very solution-focused. Ketil, John, Inge, Harald and I are the A-team. The start has been bad, so it can only get better. As the leader I should probably have been more pushy, but luckily the guys lack neither initiative nor ideas.

Everyone has started eating seal meat, which we were joking with Ketil about before we started.

DAY 5
Accident tonight. A big pan of water fell over when Inge and Ketil were trying to get the snow off the sidewall of the tent. Mine and Harald's sleeping bags got wet in the tsunami. Out to dig away the snow while Ketil was sorting things out inside. Small but annoying events. The day looks promising, though. The snow has become firm and there's a mild wind towards us. We're far behind schedule, but I guess it's just to be expected that there will be stops; it just came very early. We've had a hard start with loose snow, breaking in the dogs – which is still going on, and then the *piteraq*. Quite a lot really for four days.

Bruce Parry's Diary

DAY 5

Alarm late.

Wind has died, but still misty. Spend the morning digging out the poor dogs (who are all present and correct, hungry and pleased to be found). Our tent and sledges are completely covered in places by drifts.

Get under way, and although I didn't know it at the time, Nick has a bad accident early in the day. Sledges are hard going in places and he's on one when it bottoms out and he gets a blunt hit to his lower chest/abdomen.

Weather comes in and all sledges having a hard time of it.

Mark has a dreadful near miss with the snow anchor, and it's a sobering tale which we all take in later. He's lacerated his leg right by his femoral artery and if it had been half an inch deeper he might well have died or at least lost his leg. Ouch! No chance of evacuation in the present weather.

Make camp.

Nick pain.

DAY 6

Set off 2 p.m.

Going better – 3.9 miles.

Wind picked up. Tents up 5 p.m.

'Got rid of Nick.'

V cold. Minus 20 degrees Celsius.

DAY 7

The dogs set off without a hitch and the going was fantastic for the first two hours. Skating along on solid crust snow was a dream … The sun got warmer and the irony of the day was that the weather beat us again. This time the sun made the crust melt a bit and the going got tougher and tougher. It slowed us down so much that unanimously we decided to call it a day at about 4 or 5.8 statute miles done.

Day 8

The going tougher than ever. Dogs not interested and just going nowhere (slow). Mark had a shit start and I walked back to meet him (1 mile).

But then he bunged Chris on to skies at midday and suddenly his team was the fastest of all. He shot ahead, sitting on his sledge using a bamboo cane to swish over the dogs' heads to chivvy them on. Brilliant. Rupert and Arthur going well too, but for some reason me and Rory having a nightmare. No leader works, and we've changed the two dominant males to no avail. Rory and me absolutely f**ked by the end, and so thirsty – not pleasant. (Others sat on sledges with occasional pushes. Bastards.

Day 9

Best day yet by a long long way … I went ahead with Chris all day. Mark gets frustrated with his lackadaisical attitude, but I've not really witnessed it yet. He certainly acts helpful and says all the right things. Not sure if it's Mark being a perfectionist and somewhat easily agitated by dog-sledging. I may soon swap tents with Mark to see how the others are doing. I feel I must do some more work with them to assess them fully for my selection of final four to pole. So far I'm favouring Mark, Dave and Chris, but if Chris proves too lazy, then Rory and Rupert are both v solid. In fact, Rory is an absolute diamond and very industrious. Chris probably my preferred company, but Rory a better expeditioner.

CHAPTER FIVE

Navigation

How do you find your way around an unimaginably large field of snow? How do you know you're going in the right direction, or how far you have travelled? How, in the end, do you locate a purely notional dot of ice lurking invisibly – unrecognizably – somewhere in a landscape whose salient feature is an utter absence of features? It may be known by its mathematical name of 90 degrees south, but how much maths do you have to do to get there? And once you *have* got there, how do you find your way back?

Long before Admiral Ross ever breached Antarctica's protective girdle of pack ice and entered the sea that would take his name, long before Captain Cook established that New Zealand was not, as previously put about, the northern tip of a vast continent at the bottom of the world, it was assumed that something was there. The Greeks – Aristotle, Ptolemy – theorized that there must be. With absolutely no evidence for it, the cartographers of the Renaissance imagined a southerly continent that, to be on the safe side, they envisaged on their maps as the biggest chunk of land on the planet. How else could the globe, newly known to be spherical, remain in equilibrium? There was all that land in the northern hemisphere, and it needed a counterweight in the south. On their maps they drafted it as white, not because they knew it must be cold, but because they had no idea what, if anything, was there. It was known as *Terra Australis Incognita*, or the Unknown Southern Land.

Incognita is largely what it still was when Scott's *Discovery* expedition reached Antarctica in 1902. By the time Scott returned on the *Terra Nova* nine years later, much more was known. Scott himself had trudged hundreds of miles towards the interior with Wilson and Shackleton. Not that, after leaving Hut Point, they ever actually set foot on land until they got back. The Great Barrier, they discovered, went on for ever and ever, until one day the mist cleared and they'd bumped into the Transantarctic Mountains. The next sledging season Scott, with the stokers Lashly and Taff Evans for company, found a glacier splicing the mountains near to the base, and went up on to the Polar Plateau.

When Shackleton returned on the *Nimrod*, he used that hard-won knowledge of the terrain to plunge into the heart of the continent. There was a plateau high on the other side of the mountainous rampart. If Scott had found a way up to it, there was no reason why he shouldn't find one too. Travelling across the Barrier, familiar to him from his journey with Scott and Wilson, he eventually came within sight of the Transantarctic range. He duly skirted along in its shadow until he chanced upon the highway he called the Great Glacier. At the top of it was the plateau, and somewhere away off in the middle of it, the South Pole.

Wherever there are landmarks, navigation becomes easier. But as the two expeditions raced south towards their goal, there was only one significant landmark: the Transantarctics. For most of their journey, the mountain range was invisible, either far in front of them, or far behind. That left just the flat, white prairie of the Barrier, and the flat, white prairie of the plateau. At least Scott had Shackleton's footsteps to tread in. Amundsen had the additional disadvantage, as he ploughed southwards from the Bay of Whales at the far end of the barrier, of not even knowing if there was a pathway waiting for him up on to the plateau.

The advantage that both Scott and Amundsen did have was years of experience of maritime navigation. The best navigators on Scott's expedition were Teddy Evans, his second-in-command on the

Terra Nova, and Bowers, though not long before they set out for the pole, the landlubber Wilson made an effort to pick up the basics. 'It will be wiser to know a little navigation on this southern sledge journey,' he wrote. Amundsen himself was an expert, and could also rely on Wisting and Hassel. There is little mention of the business of navigation in any of the private or published diaries. The 1911 teams took their skill for granted, and can't have thought it worth dwelling on. The only time either expedition engaged in a prolonged stint of position-finding was when they got to the pole. Amundsen spent an intense 24 hours just taking readings and doing maths, simply to ensure that he could proclaim to the world to have been where he thought he was. A month later, Bowers could find no fault with his calculations.

As at sea, they navigated by the sun. (Technically, while on the Barrier, they still were at sea.) To get a reading off the sun they needed the appropriate piece of equipment. In Scott's case, it was a theodolite, a heavy and vulnerable bit of surveying kit stored in a large wooden case. Amundsen, who was not remotely inter- ested in surveying the land he raced across, also brought a theodo- lite, but it broke on the depot-laying expedition. Thereafter he relied on a pair of ship's sextants.

But readings off the sun were irrelevant without access to the time. Scott makes reference to a chronometer room in his diaries, which implies he had a lot of them. Amundsen took three chrono- meters on his journey. These timepieces were pocket descendants of the series of bulky chronometers developed by John Harrison in the eighteenth century to measure longitude accurately. In the days before quartz and batteries, they required regular winding.

The modern teams have many advantages over their pre- decessors whose journeys they are attempting to re-enact. Principal among these is the almost certain knowledge that, unless they get run over by a bus (or the Greenlandic equivalent: fall unroped down a very deep crevasse), they are not going to die. Among the disadvantages – intolerance of the 1911 polar diet, unfamiliarity with the equipment – there is one that overarches all the others, and it is a glaring practical one. However hardy the Norwegians are, however much they know about dogs, however much the British team laugh in the face of adversity, none of them knows anything about nautical navigation across a completely blank sheet of paper.

Before they fly to Greenland, Bruce Parry is accompanied by Mark Anstice, Dave Pearce and Chris van Tulleken on a course at the Royal School of Military Survey in Berkshire. Their job is not only to learn the rudiments of astronomical navigation, but also to teach the rest of the team to understand the arcane language of degrees, minutes and seconds.

A theodolite measures an angle on a horizontal plane and on a vertical plane. (The British team don't need the horizontal plane because, unlike Scott, they are not actually surveying the landscape through which they pass.) It allows the user to take measurements from the sun, the moon, the visible planets and those stars by which navigation is possible (there are 57 of them). But as the British team travels in 24-hour daylight, just as the explorers of 1911 did in the Antarctic summer, they take their readings solely from the sun.

'The 1922 theodolite comes in a nice wooden box with leather straps,' says Mark before departure. 'It weighs a ton. Setting it up so it's all level and perfectly rigged to measure the sun and then getting five readings from it is taking us half an hour at best. You then take an average. If you have one reading and get it slightly wrong you are not going to get a good fix. If you do two readings, you don't know which is slightly wrong. You need a minimum of three. Generally, you take five because you might get one wrong anyway and you might have to discard one a bit later. Five is easier because to take the average from them you multiply by two and divide by ten, rather than dividing by four.'

Both theodolite and sextant give the angle between the Sun and the Earth. The team then needs to know the time relative to Greenwich Mean Time, which is where the chronometers come in. Both teams are using vintage Omega chronometers made in the early twentieth century. They may be beautiful to behold, but the navigators need them to be accurate. 'They are that old,' says Mark, 'I don't know if anyone has replaced the springs. We've got four of them, but one has gained seven minutes in a week, and that would be fine if it was steady each day, if you could say for sure that this watch gains fifty-three seconds every day from 7.30 one morning to 7.30 the next. Unfortunately, they don't even do that. They might gain forty seconds one day and one minute seventeen seconds the next day. They are well out. All we need is one steady watch that will drift in a steady fashion. But if we've only got one, if it suddenly goes wrong, we've got no way of knowing. We really need three to drift in a steady fashion. If two drift in a steady fashion and one goes wrong, you still don't know which one has gone wrong.'

Sure enough, by the time they get out on the ice, they realize the watches are too erratic to be of any use. 'We are cheating on the time,' admits Chris. 'Scott had his watches for six months before and set them at Greenwich and watched the drift, then got a chance to reset them in Auckland and knew exactly how those watches behaved. These watches we've had for a matter of weeks, which isn't enough to draw a good graph. They lose or gain a minute and a half a day. They are a bit hopeless really.'

Armed with the time, it is only now that the real work actually starts. With those readings off the sun, and using a combination of mental arithmetic and the *Nautical Almanac*, they work out a series of angles: the Greenwich hour angle, the local hour angle, adjustments to be made for declination, refraction, air temperature and air pressure. The actual angle needs to be measured from the centre of the sun, but as the theodolite measures it from the edge, they need to know the diameter of the sun according to where it is in the sky at the time (the sun gets bigger and fatter the lower it is in the sky).

'It basically takes two A4 pages of sums plus another page of workings,' says Mark, 'to get one line which you can then draw on a plotting chart. You are somewhere off that line. You know which side but that's it. You have no idea where you are on that line unless you have a dead reckoning position.'

This evocative nautical term, which has its first use in late Elizabethan seafaring, is a colourful euphemism for an educated guess. In effect, it is the business of navigation without the use of astronomical observation. On the ice, it comes down to knowing how far you have travelled and in which direction, which is why, rigged to at least two sledges in each team, there is a quaint Edwardian contraption known as a sledge-meter. A bicycle wheel with a counter attached, it measures the mileage covered.

This information is useless without an accurate bearing. For both teams, keeping to a direction is a collaborative business. In front, as often as not, is the trail-breaker on skis, who finds some form of landmark in the appropriate direction and heads for it. Landmarks being few and far between, it may be the merest undulation in the snow. Behind him someone with a second compass checks the course he's following. Amundsen liked to go at the back and keep tabs on the straightness of the procession in front of him. In the modern Norwegian team, Ketil Reitan on the first sledge checks the direction taken by Inge Solheim against his own compass. After a couple of weeks the British team have still not worked out why they keep bearing to the right.

'It is no easy matter to go straight on a surface without landmarks,' Amundsen explained. 'Imagine an immense plain that you have to cross in thick fog; it is dead calm, and the snow lies evenly, without drifts. What would you do? An Eskimo can manage it, but none of us. We should turn to the right or to the left, and give the leading dog-driver with the standard compass endless trouble. It is strange how this affects the mind. Although the man with the compass knows quite well that the man in front cannot do any better, and although he knows that he could not do better himself, he nevertheless gets irritated in time and works himself into the belief that the unsuspecting, perfectly innocent leader only takes these turns to annoy him; and so the words "A little to the left" imply the unspoken addition – perfectly understood on both sides – "Duffer!" I have personal experience of both duties.'

In order not to rely solely on the intersection of one plotted line and the position according to dead reckoning, it is necessary to put more than one line on the chart. So they need to wait for six hours till the sun is in a different place and take another reading, which after another stint of mental arithmetic and table-reading will give them a second line that will cross the first line. 'It would be nice to believe that where those two lines cross is your position,' says Mark, 'Not nearly the case. It'll give us a vague position, but really very vague. A third line will give you a more accurate position.'

The problem is that the work is time-consuming. The half-hour required to come up with the theodolite readings – a job that can't be done with heavily mittened hands – is only the preliminary. Then there is the working out. Each line requires an expenditure of about two hours. In other words, every time you want to find out even roughly where you are, you have to sit a maths 'A' level. And in this 'A' level you have to get 100 per cent. 'Every single sum you do there's just massive room for error,' says Anstice. On a pre-expedition get-together in Northumberland five of them try to plot their position. Calculations put them in North America, the second set south of Birmingham. The third set put them a mile and a half from Alnwick. At least this proved that they can do it.

In the event, it is Chris and Rupert Elderkin who take on the navigational duties: they turn out to be the ones with the most efficient mathematical brains. On the smaller Norwegian team there is no division of labour. Although Rune does some rudimentary training, the navigation by sextant falls to Harald Kippenes, who is just as worried about this aspect of the reconstruction. 'We will never know 100 per cent that we are where we think we are,' he says darkly. In the calm aura of certainty that emanates from the Norwegian camp, like an air-conditioning system pumping unvarying measures of cool air into the atmosphere, this is a rare note of alarm.

But both modern teams have already determined before they set out that they will not even attempt to scale such a mountain of maths every day. There simply won't be the time.

* * * * * * * * * * * *

'While the sun is shining,' wrote Bowers with the pole still more than 600 miles away, 'we have an excellent little sundial – an excellent idea of Captain Scott's. You set the shadow to the time and there you are – it is the simplest device imaginable and useful in many ways besides being the best thing to steer by.' In this instance,

Bowers's customary bounciness carried him only so far. Soon the clouds came over, consigning the Scott party to a white-out for much of the Barrier journey. Of course, if there's no sun, there's no reading angles off it, and dead reckoning becomes the only tool in the navigator's locker.

Maintenance of the equipment was vital. Out on the Barrier, Bowers writes proudly of how he 'took my sledge-meter into the tent after breakfast and rigged up a fancy lashing with raw hide thongs so as to give it the necessary play with security'. Christopher the horse damaged one of the sledge-meters, and Bowers stayed up half the night mending it. 'We started late,' wrote Scott of one morning on the glacier, 'for Birdie wanted to get our sledge-meter dished up. It has been quite a job today getting it on, but it rode well this afternoon.' But however fancy their lashings, sledge-meters refused to work in the deep snow at the base of the glacier. Sometimes, especially towards the end when they were exhausted and desperate, their dead reckoning became unreliable: they thought they'd marched a certain distance, and it turned out to be less.

Whenever things went wrong, the unfortunate Bowers was somewhere in the thick of it. Thus Cherry-Garrard on 20 December: 'At lunch Birdie made the disastrous discovery that the registering dial of his sledge-meter was off. A screw had shaken out on the bumpy ice, and the clockwork had fallen off. This is serious for it means that one of the three returning parties will have to go without, and their navigation will be much more difficult. Birdie is very upset, especially after all the trouble he has taken with it, and the hours which he has sat up. After lunch he and Bill [Wilson] walked back near two miles in the tracks, but could not see it.' A similar gremlin visits Harald in the modern Norwegian team. One day his sledge-meter is dragging flat along the surface without rotating, rendering the clock-counter useless. Eventually it falls off, and as he is on the rear sledge, he is the first one to notice and has to walk back and retrieve it. He has more luck than Bowers.

One day up on the plateau, Bowers contrived to break the hypsometer, a thermometrical gizmo used for measuring altitude according to the temperature at which water boils. As they started out at sea level and reached a height of 10,000 feet, knowing the altitude was an important part of the navigational equation. Another day it was discovered that Bowers had allowed his chronometer to lose time and 'got an unusual outburst of wrath in consequence, in fact my name is mud just at present. It is rather sad to get into the dirt tub with one's leader at this juncture, but accidents will happen.'

The modern team's sledge-meters also turn out to be unreliable. On Day 13 members of the British team note that one of theirs says they have done only 41 nautical miles when their others record a distance of 60, which is duly confirmed by their navigation. On Day 10 the Norwegians discover that they have outstripped both of their sledge-meters. 'They are showing less than we are travelling,' says a baffled Rune.

* * * * * * * * * * *

Scott and Amundsen had another advantage over their modern counterparts. They were heading due south (and then due north). In order to create a journey over comparable distance and terrain in Greenland, it was not possible to devise a route that sent the British and Norwegian teams due north (and then south). In the early part of the journey – the equivalent of the Barrier – they change direction. After the glacier – the plateau section – they are never heading due north. So they have more fiddly calculations to make when it comes to setting directions.

The ultimate use of accurate navigation was, and still is, to direct the expedition towards the pole. But even if all else failed, they still had to eat. Out in the blasted wastes of the ice, their navigation had to bring them to their next meal.

In 1911 they made it as easy for themselves as they thought necessary. Amundsen thought it was a lot more necessary than Scott. Before the winter, the Norwegians made three journeys on to the Barrier, partly to take supplies out, partly to see the lie of the land. According to Johansen, each was a 'combined reconnaissance and depot-laying journey'. As the Norwegians successively skied back and forth to 80, 82 and again 80 degrees south, taking huge quantities of dog pemmican, seal meat and paraffin on to the Barrier, Amundsen marked the trail with bamboo sticks. There was one every 8 miles, each topped by a black flag, each numbered. Four times in every mile he also deposited stockfish in the snow to give the dogs something to aim at. On the first journey Amundsen's theodolite broke, so they had to use dead reckoning to get to what they thought was 80 degrees south. When they came back in the same direction the sextant confirmed their accuracy.

As for the depots themselves, he went to extraordinary lengths to ensure he'd find them. Either side of the depot ten more bamboo sticks were planted laterally at a total breadth of 10 miles, again with numbered flags. It was only because he had skis and dogs that this was possible. If they found a flag, it would tell them exactly where the depot was. The flagging for the depot at 82 degrees verged on the neurotic: 60 flags in all, spanning 10 miles across their route. Every 8 miles or so the dog teams would pull to a halt for a much-needed rest while their masters would build a 6-foot snow cairn. In all, they built 150 of them out of blocks of snow. Ever the stickler for detail, Amundsen even knew how many blocks they'd used: 9000. At the top of each cairn was a slip of paper noting the distance to the next cairn, and the direction in which it lay. 'One could not be too careful on this endless, uniform surface.' He would have to go dramatically wrong to miss a depot. When they found the depot at 82 degrees south, more than 200 miles from Framheim, it was 'an unspeakable relief,' wrote Amundsen, who now had a huge surge in confidence. 'The victory now seemed half won ... There they stood, flag after flag, and the little strip of black cloth seemed to wave quite proudly, as though it claimed credit for the way in which it had discharged its duty.'

The most thorough marking was reserved for the last depot before the pole, where they used 'a system of marks that would lead even a blind man back to the place. We had determined to mark it not only at right angles to our course – that is, from east to west – but by snow beacons at every two geographical miles to the south.' He noted, incidentally, that the snow at this extreme latitude was 'ill-adapted for building, but we put up quite a respectable monument all the same'. It must have been a laborious business to stake out 60 splinters of black packing-case, 30 either side of the depot and each separated by 100 paces. Every one had a shred of black cloth on the top. As a final attention to detail, the splinters on the east side were all marked 'so that on seeing them we should know instantly that we were to the east of the depot'. And still Amundsen took more food than he needed, just in case they missed the depot on the way back.

He was right to be so strenuously careful. For all these precautions, Amundsen was the one who sailed straight past one of his glacier depots on the way home. Two men were sent back to retrieve the food.

Compare and contrast with Scott's single flag fluttering atop the pile of boxes at One Ton Camp. Instead, his team built snow cairns, of which the 15-foot Mount Hooper at the Lower Barrier Depot was easily the most impressive (but then its builders did have six days of waiting to work at it). They built double cairns each time they camped, and single cairns at each lunch stop. Cherry-Garrard also says that they built a cairn every day after the first 4 miles.

＊＊*＊*＊*＊*＊

On Day 12 Bruce's team reach their first target point and plan to make for a depot they have called One Ton, after the main deposit of food and fuel left by Scott out on the Barrier before the winter set in. Rupert and Chris laboriously go to work with the theodolite, despite the lack of reliable sun sightings. The day is bitterly cold and they have to be careful as their eyes can freeze to the scope; when they breathe near the lens it gets covered in moisture. But the readings have to be done.

'It seems to have fallen to Rupert and me to crack on with the maths,' says Chris, 'which I'm sure my mother and maths teacher would be very surprised to hear. There are literally a hundred points where error can creep in which will put us 100 miles out. So it's important one person doesn't have sole responsibility for the maths. It took us six hours of maths, including a couple of severe cock-ups. We thought that GMT was BST. We had the time wrong by an hour which put us somewhere in northern Canada, which wasn't much use.'

On Day 15, the British caravan heads in the bearing they hope will bring them to One Ton. Despite a much sunnier day, they are not confident of finding it. 'It's 6.8 miles according to our calculations,' says Rupert, who is out in front on skis. 'That could easily be 2 miles out. Two miles out would be quite good. As soon as we get to 4 miles I'm going to start scanning the horizon.'

As they didn't lay the depot themselves, they have no idea what it will look like. 'It's quite challenging to stay on your bearing today,' says Bruce, who is leading from the front. 'There is no shadow cast on the ground. It's like a carpet of white with no small features. We've been dealt another card in the weather. From temperatures of minus 40 and horrendous storms to a day like today which is just baking hot. For the first time we've got hats and gloves off, and I've even got beads of sweat on me, but the consequence of that is the snow is like porridge. It's really hard trail-breaking, particularly with these period skis which have got no give in them whatsoever.'

Several hours later Dave Pearce spots a faint interruption of the monotonous topography somewhere in the distance and thinks it might be One Ton. They head for it and, sure enough, a fluttering flag comes into focus. 'The honest truth is I'm absolutely gobsmacked we're here,' confesses Bruce. 'It's a very inexact science and we never in our wildest dreams thought we'd walk straight to it. There must be luck involved in this. Even the best navigators can only get to within a mile using the techniques we have. It's just fantastic to be here.'

But when they pull into One Ton, not all of Bruce's team are able to fall in line with his enthusiasm. 'Well, what an anticlimax,' says Mark. 'Of all the shit places to get to.' The problem comes when they open the boxes of supplies. 'My God,' marvels Dave, 'there's roast beef and Yorkshire pud here.' There isn't. 'It feels like we should look forward to it but it's extraordinarily disappointing to find more of the same crap,' says Chris, unloading the boxes. 'I guess there's nothing positive about this depot at all. It's an entirely negative experience of increasing weight [on the sledges] and the same disappointing food. Maybe there'll be more raisins. Our treats are raisins and chocolate. They are the stuff we like eating. The biscuits are becoming bearable, but the pemmican remains purgatory. I keep predicting that we're going to start craving the pemmican, but I've been wholly disappointed so far.'

However, they now know they can navigate their way to the pole.

No such certainty attends the Norwegian journey. Somewhere else on the ice, Day 10 also finds them looking for their first depot. Harald has been religiously making his three observations in different parts of the day. Rune says, 'We are doing this every day and if we don't find the depot we need to know where we are.'

As they approach the first depot, they have cause to be thankful for Amundsen's neuroticism. The flags planted across the line of the depot at a 90-degree angle mean that Inge, breaking the trail out in front, finds a note telling him exactly where they are in relation to where they want to be. Unfortunately, they are not where they thought they were. The note reveals they are approximately 4.2 nautical miles to the west of the depot. 'Even with a short stop, we will be there in one and a half hours,' he says breezily. 'I thought we were more spot on our line.'

So did Rune, who is dismayed at the error. 'We are west and I thought we were east of there,' he tells Harald. He asks Kippenes to guess how far out they are. He can't. The error is not just in the direction but in the distance. Having thought there were 9 miles left to the depot, the flag tells them otherwise. The problem is partly down to the unreliability of the sledge-meter. The dogs have been pulling the sledges so fast over bumpy terrain that the wheel is missing the distance between the ridges. Some of their mileage is unaccounted for by the dead reckoning.

'We nearly missed the flag line altogether,' says Harald. 'Luckily we didn't. But it is a challenge to do this and we are still learning. We were lucky this time and hopefully we won't have to rely on our luck in the future. We are getting more and more into it but it's definitely a challenge. I'm quite amazed how all the explorers a hundred years ago managed to navigate. But they were really used to this equipment. That was what they had. I'm very impressed by them. It's understandable that Columbus thought he was in India when he had actually reached America.'

Rune is less inclined to joke about it. 'We can improve. Amundsen had sailors in his team, so they were all good navigators. They were much stronger navigators than us, definitely. We would have been looking for the depot 10 or 11 miles further north. Today we would have missed it. It's annoying that something that should be very accurate is quite inaccurate.'

For the navigators, the next stage of the journey will bring respite. With mountains to take readings off, it will become much easier to find their way around. Almost everything else, however, becomes much harder.

Rune Gjeldnes's Diary

DAY 10

Looks like it's going to be a great day. Some wind, but the view is good. Hoping to get to Depot 80 degrees today.

Yes, we managed our depot today and a bit further. Were there at 15.00. Packed for two hours, and did one and a half hours and 6.5 nautical miles. Have celebrated a bit this evening. Coffee and a bit of aquavit and good pipe tobacco. Now the mountains are waiting. Will get through them quickly. We'll need time on the next part of the journey. But the last couple of days we've shown what we're able to do on good days. We won't get real speed before we're up on the plateau.

Miscalculated on depot with 4.2 nautical miles and we were wondering why. The explanation turned out to be that the depot was moved during all the changes that have happened over the last few days, and Harald had plotted the depot and other positions before the changes. We didn't know that. But we're keeping a very good course, which is reassuring.

Harald is not pleased with the navigation today. None of the three readings were any good. Two don't work, and they all give the wrong answers. If we have another couple of good days, we'll be on schedule again.

DAY 12

New day, new opportunities.

The equipment that we've got we haven't even had the chance to test, and a lot of or some of the equipment isn't even made for this kind of expedition at all. It breaks. To set off on an expedition of this kind, one should have tested the equipment over a long time and had a chance to correct the flaws. That's what we're doing now, on the actual expedition. Crazy! Preparation is everything. If you haven't got that sorted, then you'll have problems when you're out.

Was tired yesterday, and tired this morning. Not much sleep lately. Normally six hours. A bit too little.

The day is over and we haven't really worked more than five hours, but did 20 km easily. Steep downhill and some areas with crevasses before it evened out, and then up again. The worst thing is that the map we've got doesn't correspond with the terrain we're walking in. My gut feeling from yesterday was right. Something was wrong. But we're now lying under the glacier. Not a pretty sight. I think I've got the route sorted.

Bruce Parry's Diary

DAY 10

Funny situation with me and Dave. I love him and respect him, but sometimes he does want to take charge. Obviously used to leading himself, he's not used to orders from younger people maybe. I tell him I'm happy for him to take charge from the rear if he wants, and generally talk about the situation a bit. Cloud instantly lifts and we're best mates again. Amazing how small things get to you out here, but can be easily overcome with tact and diplomacy.

Cold, cold wind: minus 15 degrees (approx minus 40 degrees Celsius wind-chill). A couple of the guys got a few cold spots, but my sex-pest balaclava is doing a good job.

Got run over today – twat. Got hit by sledge. Didn't hurt at all – shame as I would have loved a heli ride home (joke). Felt a bit silly.

DAY 11

Wake to obvious blizzard outside. Not going anywhere this morning. Turn over and go back to sleep. Good chats all day and finally wind drops around 2 p.m. and chat to Mark about options. It's a lovely day for sledging, but decide to stay put for morale reasons.

Mark makes wind barrier shit house and looks like Robinson Crusoe with rags about him.

Dodgy dreams, can't sleep – pemmican overload.

DAY 12

Our daily average for this first leg is 4.5 nautical miles per day. Our optimum rate was 9nm/day in order to get back to One Ton in 99 days. We're having to rethink. … Anyway what a fantastic day. Total whiteout. Could not see up or down or any perspective at all. Absolutely no shadow and so could not see what was a rise or a dip in the ground. Everyone falling over everywhere.

DAY 13

V cold start: minus 20 deg Celsius. My hands are totally frozen. I try out my reindeer fur mitts. Fiddly shit with metal compass doesn't help my fingers any, so not the best start. Dogs seem on excellent form and catch us up really quickly. It turns out to be a record-breaking day – 12 statute miles. Not bad. V flat light. Falling over all day. It's totally surreal and like being in a whitewashed film set. I can't work out my sense of perspective at all and become easily disorientated on all three planes. Quite bizarre. We can see the mountains in the distance.

DAY 14

Mark's boil was lanced first thing this morning. Both docs enjoying a bit of puss and pain, with blood and blasphemy to boot, while Mark bent somewhat compromisingly over his sledge. Mark was in obvious pain but braved it out well. It looked f**king sore and everyone was impressed. I gave him some recreational pain relief from my personal supply of opiates as a mark of respect.

I was on nav and it proved a f**king nightmare. Kept veering right for some reason and just couldn't keep on a bearing except by looking down compass literally all the time. To take one's eyes off it for one second spelt instant disorientation as there were absolutely no landmarks in front at all. Complete white-out at times.

DAY 15

Up to a magnificent sunny day. Too hot really. Chris and Rupert did theodolite reading to good effect. Added their calculation to my accumulated dead reckoning and was v happy with answer. Set off about 1 p.m. Was most surprised, in fact didn't believe it, when Dave announced that he could see something on the horizon which was directly on our bearing. Sure enough, as we closed it in, it was an obvious cache, and on arrival it was none other than our One Ton Camp. Amazing to walk straight to it. Wasn't expecting anything like that level of accuracy. All suitably impressed with navigation.

CHAPTER SIX

Glacier

WE ... GOT INTO A PERFECT MASS OF CREVASSES IN WHICH WE ALL
CONTINUALLY FELL; MOSTLY ONE FOOT, BUT OFTEN TWO, AND
OCCASIONALLY WE WENT DOWN ALTOGETHER, SOME TO THE LENGTH
OF THEIR HARNESS TO BE HAULED OUT WITH THE ALPINE ROPE. MOST
OF THEM COULD BE SEEN BY THE STRIP OF SNOW ON THE BLUE ICE.
THEY WERE OFTEN TOO WIDE TO JUMP THOUGH, AND THE ONLY THING
WAS TO PLANT YOUR FEET ON THE BRIDGE AND TRY NOT TO TREAD
HEAVILY. AS A RULE THE CENTRE OF A BRIDGED CREVASSE IS THE SAFEST
PLACE, THE ROTTEN PLACES ARE AT THE EDGES. WE HAD TO GO OVER
DOZENS BY HOPPING RIGHT ONTO THE ICE. IT IS A BIT OF A JAR WHEN
IT GIVES WAY UNDER YOU, BUT THE FRIENDLY HARNESS IS MADE TO
TRUST ONE'S LIFE TO. THE LORD ONLY KNOWS HOW DEEP THESE VAST
CHASMS GO DOWN, THEY SEEM TO EXTEND INTO BLUE BLACK
NOTHINGNESS THOUSANDS OF FEET BELOW.
Henry 'Birdie' Bowers

When Ernest Shackleton chanced upon the Great Glacier three years
earlier, he called the path leading up to it the Gateway. The name was
not conferred without irony. For all the solidity of the ice, this was
where frozen sea met frozen land. The glacial mass tumbling down
into the Barrier made for an epic collision of forces, and the route was

verging on impassable. Everywhere there were pressure ridges, vast walls thrown up when kinetic blocks of ice barged into each other like clashing titans. Most unnavigable of all was a so-called 'shear crack', a gaping fissure formed where the glacier loosed its bonds with terra firma. But Shackleton found a rocky hillock bridging the two. Amid all that tumult, it must indeed have resembled a gateway.

Bruce Parry's team has its own equivalent that, with rather less cause for melodrama, it decides to call Hell's Gate. The name would imply that the men are not looking forward to the next phase of the expedition. But they already intuit that once they are through the mountains and out on the infinite pasture of the ice cap, they will look back with fondness on the glacier. It may be steep. It may be slotted with crevasses. But at least in the majesty of the surroundings there is something to take the mind out of itself. After the Beardmore, Bowers wrote fondly of 'the distant mountains which have so recently been our companions'. (In much the same place, but many weeks later, Scott said returning from the pole to the mountains was 'like going ashore after a sea voyage'.)

The mountain range in Greenland materializes in front of them after One Ton Depot, but remains tantalizingly out of reach for days. 'It's just never-ending,' says Dave Pearce. 'The scale of this place is immense. You see a feature on the horizon and think we'll go there, but it takes you two or three days to get there. We've been looking at these mountains for three days and they still look a fair way off. Good to see a change in scenery, to be frank. White frozen desert can slowly drive you insane.' Cherry-Garrard's similar sentiments have echoed down the century: 'The great jagged cliffs of red granite were welcome to the eyes after 425 miles of snow ... a wonderful sight indeed.' Amundsen was even more effusive: 'Each day we drew considerably nearer the land, and could see more and more of its details: mighty peaks, each loftier and wilder than the last, rose to heights of 15,000 feet ... I do not think I have ever seen a more beautiful or wilder landscape.'

A glacier shimmers in the distance, beckoning innocently. A shallow slope between two rocky walls, it rises at a gradient that seems gentle enough, but the closer it comes, the steeper it looks.

Disturbances in the snow's surface – ridges, ribs – hint at the peril that awaits. 'The first little glacier we're going up is full of crevasses,' says Bruce. Cherry-Garrard noted: 'From Shackleton's book we gathered that the Beardmore was a very bad glacier indeed.'

There are enforced dissimilarities between the original journey and its re-enactment. Scott reached the Gateway on 4 December, the thirty-third day of the journey, and sent Meares and the dogs back a week later once they'd negotiated their way through it and up on to the glacier. Bruce's team have pledged to keep the dogs until Day 40, but reach the base of the mountains on Day 17. They will thus have the dogs to help them up the hill, a luxury Scott chose to forego. By now the original team members all knew that they had missed a trick with the dogs – their diaries and letters frequently admit it. But Scott didn't trust the dogs not to fall down crevasses and take a whole sledge with them, as nearly happened with one of the ponies at the Gateway. Dogs, says Rupert Elderkin laconically after his own team drags the sledge into a maze of crevasses, 'don't have a huge knowledge of mountain safety.' And although Scott's orders for them kept changing, he needed the dogs to do more work back on the Barrier. 'Other than that, the slog that we've got compared to the slog that he had is going to be pretty much the same,' says Bruce. 'We'll just get stuck in and see how the dogs cope.' At least their slog is shorter and more varied. The medley of glaciers to be crossed includes some downhill sections, and covers about 40 miles.

Scott and the 11 men who were still with him had a rather harder task ahead. The Beardmore, named after one of Shackleton's expedition sponsors, has since turned out to be the biggest glacier on the planet: 40 miles wide and 120 miles long. It was an Amazonian cascade of ice.

'Its very vastness ... ends to dwarf its surroundings,' noted Cherry-Garrard, 'and great tributary glaciers and tumbled ice-falls, which anywhere would have aroused admiration, were almost unnoticed in a stream which stretched in places forty miles from bank to bank. It was only when the theodolite was levelled that we realized how vast were the mountains which surrounded us: one of which we reckoned to be well over twenty thousand feet in height, and many of the others must have approached that measurement. Lieutenant Evans and Bowers were surveying whenever the opportunity offered, whilst Wilson sat on the sledge on his sleeping-bag, and sketched.'

No wonder, after all that ice, the modern British team brims with anticipation of its own mountain stage. 'Now we're here it's awe-inspiring, it's quite intimidating and also really exciting,' says Bruce as they camp at the foot of Mount Forel. 'We've got quite a tricky route ahead and it'll be a real challenge. I think it'll be the most exciting part of the whole expedition. I think we can cope with anything that's thrown at us, but we will have to have our wits about us because there are some real dangers.'

Led by the ex-marine Dave, the three roped-up skiers discuss safety routines. But it's not the skiers who are the real issue. As they pull up in front of the glacier the worry is whether they can control the dogs and sledges in an area of hugely increased danger. So significant is the concern that the safety expert is initially adamant that the risks are too great and that he cannot allow the glacier stage to go ahead. A debate ensues that Bruce somehow contrives to win on the grounds that no such option was available to Scott. A reconstruction of his journey with the one genuine element of jeopardy removed, leaving only days of unabated trudging, would by common consent render the experience less worthwhile.

However, one dissimilarity they *are* grateful for. When Scott reached the Gateway on 3 December, he was promptly engulfed in unseasonal bad weather. It was warm and therefore wet, dampening both clothing and spirits. Just when they needed clear visibility to lead the five remaining ponies over the last few miles to where they hoped to make the next depot, they were stalled. The glacier was 9 miles away, and so it remained for four days as they sat in their tents while the snow deepened around them. The weather was in every conceivable way a disaster: it lost them valuable time, forcing them to break into rations reserved for the glacier, and it deposited a thick blanket of soft snow over the ice Shackleton had gratefully found three years earlier.

For the ponies the last day's march, on 9 December, was the most desperate yet. Fortified by some extra Huntley & Palmer biscuits, they were dragged on for a dozen miles, sinking up to their bellies. 'Hour after hour we plugged on,' wrote Cherry-Garrard. 'We dare not halt for lunch, we knew we could never start again. After crossing many waves, huge pressure ridges suddenly showed themselves all round, and we got on to a steep rise with the coastal chasm on our right hand appearing as a great dip full of enormous pressure ... Every step we sank fifteen inches ... Snippets nearly fell back into a big crevasse, into which his hind quarters fell ... '

Meares left after two extra days on 11 December, and they depoted more food at the Lower Glacier Depot. Now, for the first time, they were alone with only their own strength to propel them: three teams of four, each hauling a sledge. Conditions were no better once they made it on to the glacier proper. If anything, with the new gradient, they were worse.

At the base of the glacier, with the sledges impacted in the deep snow, they resorted to relaying. It was a time-consuming business. Needless to say, the sledge-meters didn't work in snow with so much give, but it wasn't hard to work out how many miles they'd travelled on 13 December: less than one in nine hours. For much of his chapter on the glacier, Cherry-Garrard makes way for Bowers's diary. Bowers, the Edwardians' Edwardian, was always one for making light of difficulty and hard work, as a result of which the Beardmore sometimes comes across as less taxing than it undoubtedly was. But even Bowers, newly strapped into a harness and pulling his own sledge, found this day brought 'the most backbreaking work I have ever come up against ... so heavy were our weights that if any of the pair slacked a hand even, the sledge stopped. It was all we could do to keep the sledge moving for short spells of a few hundred yards, the whole concern sinking so deeply into the soft snow as to form a snow-plough. The starting was worse than pulling as it required from ten to fifteen desperate jerks on the harness to move the sledge at all ... I have never pulled so hard, or so nearly crushed my inside into my backbone by the everlasting jerking with all my strength on the canvas band round my unfortunate tummy.'

They lived more or less by the hour in these days. One morning they tracked the recession of the glutinous snow, and the emergence of the blue ice beneath it, until their feet – or skis if they were wearing them – sank in only 6 inches. 'The great thing is to keep the sledges moving,' wrote Scott on one of these days, 'and for an hour or so there were dozens of critical moments when it all but stopped.' And as he strained every muscle, he succumbed to the realization that he could have had help: 'certainly dogs could have come up as far as this', he said halfway up.

They tugged and sweated and tore off their layers, and froze when they stopped. Every so often they stopped to tip over the sledges and rake away the build-up of ice on the runners, formed when friction melted the soft snow, only for it to freeze and impede the glide. They used the sides of their knives, noted Bowers, 'so as to avoid any chance of cutting or chipping them'. In the nine-and-a-half-hour marches, dehydration bedevilled them constantly. 'Tea at lunch was a positive godsend,' enthused Cherry-Garrard.

Every day was different and the same. The conditions varied, as did the weather, the undulations of the snow's surface known as sastrugi, the size of the pressure ridges. And yet progress was somehow made. Their diaries note the gradual ascent: 2000 feet, 2500 and, halfway up, 3600, where they made another depot. 'December 19,' says Cherry-Garrard's diary. 'Total height 5800 feet. Things are certainly looking up, seeing that we have risen 1100 feet, and marched 17 or 18 statute miles during the day.'

All the way up, the same dangers lurked underfoot. 'There were countless cracks and small crevasses,' noted Bowers, 'into which we constantly trod, barking our shins.' Spotting them was not made any easier by the fact that for four days on the bottom half of the glacier there was a mass outbreak of snow-blindness. Where there was blue ice, the snow usually designated a bridge concealing a crevasse. They stepped over them unruffled, apart from Bowers. 'With my short legs this was strenuous work, especially as the weight of the sledge would often stop me with a jerk just before my leading foot quite cleared a crevasse, and the next minute one would be struggling out so as to keep the sledge on the move … Of course someone one often gets so far down a hole that it is necessary to stop and help him out.' In the area of huge disturbance near the mouth of the glacier, Lashly fell down a crevasse on Christmas Day, his forty-fourth birthday. He hung in his harness till they could lug him out. 'It was not a very nice sensation,' he confessed. 'It seemed about 50 feet deep and 8 feet wide, and 120 feet long. This information I had ample time to gain while dangling there … it seemed a long time before I saw the rope come down alongside me with a bowline in it for me to put my foot in and get dragged out. It was not a job I should care to have to go through often, as by being in the crevasse I had got cold and a bit frost-bitten on the hands and face, which made it difficult for me to help myself.' When they pulled him up, Crean wished him a happy birthday.

They made the Upper Glacier Depot on 21 December, 11 days after the Lower Glacier Depot. They had done the Beardmore. For all three returning parties, the descent would be even more taxing. In less than half an hour Pat Keohane would tumble into crevasses the full length of his harness no fewer than eight times. 'And Atkinson went down into one chasm head foremost,' noted Cherry-Garrard: 'the worst crevasse fall I've ever seen.'

* * * * * * * * * * * *

The modern British team also make faster work of their mountains than the ten days they have anticipated. This despite the fact that, like Scott, they have to resort to relaying up some of the steeper slopes. Although they have sweated and toiled to control the recalcitrant dogs in the early days of the journey, now is the first time they have to propel the sledges for any length of time. The work is every bit as back-breaking as Bowers found it, the only difference being that the dogs are pulling from the front and, initially, as many men as possible are pushing from the rear. Only short bursts of shoving are manageable. They soon give up on this. When they go down for the next sledge they put on their harnesses and pull with the dogs. It is their first experience of man-hauling.

Their footgear deprives them of real purchase in the snow. The *finnesko* are slippery and the crampons are, in Mark Anstice's pithy description, 'crap'. The dogs are also overheating.

'It's hard work,' says Bruce. 'It's really hard work. Even on a slope you get slight rises, little bumps, and it takes it out of you. Grinding to a halt is the worst thing you can possibly do.'

In order to limit the dangers of crevasses, he has decided to travel at what passes for night. Out on a path-finding recce, Dave has spotted snow bridges over hidden crevasses melting in the midday sun. Although the sun never sets, the temperatures sink low enough at night for surfaces to harden and make the snow both easier and safer. But there is no avoiding danger altogether.

At this stage in the journey Scott had an advantage over his successors. With the log of Shackleton's expedition written by Frank Wild to guide him, he had a shrewd idea of where the crevasses were. Bruce's team, relying on an inaccurate 70-year-old map and aerial photographs, are taken aback when Dave, out in front, discovers far more crevasses at the mouth of their first glacier than expected.

At one point on the glacier they are obliged to deviate from their planned route to navigate around a river. When they eventually cross it, the sledges go first. Bruce and Chris van Tulleken, without skis to distribute their weight, get their feet wet when the carapace of snow crumbles away under them. (It was too cold for streams on the Beardmore.) One day they even come across a lake.

At times they come much closer to danger than they realize. Once, when they begin the night's journey, they cannot dislodge one of the sledges. This time it's not just that it has sunk into deep snow. Unbeknown to them, it has become wedged in the jaws of a crevasse. When they toss shards of ice into the hole to see how deep it is, it takes 20 seconds for the sound to reverberate back up to them. It is as deep as a mountain gorge. Arthur Jeffes notes that he has been innocently sitting on the sledge the entire time. It will not be his last flirtation with gravity.

But there are rewards. At the end of Day 25 they have reached the top of the mountain section and are able to sit on the sledges and simply slide down what Rory O'Connor calls 'a massive slope'. 'We came out on the long undulating plain. The first part was the downhill section. The dogs really enjoy it. There is less weight on the sledge and they were going full tilt. I was sitting on the sledge thinking, this is fantastic.' It is at this point that he has his near-collision with Mark Anstice's sledge. They take greater care on the next run, which Chris describes as 'good fun. We had a couple of hairy moments but Art has cleverly devised these rope breaks that we flick under the runner and takes some of the speed off so I can jump off and use the claw. When it's going well, it's good fun, real sensation of momentum. We try and leave a long distance between the sledges ahead.' Before they entered the mountains it was Chris who argues for ditching the dogs. 'Glad I was wrong,' he concedes. 'I couldn't imagine the horrors of man-hauling all of that.'

On Day 23 they come across the tracks of the Norwegians. Bruce puts a brave face on it. 'It doesn't bother us. They had a slightly shorter route than us on the way here, and they've got more dogs. When we start pulling we can put the hours in and they're limited by how many hours they can work the dogs. It's all to play for.'

* * * * * * * * * * * *

Perhaps it would have been kinder on Scott to have found Amundsen's tracks. It might have reduced the misery that attended the discovery of the black flag at the pole. Their assumption was that the Norwegians would have to clamber up to the plateau via the route pioneered by Shackleton, and it was a fair one to make. When Campbell admired the abundant library at Framheim, he would have found among it Shackleton's account of the *Nimrod* expedition, *The Heart of the Antarctic*. (He would also have found Scott's *The Voyage of the 'Discovery'*.) Only when they came upon Amundsen's tracks at the pole did they realize that he had approached the common goal along a different meridian.

From reading Shackleton, who got to within a degree and a half of the pole, Amundsen guessed that he would face a climb at some point. He didn't know for certain until the morning of 11

November, when the clouds cleared and there, bristling from one edge of the horizon to the other, was a long rampart of peaks. 'The land looks like a fairytale,' he enthused, but it was real enough. Somehow he had to find his way through it. He didn't know it, but he was to encounter the mountain range at its narrowest. The peaks were intimidatingly high, but only 40 or so miles would separate the Norwegians from the plateau. He was 250 miles to the east of the Beardmore.

Two days later Amundsen found a bay and ploughed on through, expecting the usual commotion caused by the collision of the Barrier and the Transantarctics. But for a few frozen waves, it was all plain sailing. Pausing to make a new depot just after 85 degrees, he reconnoitred to the south, skiing slowly up and then rather more rapidly down 2000 feet. The slope was forbidding, but the crevasses were not. This was the first time they had done significant exercise without the dogs, and noted that they were out of condition. The next few days would soon knock them into shape. They were relaying on 18 November for the first part of the climb, but still managed 10 miles and 1500 feet. They found themselves using rope brakes on the runners on a dramatic descent before they could go up again. On the next ascent the entire team of 42 dogs strained every sinew to drag the sledges in relay, only to run into another slope. Bjaaland found it 'more violent than the first, so dogs and sledges ran into each other. Broke the bow of my sledge and the stern of Hassel's.'

At the bottom they found their path blocked by their biggest crevasse. Their only alternative was to make for a forbiddingly steep glacier. To reach it they chose a route that found them plummeting through 2000 feet, keeping control of their cross-country skis, the sledges and the dogs, then climbing back up even higher through near-impassable ice falls, seracs and crevasses. They persevered, stopping to reconnoitre. The third afternoon brought them up against the most obstinate barricade so far. 'Enormous blocks of ice, mighty abysses and wide crevasses blocked the way everywhere.' They camped that night among crevasses 'thousands of metres deep', noted Bjaaland, and woke up the next morning to their most gruelling day yet. It would take them up to 8000 feet and on to the plateau. Not given to overt displays of enthusiasm, Amundsen was nonetheless exultant. 'It was a sheer marvel ... what the dogs accomplished today,' he wrote that night. '17 miles, with 5,000 ft climb. Come and say that dogs cannot be used here.'

They were often hot. 'We sweated as if we were running races in the tropics,' said Amundsen, who had been blessed with clear weather throughout. Imperious peaks frowned on the Norwegians from all sides, and he had the pleasure of conferring names on them, like a farm girl strewing chicken feed from her basket. One acquired the name of his old nanny, another of a financial backer, while the tallest mountain became Mount Fridtjof Nansen. As for the glacier, he called it Folgefonni after a glacier back at home, though the pragmatist in him later relented and named it after a sponsor: Axel Heiberg.

* * * * * * * * * * * *

The tracks found by the modern British team in the snow were left five days earlier. The Norwegians have started to move at pace, and nowhere is their advantage more evident than in the glacier region.

Not that their path through the mountains is entirely characterized by grinding efficiency. Camping the night before they head up, Ketil Reitan keeps the tent door open so that he can drink in the view. Inge Solheim has problems with his feet on the glacier, but deems it churlish to complain when surrounded by the most beautiful landscape he has ever seen. These experienced Arctic travellers still have a sense of wonder. Or some of them do. After two days of glacier travel Harald Kippenes looks forward to getting away from the slopes and up on to the flats of the plateau.

Rune Gjeldnes sets out on Day 15 with the aim of climbing the team's first glacier – a rise of about 3500 feet in 10.5 miles – with a long rest for the dogs in the heat of the midday sun. It doesn't pan out that way. The dogs struggle to pull the sledges uphill through the sludgy snow. Their drivers dismount to ease their burden. Their progress is also impeded by the meticulous route-checking Inge is asked to do out front by his leader. Eventually they stop short of the top of the pass for the night. The next morning Rune is fretting about the micro-climate that clusters around Mount Forel. He doesn't want to set off only to be forced back down by a white-out. But caution is the theme of the Norwegians' trek through the mountains. They are taking no risks. Somewhere in these mountains they also have to find their next depot.

But they set off, less impeded by the weather than by a steep hill. The snow is melting again under the runners and Inge's skis, causing ice build-up, which they have to stop and scrape away. This time they are not just off the sledges; they are pushing them. After two days – two fewer than Amundsen – they are nearly out of the mountains, but as the weather closes in, they stop an hour short, partly to protect Rune's feet, which are wet and vulnerable to the cold.

With a final climb, they are out of the glacier system the next day. There are still some big crevasses en route, so they have to be careful, but with skilful navigation they avoid them. They are still inconvenienced by warm temperatures they hope to leave behind when they gain some more altitude. So when Inge says, 'You get a sense of the steep climbing Amundsen had to do in the Axel Heiberg,' a sense is all it is. Rune has found one of the glaciers 'much easier than I thought'. Harald has found the navigation 'fairly easy'. Even Amundsen, who also had clear weather and mesmerizing views on the glacier, never had cause for such nonchalance.

* * * * * * * * * * *

Bruce imagines the glacier will take his team ten days. In the end it takes them five. But there is a sting in the tail. Those who have recently travelled through a mountain range do not leave its force field as quickly as they imagine. One member of the team finds himself inadvertently reconstructing an element of Amundsen's journey.

With the mountains far behind them, the Norwegians found themselves virtually trapped in a sea of crevasses that their leader named the Devil's Glacier. It happens rather sooner to Arthur Jeffes.

A day or two earlier he has been talking about his unique relationship with the original expedition, as the great-grandson by her second marriage of Kathleen Scott. 'You can read the diaries,' he says, 'but it's history rather than real people. So coming out here and doing this and missing my girlfriend horribly you start to glimpse what might have been going on in their heads. Some things don't change. Tough aspects of dragging stuff about in the cold is pretty much the same. It puts flesh on the bones of the story.'

But nothing puts flesh on the bones of the story quite as efficiently as what happens to Arthur on Day 27. Pulling away from the mountains, they struggle to haul the sledges over a series of sastrugi. Arthur, like the others, is always off his sledge, pushing, and one day feels his feet sliding away under him. 'I just wandered round to the back of the sledge with a hand on the back of the tent sort of out of habit, stood there and looked down and noticed there was a little black hole. Then the whole ground gave way and I was just scrambling out as the ground goes, trying to get back up to the sledge. Horrible feeling. You start to go down. Doesn't feel that fast. Very nasty.'

He has no harness on. As the snow bridge falls away, a full panoply of horror opens up beneath him. He grabs on to the sledge and manages to scramble out, kicking away snow from the edge that tumbles soundlessly into what he has no hesitation in calling 'the black abyss of death'. He is extraordinarily lucky. 'Probably would have died,' he says straight after. 'It's pretty f**kin' horrible. Not something I want to repeat. I wanna go home, I've come much closer to death than I was planning on coming this morning, or this year.'

Arthur is the quiet one of the party, and certainly the least experienced in any form of expeditioning. A brush with death has made him talkative. 'I imagine in a few days I could tell the story with a bit of relish, but at the moment I'm a bit shaken up, it's just not something you wanna be doing. It's all a little bit dangerous. It's happened three times now. Ridiculous! First time I went into a crevasse, just up to the thigh, it was a bit of fun, you could see the bottom – it was about 3 feet deep. Then at the top of the first glacier, when Rupert and Mark had gone on a sledge along a snow bridge, we popped on to it and the sledge basically sank about a foot. We looked under it and there was basically a bottomless pit and I was sat on the sledge when that happened. And that was my third crevasse incident and they're getting worse. It sucks. I hate crevasses. What was flashing through my mind was "Is that a dog poo or is that in fact ... " and then it all started to go. You start to fall down and you think it can't be that deep, then you go, "Of course it can, it's a f**king crevasse!" If I hadn't held on to the sledge, I would have gone. I'm pissed off more than anything else. Pissed off with ice for having crevasses and being dangerous instead of fluffy and fun to run a sledge on, and 10 per cent pissed off with myself for getting into that position. One hand on a sledge isn't enough. You don't really expect it to happen, so you don't put 100 per cent into protecting against it.'

Part of the reason for his accident is a slightly casual attitude to the safety expert's advice. Arthur says that Scott's team was always falling into crevasses on the Beardmore Glacier. He mentions Lashly. He doesn't mention that none of them died and that all of them were wearing man-haul harnesses: they were attached to a heavy sled. Arthur was attached by his hand. Perhaps Scott was right after all to do without dogs on the glacier.

Chris, who has been pulling at the front of the sledge, approaches the edge of the crevasse. He can see perhaps 60 feet down, but can't see the bottom. 'I've never been in such close proximity to someone who was so close to death,' he says. 'In some ways I slightly envy Arthur his near-death experience. But I wouldn't envy him his death experience. It must be rather fun to come that close.'

Arthur interrupts. 'I can assure you, Chris, that the fun is ... '

'Retrospective?'

As if they didn't know it already, this is no tame reconstruction. Death came to claim Scott and four of his men. One sunny afternoon on the Greenland ice cap, with the danger apparently behind them, it nearly came for the great-grandson of his widow.

Rune Gjeldnes's Diary

DAY 13

Excited about today. Going to get through one of the greatest challenges of this journey today. First time on a steep glacier with dogs and lots of kit. We went like the wind up through the first gorge and Inge found us good routes through, but it was very steep. Completely amazing that the dogs managed to pull all the stuff up those slopes. No big crevasses in the ice today, but John put his foot through the ice and so did I. Not more than can be expected. And the dogs … they did a fantastic job today. My team were tired at the end. Very tired and I had to go and push the sledges too. Good for me. The sun is burning as well. Far too hot, especially for the dogs. Anyway, we named the glacier today: Hot Dog Glacier. Magical landscape.

Bruce Parry's Diary

DAY 17
Our gear is not lasting.

Set off roped up. Can see the mountains looming large and ominous. Got so hot that Mark called a halt for the sake of his dogs at about 4ish. Good call as all were v hot, sunburnt and dehydrated.

DAY 19
Happy birthday, Mark. He's outside feeding the dogs again – great guy – so industrious and never complaining – an absolute must for the final four. Great going at first including some magnificent slides downhill, but the sun was so strong that soon enough the dogs were really too hot. Some trouble finding the best way to avoid crevasses, and I and a few dogs at least found a few ones to thigh depth or so. Come 1 p.m. we called it a day midway across the glacier in favour of trying nights instead. I faked an injured leg so that Mark would head off with Dave on a recce. Meanwhile, we pooled presents, made a pemmican cake that looks like a dog with candles – blew up balloons, put brandy and vodka on ice. On his return we sang 'Happy Birthday' and basically started getting pissed. He was genuinely touched, and chocolate truffles and tobacco went down well. I broke out some tramadol (painkillers) to add to the fun. We'd decided to get up at 10 p.m. and a few of us were still supping brandy at 8ish. Finally got some kip for an hour or so before being woken up again by Mark (legend) to set off. A few bleary eyes and most of us

on autopilot. Brilliant idea to do nights as it was still v bright despite no sun but the ground was firm and icy. Beautiful, beautiful night and the going was fantastic.

DAY 20
Without doubt the best day yet. The glacier valleys looking so impressive as your view changed the perspectives. The vastness of the surroundings was hard to take in at first. Even the distances that looked like just a few hundred yards took hours and were in fact often a few miles. Had some fun river crossings which ended up with me and some others getting our feet quite wet.

DAY 21
The journey up is magnificent. Blocks of ice and obvious crevasses strew the way, but water was our nemesis. Rory takes a full dunking, but he stoically offers to carry on and dry out walking. Near the top Arthur is sat aside his sledge when it drops a foot or two into an obvious crevasse.

DAY 22
Routine is v ordinary now, and some tasks which I previously loathed are just normal tasks now. Still it takes us 4 hours before we are ready at 1 a.m. to go.

DAY 23
Hilarious moment when Mark's sledge careered off the wrong way. Lovely moon still up and colours just warm and surreal everywhere. The great advantage of travelling at night is that the contrasts are so fabulous. Almost ethereal texture to everything. Watching the sun come up is also always a treat as it slowly catches the tops of those magnificent sharp peaks first (quite the most impressive small mountains I've seen for many years), and then we expectantly wait for the warmth of the sun's rays to reach our cold bodies. It takes a good hour or two before it does any warming … great campsite view and everyone happy.

Day 24
The Paris Glacier offers a long downhill stretch, and soon enough the boys are careering down a steep section behind us. Keep to the middle and criss-cross the Norwegian team's tracks all day. I cannot keep my fingers warm at all. I can't grip my ski sticks and soon enough fall over my crossed ski tips. V frustrating. The mountains are simply majestic. A wonderful day to be out and we truly are very lucky.

The last glacier is v steep. Push everyone quite a lot and Mark's team suffering. Towards the end of the day I promise just one more bit to the base of a slope which seems some way off. It ends up being v close, so I decide to go up the incline. This turns out to be like a 3-mile horror and I'd promised Mark I wouldn't push his dogs so far. I feel so guilty at pushing them so hard at the end of an already long day. We decide to go for it, and although it requires a mammoth effort, we finally get to flatter part near the entrance to our final glacier. Great day. Big day tomorrow. After that it's the ice cap again and back to abject boredom.

Day 25
Oh my God, oh my God, what a fantastic day! It had it all – tension, jeopardy, physical exertion and emotion and tears and happiness. Wow! The epic of all time. We knew this was our nemesis day and we needed tiptop dog teams.

The twilight made every slope absolutely impossible to figure out its length and steepness. Every little slope turned out to be a 3-mile epic. Potentially disastrous for the boys and dogs but it just seemed to bolster their resilience and resolve. Awesome.

The first slope took a few hits with fresh dogs, then turning a wide left to avoid confluence crevassing, we were faced with our final slopes. At first it seemed all quite easy until we got started. F**k, then we knew what was ahead. We decided to hit the slopes in the sledge teams as we were, and try and get as far up them as possible, then rethink. This worked and we got a small distance up some monster incline, then got all loads on to Chris and Arthur's sledge, harnesses at the ready and six guys struggled valiantly to get the thing going – lots of problems with dogs being distracted by us, and us not being very efficient in pushing and pulling (no ski poles and wrong footwear etc) but we got it up to the lesser slope. Had minor disagreement with Chris about going on or going back for the others. Both of us backing down amicably.

Next two sledges were much easier, as we'd learnt to extend the dogs with an extra trace to avoid tangles with us, and put man-haul traces on to the sledge to add to our purchase. One person led the team with a harness, and one followed at the rear to lessen slide. It worked a treat and almost got us up the hill to the other sledge in two hits. We then split our efforts and had two sledges move simultaneously. I was with Mark's team and they were hilarious; they always start so fast I could hardly run fast enough with my ski poles pumping ahead of them. Then we'd grind to a halt, having reached our anaerobic threshold so rest and start again. Then back for Rory's sledge. V hard work for everyone. We then went back to individual sledges and tackled the last few slopes. Finally got to the top. Elation, but windy and cold. The next depot was potentially in reach. I was up for stopping but thought I'd offer a deal to the gang. If we pushed on, I'd consider a day off. The gang agreed and the few miles actually flew by with us all sitting on the sledges with fantastic ice conditions and the dogs going for it. How they had the energy left I don't know.

DAY 26

Day off. Truly this was a day off covered up as a day of admin, navigation, stock check. Reassess our expedition goals. I suggested that One Ton was unachievable. We decided that we'd go on till the end regardless. I sat with Rupert and Chris to organize the depot points, distances and food allocations. It soon became apparent that we could keep the final guys on for a bit longer. So we decided that we'd keep the dogs for the same 40 days at 10 nautical miles per day. This will take us to the same distance from the pole as Scott (in his first phase) for our man-hauling phase. After that I want a geographical location to aim for within the 99-day parameter. Scott reached Upper Glacier on Day 99, so maybe this will work for us.

DAY 27.

Icy icy. Had an abortive dump in the tent before it went down. V cold nose, hands and knob on the march.

CHAPTER SEVEN

Attrition

THE BACK TENDON OF MY RIGHT LEG FEELS AS IF IT HAD BEEN
STRETCHED ABOUT FOUR INCHES. I HOPE TO GOODNESS IT IS NOT
GOING TO GIVE TROUBLE.
Laurence 'Titus' Oates

One day, while still in the early part of the Barrier journey, Scott's team came across a cairn they had made on the depot journey. It stood just as they had left it, with only one spectacular change. The prevailing wind had sculpted an accumulation of loose snow against its side. The result, noted Scott, was 'a big tongue of drift, level with the top of the cairn to leeward, and running about 150 yards to N.E., showing that the prevailing wind here is S.W.'

For all the miles they covered, for all the treacly snow they slogged through, for all the misery they suffered in the extreme cold, it is hard to find a more succinct image of the unrelenting harshness of the Antarctic climate. Here, in a single, immensely long tapering wall of snow was an illustration of the odds stacked against the possibility of a comfortable journey. Those pictures of men standing at the pole, however exultant or morose the figures themselves may happen to be, have one thing in common. A vigorous wind is always snapping the flag to attention.

Not that they could always rely on it to howl at them from the same direction, despite the evidence of the 150-yard tongue of drift. One day they built snow walls to protect the ponies from a prevailing north wind, only for it to swing round overnight and assault them from the southeast.

The diaries noted its force. Gale force 5. Force 8. Of course, for those being pulled by dogs, the deleterious effects of a howling gale on mind and body were much less imposing. This is why members of Scott's party seem to rail at the heavens as if collectively afflicted by a (rather unattractive) victim complex. It was easier for Amundsen and his men to shrug off the incursions of snow, wind and white-out. They were, for the most part, sitting on sledges, or gliding through the snows on skis. 'Today we have had a lot of loose snow,' Amundsen enthused on one of his depot journeys. 'For us on skis it was the most magnificent going.'

More than anyone's, the diaries of Bowers fixate on the conditions underfoot and overhead. He was a practical young man, and was charged by Scott with keeping the meteorological record. When adverse weather threw up actual barriers in his path, he chafed against them. 'We have now run down a whole degree of latitude without a fine day, or anything but clouds, mist, and driving snow from the south ... The weather was about as poisonous as one could wish; a fresh breeze and a driving snow from the E. with an awful surface.' One day he complains that 'the light was so bad that wearing goggles was most necessary, and the driving snow filled them up as fast as you cleared them ... At the four-mile cairn I was about fed up to the neck with it, but I said very little as everybody was so disgusted with the weather and things in general that I saw that I was not the only one in tribulation.' So it goes on.

And Bowers was one of the more cheery souls under Scott's command. If the weather could turn him into a misanthrope, its effect on his leader was exponentially worse. Scott would dwell on the cards dealt him with a steadiness of purpose that has yielded criticism. 'Our luck is preposterous,' he grumbled at the foot of the Beardmore Glacier. And then again, as he sat rooted to the wet floorcloth of his tent, waiting for the blizzard to pass: 'What on earth does such weather mean at this time of year? It is more than our share of ill-fortune ... How great may be the element of luck ... It's real hard luck.' When sending back a letter with one of the returning parties, a letter to Cape Evans concluded thus: 'We keep our spirits up and say the luck must turn.'

In this unceasing mantra, Scott reveals a gift for self-pity, but it is interesting to note inadvertent echoes of his exasperation in Bruce Parry. 'Luck plays a big part in these things,' Bruce says before setting out. He has clearly bought into the idea that Scott was felled by misfortune rather than incompetence. After the terrible early days when it seems the modern British team have bitten off far more than they can chew, he attributes all their troubles to a bad hand rather than the more obvious fact that, through no fault of their own, they are insufficiently prepared for the task. 'I actually think that we are just having a lot of bad luck,' he says. 'It's been really turgid snow that's like treacle syrup and the weather has been bad and we're slow. Scott had it at the base of the Beardmore. We're having it in the first few days. It's just tough going.' The real stroke of bad luck is the injury that removes Nick Akers from the expedition.

Later Bruce returns to the theme at the base of the glacier. 'Scott was in the Antarctic in one of the worst summers that has ever been. He had an immense amount of bad luck, and some of that was the weather. We've shared some of his bad luck. It makes you realize how tough they were back then. They were really quite hardcore. And we haven't even started man-hauling yet.'

There is scientific proof that Scott was indeed unlucky. It has been demonstrated by a comparative study of Antarctic weather patterns that the four-day blizzard at the base of the Beardmore was, for the time of year, a meteorological freak. Unluckily for Scott, it came just when he didn't need it. Amundsen was also tent-bound for four days, and his admirers pat him on the back for not moaning about it. But perhaps he really was lucky that when the weather turned foul, it couldn't have come at a better time. He happened to be at the top of the glacier, and was badly in need of a few days' rest and a period of acclimatization to the new altitude.

Scott was prone to moods anyway, but at times his men seemed to travel in a permanent state of seasonally adjusted depression. Thus Scott, early in the journey: 'The weather was horrid, overcast, gloomy, snowy. One's spirits became very low.' Or, 'I expected these marches to be a little difficult but not near so bad as today.' 'Miserable, utterly miserable,' wrote Cherry-Garrard in the blizzard at the Gateway. 'We try to treat it as a huge joke, but our wretched condition might be amusing to read of later. We are wet through, our tents are wet, our bags which are our life to us and the objects of our greatest care, are wet ... our food is wet.' By the time he came to write *The Worst Journey in the World*, he had read up on everyone else's response to adversity too. 'It is curious to see how depressed all our diaries become when this bad weather obtained, and how quickly we must have cheered up whenever the sun came out.'

He wasn't being quite accurate about the benign effects of the scattering clouds. Problems with visibility led to problems with navigation. But when the white-out dispersed and the sun reflected off the glaring whiteness all around them, it was sometimes even harder to see. Snow blindness came down like a contagion on many of them. At the start of the Beardmore they suffered from it dreadfully. 'I am afraid I am going to pay dearly for not wearing goggles yesterday when piloting the ponies,' wrote Bowers in the Gateway. 'My right eye has gone bung, and my left one is pretty dicky ... it is painful to look at this paper, and my eyes are fairly burning as if someone had thrown sand into them.' For the next four days he didn't bother with his diary. It was all he could do to haul, eyeless, on to the glacier.

It was worst when they switched from night travel to day on the glacier. The sun was suddenly brighter, and it took them by surprise. They had a variety of remedies in the medicine bags of the two doctors, Wilson and Atkinson. They approved of the cocaine and zinc sulphate tablets, but also resorted to a more organic cure. Someone had the bright idea of placing discarded tea leaves over the eyes. With a bit of cotton and a knotted handkerchief, they found a way to keep them in place while hauling. Bowers stuck plaster over his glasses, leaving only a small pinprick of visibility through which he could make out the tips of his skis at such moments as sweat hadn't clouded the glasses. He couldn't wipe them off because no one would risk bringing the sledge to a halt in the deep snow. It was at times like this that Cherry-Garrard must have minded less about being short-sighted: while the sun scorched the corneas of all around him, so everyone else was similarly disadvantaged.

Wilson would suffer just as they turned away from the pole. 'Had $ZnSO_4$ and cocaine in my eyes at night and didn't get to sleep at all for the pain.' Cherry-Garrard theorized that Wilson was particularly prone to snow-blindness on account of 'his anxiety to sketch whenever opportunity offered, and his willingness to take off his goggles to search for tracks and cairns'.

One of the ways in which the reconstruction veers away from accuracy is in the business of health. There were no UV filters in 1911, but all the modern explorers have been supplied with up-to-date lenses in their period goggles, as well as sun cream and lip balm. The medical kit is also historically inaccurate. Wilson went to the South Pole with a variety of compounds containing arsenic, lead and mercury. Once the poisons have been removed from the period bag, the modern British team is left with a quarter of what Wilson took.

But there is fidelity in other areas. They have problems with the goggles, which freeze up and are difficult to see through. Their eyes take a particular battering whenever they have to navigate out in front. The difficulty is partly down to the inadequacy of their compasses, which means that they have to navigate by picking a point on the horizon and aiming for it. But once they reach the ice cap, there are no points on the horizon, and often they find themselves navigating by cloud formation. On Day 48, Bruce's eyes are 'screaming' from the incessant effort of trying to make sense of constantly evolving cloud shapes. 'An absolute nightmare,' he concludes. 'Really horrible, double vision pain, nasty. It's not pleasant.'

Amundsen's men all fashioned their own goggles, and only Bjaaland suffered from snow-blindness. Amundsen himself never used goggles, relying instead on a pair of open-sided yellow-tinted spectacles. When it came to health, Amundsen seemed to trust to his instincts. For some reason, he was suspicious of medical expertise. As a young man, he had dropped out of university, where he had begun to study medicine, the instant his mother died. Clearly, he thought that he'd picked up enough to be going on with because he took no doctor south with him. He sounded proud of it. 'We took a little travelling case of medicines from Burroughs Wellcome and Co. Our surgical instruments were not many: a dental forceps and – a beard-clipper.' They used the beard-clipper every Saturday night in the tent. The forceps were used to extract a tooth of Wisting's.

In the interests of accuracy, the modern Norwegian team in Greenland travel with the same number of medical qualifications as Amundsen did: none. And it turns out that, just like Amundsen's men, they have little need of medical attention. Both Rune Gjeldnes and Harald Kippenes suffer from cold feet when their unproofed snow boots get wet in the slushy snow on warm days. But that, remarkably, is it. Amundsen was similarly unafflicted. He had his warning when he set off for the pole a month too soon. Hanssen went home with a particularly frostbitten heel that Amundsen compared to the colour of tallow, but others were affected too. Their boots, which were too stiff, provided insufficient insulation. Four of the party were bedridden for ten days.

Bruce is even better supplied with medical expertise than Scott, as the doctors Rory O'Connor and Chris van Tulleken make up a quarter of the entire party. Until Atkinson turned for home at the top of the Beardmore, Scott had two doctors for a dozen men. Thanks to the style of travel, and the inadequacy of the equipment, Scott would need his doctors. By the end of the Barrier he remarked on 'a run on the medical cases for chafes and minor ailments'. Muscles, joints, limbs creaked and groaned under the strain. Scott complained of a troublesome heel, and bruises on his knees and thighs. Oates's old bullet wound from the Boer War started to play up.

But they didn't just suffer from the sheer punishment meted out to their bodies on the long march through difficult snow. The cold, as much as the physical exertion, took its toll. Neither allowed ailments and wounds to recover. In the case of Taff Evans, this would prove extremely serious. While shortening the sledges from 12 feet to 10 with Crean at the top of the glacier, he cut himself on the right hand. Somehow he managed to conceal the injury from Scott.

He nursed the ambition of running a pub once he'd returned to South Wales. A landlord sent home before the final assault on the pole would hardly be as magnetic a draw for Swansea's drinkers as the only man from the ranks to stand with Captain Scott at 90 degrees south. Perhaps he talked about his dream with Crean while they doctored the sledges. Being sent back before the pole would not stop Crean from going home to the west of Ireland and pulling pints at the South Pole Inn, though his even more dramatic adventures on Shackleton's *Endurance* expedition were still to come.

Under foot there were more hazards than just hidden crevasses. 'The surface was very slippery in parts and on the hard sastrugi it was a case of falling or stumbling continually.' If the surface wasn't too soft, it was as often as not too hard. On the glacier they came across rippled blue ice, which caused the sledges to skid and capsize. Their feet took a pounding. Now, as then, the inadequacies of the *finnesko* footwear are exposed by the different conditions. Bruce is affected by a dose of trench foot, which comes on quickly because so much of his previous travelling experience has been in swamps. A sudden drop in temperature would cause him difficulties. But the *finnesko* is better suited to sustained cold. 'I much prefer colder temperatures,' says Rory. 'Your feet stay in better condition.'

It goes without saying that in 1911 their exposed faces and lips were all burnt to a crisp. 'One's nose and lips being chapped and much skinned with alternate heat and cold,' wrote Scott at the Upper Glacier Depot, 'a breeze in the face is absolute agony until you warm up.' It was just as bad for Amundsen's men on the sledges. 'The left side of our faces was one mass of sore, bathed in matter and serum. We looked like the worst type of tramps and ruffians ... These sores were a great trouble to us during the latter part of the journey. The slightest gust of wind produced a sensation as if one's face were being cut backwards and forwards with a blunt knife.'

Up on the ice cap the modern British team briefly change from day to night travel, but decide after two days that the risk of frostbite on the face, especially for those working the sledges, is too great. Chris describes sledging in extreme cold as 'purgatory'. 'You can't breathe well enough to run with the balaclava pulled down around your face, but you still get very cold and are very susceptible to frost-nip when you are sitting on the sledge not doing anything.' To prevent frost-nip, in colder temperatures Rory takes the precaution of stopping every ten minutes to warm up parts of his face. Then he has to coax the circulation back into his hands.

Scott's men didn't write about the sensation of frostbite, other than to report they suffered from it. Within the parameters of the experiment, as much care as possible is taken to ensure that no one is in a position to find out what it's like. But Mark Anstice spends so much time in the first two weeks doing fiddly jobs with the dogs that it is quicker to remove his gloves. The result is that up on the ice cap he sometimes loses circulation in the top two joints of fingers and thumb on his right hand. 'It starts off on the backs of the fingers and is like a burning sensation and then it very quickly goes. It's really hard to get back circulation in the right hand, and when it comes back, it is just painful.' Whenever frost-nip strikes, he rotates his arm to increase the flow of blood.

At least Mark has not emulated Scott. He tells his sledgemates that Scott got his first taste of frostbite when he overdosed on curry powder in his pemmican, and had to dash out of the tent in the middle of the night. It is a little remarked footnote of the race to the pole that both leaders were martyrs to their bowels. Amundsen suffered from some form of haemorrhoidal complaint throughout the first depot-laying journey. The pain was so excruciating that he felt obliged to withdraw from the third one. Meanwhile, there are occasional references – though not in his own diaries – to Scott's indigestion.

The pemmican plays merry hell with the innards of Bruce's team. Mark and Dave Pearce both suffer at one point from diarrhoea. Inconvenient enough at the best of times, it is infinitely worse when they know that answering the call of nature will result in instant frostbite. In Tassilaq they make a loose plan to take turns to defecate in the tent each morning before they set off. Whether or not this turns out to be too time-consuming, by the middle of the journey the tent-mates Rory, Mark and Bruce are no longer standing on ceremony, and just squatting all together. The morning ritual is to remove the ground sheet, defecate into a snow hole, and light a communal pipe to clear the aroma. Then they strike the tent. At the lunch break they will happily squat by the side of a sledge and simply defecate there and then. Nothing was quite as easy in 1911, or certainly not in Scott's tent. Such was his squeamishness that Scott's tentmates felt obliged to leave the tent, whatever the weather, rather than defecate or even urinate in his presence.

* * * * * * * * * * * *

Gradually the inventory of physical depletion built up, and as Scott's men successively turned for home, the ailments would become less minor. Eyes, fingers, feet, guts – these were the parts of the body that objected most strenuously to the punitive regime of polar travel. In time the cold and the limited diet would make more serious claims on their physical resources. On his way home Teddy Evans would succumb to scurvy and have to be hauled home over the final furlongs. Oates's leg and Taff Evans's hand were specific injuries. One of them was old, picked up in the Boer War, and was reopened by the cold; the other was new, and in the cold wouldn't heal. And then their feet, in those *finnesko* slippers, started to be permanently damaged.

In Bruce's team, the one to be felled next is a surprise. Dave Pearce came into the expedition with more experience of cold-weather survival than anyone else on the British team. His 24 years in the Marines included a huge amount of Arctic training, and summiting on Everest. The problem is that his knowledge of cold climes comes at a price. His fingers are more prone to frostbite than, at the other end of the scale, Arthur Jeffes's, who has no cold-weather experience outside the Alps, and whose worst cold-weather injury is also the most bizarre. He is not used to having a beard, and habitually licks it until his tongue starts to hurt.

Since Day 1, Dave has been out in front, navigating, his fur-mittened hands gripping ski poles. Around Day 30, soon after they have emerged from the top of the glacier system, a cold fog descends one morning. The index finger on his right hand, as well as his thumb, get badly nipped. For the rest of the day he finds it difficult to keep his fingers warm, and for the next few days he complains of numbness and tingling. Rory inspects the hand, stroking the fingers and prodding them with a needle to check for feeling, and is not too worried. 'He has probably affected a nerve in the finger. It still has a good blood supply. He is not going to lose tissue, but it gives an indication of severity.'

But there are two problems. On the ice cap further cold temperatures cannot be ruled out. And now that he is worrying about his finger, Dave clearly has a reduced appetite for the long goalless slog over the ice. He describes the sensation of losing feeling in the finger as the cold constricts it, only for feeling to flood back in the form of pain when blood pumps back into it. In the circumstances, the pain is a relief.

Bruce is presented with a dilemma. On Day 49, according to the road map for the re-enactment, he must reduce the expedition to four team members, just as Scott shed numbers in his team as he advanced towards the pole. Although he has kept his cards close to his chest, it is a surprise to no one that Bruce would have had Dave in his final four. Dave is equally aware of this, and admits that if left to make his own decision, he would probably subordinate his own interests for the good of the team. He is relieved, therefore, when Bruce chooses to take the decision out of his hands because it really is clear that he'd much rather go home than sacrifice a finger or two to what is, in the end, a facsimile of a great adventure. Fresh out of the Marines after nearly a quarter of a century, he has a career in mountaineering to forge. It won't happen without a full complement of fingers.

'If I was Scott, or if this was a British attempt to get to the South Pole, I might not look at it in the same way,' says Bruce. 'I might say we're willing to run the risk of losing a finger because we've got bigger things going on here. But I don't think there's any need for anybody to get long-term damage because of this expedition. It's my responsibility that he goes home safe. Of course, he is the sort of guy who would want to soldier on till the end. He's solid, one of the strongest. He would undoubtedly be in my final four but I have a responsibility. I don't want to mess up his future career, which depends upon him not having hands which are trashed by cold. I want to shake his hand in a year and say "How's the climbing career?" Not "Sorry I trashed it for you." '

For two days Bruce thrashes the issues around in his mind. It is clear that he relishes having something to think about other than the daily routine. He seizes on the opportunity to show decisive leadership. More than once he says he doesn't mind making the big decisions ('I'm used to it'). It's also clear that the idea of having someone else's future in his hands appeals to his innate sense of drama. 'Every time I see him swing his arms it kills me inside,' he says at one point. 'I think, I have the power to stop your pain.'

Among the things to consider are the timing of the injury. Dave's problems surface in the run-up to Day 40, when a plane will fly in and take the dog teams home. Thus there are three viable options: to keep Dave till the bitter end, scheduled for Day 99; to send him home 50 days earlier, when Bruce reduces the team to four; or to put him on the plane with the dogs.

None of the choices makes complete sense. Clearly, if he has a cold-weather injury, it is best to get him out as soon as possible. If he can stay till Day 49, why can't he stay till Day 99? But only once the dogs go home on Day 40 will the man-hauling begin in earnest, and Dave is keen at least to sample the joys of polar travel as exemplified by Scott and his men. Nor does he want to shoulder the guilt of leaving the six remaining men in the lurch, with two full sledges to pull. They have already lost Nick, and if they lose Dave as well it will mean one less man on each of the two remaining sledges. Bruce is grimly aware that three men to a sledge may translate into only a couple of miles of progress a day. Knowing that Dave wants to get into a man-haul harness, Mark suggests that 'we take him to Day 49, and if it does come to a white-out, we police him'.

But Bruce is aware that deep down this is not just about a frostbitten finger. There is a motivational issue at work as well. Dave is by some years the oldest of the group, and his priorities are different. 'If it was one of the younger guys who desperately wanted to be here,' says Bruce, 'I would probably allow them to continue because they really wanted to be here and I would say the risk was acceptable.' Alone among the team, Dave has children at home – three daughters – who are waiting as usual to shave off his beard when he walks through the door. 'Everyone finds [motivation] in different ways,' says Bruce. 'Some have pride and they'll get on with it regardless; Scott had fame and fortune potentially and on the way home he had life. We're trying to have a taste of what he went through. I am not very motivated by this place, I find it mind-numbingly dull. The end is months away and I've better things to do with my life.' He adds that 'Dave's quite similar to me and Mark in that this isn't really our cup of tea. He probably doesn't enjoy it, and deep down will thank me for sending him home. If I offered him that ticket, he won't be crying all the way home.'

In the end, he does offer Dave the ticket. And he's right. Dave doesn't seem too concerned to be put on the first plane home. At no point can he admit it, but perhaps the flaring-up of an old finger injury is his deliverance, not so much from pain, but from unadulterated boredom. There is certainly a mixed message in his parting thoughts. 'It's rational and sensible,' he says. '[Bruce] knows I'm concerned. I'm more than happy ... The alternative task of going home to wife and kids is hardly onerous. I take my hat off to polar explorers who trudge on the ice cap for months. I would have liked to have been with the guys for a bit longer. But it's not the end of the world. I like calculated risks. The goal would have to be significant – the real pole or mountain, stepping into the history books. This is not worth that. I've done expeditions where people have kept things hidden and it's put us in a serious situation. You've got to be absolutely honest. Tell everyone so everybody knows. It doesn't help anybody by hiding these things.'

The historical parallel is compelling. When Taff Evans managed to conceal the cut to his hand, he did so because he knew that to reveal it would have found him harnessed on to the first sled home. He would not step into the history books, so he kept quiet and, it could be argued, signed his own death warrant. He was the first man to die on the long way home. Had Scott taken the redoubtable Crean instead, the man with whom Evans customized the sledges, might they both have survived to open a pub?

Parry's Diary

DAY 28.

It seems others are getting cold fingers too, but mine are definitely worst in the mornings.

I enjoy walking with Rory as he's so easy-going. Dave with Mark's dogs – funny and not entirely compatible. He gets quite irate and makes me laugh (but not the dogs!!). Spent some time with Chris too on his sledge. What a difference. Sat chatting most of the way. Remarkable. Smallest dogs, biggest sledge and heavy loads, and still the fastest sledge when we're sat on it and others run.

Chris had brainwave of dragging a bag of food for dogs to follow. It worked really well!

DAY 29

Three of us sat in the tent this morning with 45 minutes to go. After some time we were all sat on our sleeping bag rolls just staring at the door in silence. Just like kamikaze pilots about to walk to their planes. To my intense surprise, it was the most glorious morning … walking alone was wonderful. I didn't use skis and it was good going. Loads of time to think and my mind went everywhere: two feature film ideas, two TVs and two books. All planned to the smallest detail. The dogs don't allow for any escapism.

We easily broke our day record – 17.5 nautical miles. Fantastic and everyone very tired but happy with a great result … We've got a good system now and it's a shame that we've only about 11 or so days of dog work left. We all hope the good weather lasts so that we can squeeze the last out of our hounds before we pick up the reins ourselves.

DAY 30

Cooker wouldn't f**king start this morning. Of all the things. Really not funny. Our wake-up normally consists of Rory's 1911 alarm clock's 10-second ring waking him up (in reality, as with this morning, he never wakes up and I check the watch round my neck and wake him up). We then shuffle about and try to light the stove, make water and doze until it's done. This is the worst time of the day by far, and that extra half-hour doze while the water is heating is blissful and full of dread too. Well, when the stove didn't light, it wasn't funny. Luckily, it was a fantastic day outside. Truly beautiful with two vertical rainbows either side of the sun. Remarkable. Also a vertical shaft of light going into the heavens. Everyone in a good mood.

DAY 31

Decided to change start time once again to make full use of cold weather because it was even getting too warm by 8 a.m., so called for an early stop and then got up again at 8 p.m. for an 11 p.m. start.

DAY 32

Dave had the shits this morning and was feeling rough. Also his right index finger had started playing up and he couldn't re-warm it.

I had a huge icicle instead of a beard, which kept sticking to my neckerchief. I rashly tried to pull it away on a couple of occasions and nearly pulled off half my face. Painful. Skiing along with only a letterbox view of my ski tips is quite meditative and I really enjoy it. Once man-hauling in a group, it will be a thing of the past. Shame, as it's very cathartic and therapeutic.

Mark put up a tent after 14 nautical miles to have a dump in to ensure he didn't get frostbite and Dave and I skied in last in time for him to use it too. Dave and Mark had held their guts in all night long to avoid a dangerous cold dump, which must have been very unpleasant, to say the least.

DAY 33

Possibly the coldest period of the expedition to date: minus 26 degrees Celsius on leaving at 1 a.m. and minus 30 by 4 a.m. I was so hopeful that the decision to persist with nights was going to turn out a good one. So days it is and now I'm sat here in my tent with 18 hours till tomorrow morning when we set off again. I've decided to move into the other tent in place of Mark with Chris, Arthur and Rupert. Quite different already. Posh and intellectual, verbose and youthful. The only drawback is the lack of space. Rory gave me two coffee sachets as a goodbye gesture, my dirty mug and spoon and that was it. I've moved to get to know the others better before I make my choice of the final four. Guys are in the middle of a theodolite maths session. Thank the lord for Rupes and Chris and their astronomical brains (bad pun!).

DAY 34

I'm looking forward to the man-hauling phase just so that we can all be doing the same level of work together again. I do feel rather guilty at times just being on skis all day and avoiding the dog frustrations.

DAY 35

Best day on the ice cap.

DAY 36

Dave is worried about his health and his future ability to work with his bad fingers, but won't volunteer to go. I, however, can send him home, but I want to maintain his credibility as a cool mountain guide and tough guy. Difficult.

The fear of man-hauling looms large. Our hard work hasn't started yet and tough it will be indeed. 384 nautical miles to go to pole from here today, and that's the same distance Scott walked from Shambles, only he had the glacier first. Hard bastards.

The dogs broke loose in camp and the whole team of us had to come out and beat them off the food box, untangle the chain and generally stop them all fighting. I'll miss them so much.

DAY 37

I'm not enjoying my new tent. I love the company, but the tent routine is almost unbearable. It's just not organized -- badly planned and very slow, and for some silly reason it's getting to me. Really I should be able to rise above it because it's not personal at all. The guys are typical untidy intellectuals and I'm almost obsessive compulsive. I hope I calm down because irrational irritability will only eat away within me. I don't think they're aware of my internal struggle. I've offered to do the in-tent routine a couple of times, but this is firmly Arthur's domain. But if I do it just once or twice, I may be able to change things a little at least. I hope they never read this because in the grand scheme of things it's so minor, and in essence the problem is probably mine.

DAY 38

The time finally came this evening to tell Dave my decision. I'd rehearsed what I was going to say all day long, but, of course, when it came to the moment, I was floundering. I asked him not to reply but to think about it overnight and he took it well. I was delighted to note he was very cool with my decision and not upset at all. He saw my position and was grateful for the time I'd spent thinking it over. He will be sorely missed.

DAY 40

Day off. Awesome.

Dave is leaving today but in good spirits. I was to find out later that Dave's hand had a complete demarcation line on his fingers. His fingertip was completely white, and even Rory was shocked, so I was definitely right, and in an awful macabre way I was quite glad of the proof. Dave left to a solemn farewell. I moved back in with Rory and now with Mark which was just what I needed. I bit my lip long enough in the posh intellectual tent about the shit routines and untidiness. Great being in a tent with Mark at last.

CHAPTER EIGHT

Strength

GRIM GRIM GRIM. BREAKING THE TRAIL REQUIRED JUST TOO MUCH
EFFORT FOR EASY CONVERSATION AND MY MIND KEPT REVERTING
TO THEIR SKI TIPS AND THEIR PAINFULLY SLOW PROGRESS ACROSS
THE ENDLESS WASTE. I HAVE RARELY KNOWN NINE AND A HALF
HOURS TO DRAG SO BADLY.
Mark Anstice

What, ultimately, is the point of man-hauling? Nowadays everyone does it, and would not have it any other way. Since the pole was claimed and Antarctica traversed, the pursuit of new polar records has usually always involved someone trying to prove he (and increasingly she) is tougher than the last man (or woman). Inevitably, that involves the purity of effort that comes with auto-propulsion across hundreds, even thousands, of miles of ice.

Things looked different in 1911, at least to one sceptic. 'It must be rather hard to have to abandon one's motive power voluntarily when only a quarter of the distance has been covered. I for my part prefer to use it all the way.' Thus Amundsen in *The South Pole: An Account of the Norwegian Antarctic Expedition in the Fram, 1910–1912*. Before and after Scott's death, the Norwegian made every effort to show his rival at least the pretence of courtesy.

But when it came to man-hauling, it was a struggle not to sound smug.

Others on Amundsen's expedition found generosity easier to express. 'It is no disparagement of Amundsen and the rest of us when I say that Scott's achievement far exceeded ours,' wrote Helmer Hanssen, Amundsen's leading dog-driver. 'Just imagine what it meant for Scott and the others to drag their sleds themselves, with all their equipment and provisions to the pole. We started with 52 dogs and came back with 11, and many of these wore themselves out on the journey. What shall we say of Scott and his comrades, who were their own dogs? ... I do not believe men ever have shown such endurance at any time, nor do I believe there ever will be men to equal it.'

On Days 40 and 41, Bruce Parry says goodbye to one man and 24 dogs. From now on, the team members will be their own dogs. From the start Bruce has been optimistic about this moment. 'I think we've got a good chance,' he says before setting out. 'The Norwegians are the obvious favourites. But man-hauling with the right team is a perfectly acceptable way of doing polar exploration. We will prove that we have the endurance to keep up.' Even when he comes across Norwegian tracks on the glacier, he does not change his tune. He clings to the belief that getting rid of the dogs will make all the difference. 'When we start pulling, we can put the hours in, while they're limited by how many hours they can work the dogs. We'll get our regain. It's all to play for.'

In theory, at least, there is something in this. Amundsen rarely travelled for more than six hours a day on his journey to the pole, and contented himself with a daily distance of 15 nautical miles. Scott could have gone further than this, and, indeed, his daily averages on the plateau were only a couple of miles short of Amundsen's. But those averages were won at an exorbitant cost in physical effort.

When Scott launched an appeal for funds for his second Antarctic expedition, he announced that the endeavour would involve dogs, Manchurian ponies and motorized sledges. There was no reference to the fact that the 12 men who made it to the top of the Beardmore would spend between a half and three-quarters of the entire journey strapped into a harness. But like modern polar travellers searching for ever more punishing ways to set records, there was a part of Scott that relished the challenge of utter self-reliance. The immensity of the task appealed to him on a moral and an intellectual level, and had done so ever since his first expedition to the Antarctic, when it weighed on his conscience that animals had suffered so that he might have it easy. 'The introduction of such sordid necessity,' he concluded in *The Voyage of the 'Discovery'*, 'must and does rob sledge-travelling of much of its glory. In my mind no journey ever made with dogs can approach the height of that fine conception which is realized when a party of men go forth to face hardships, dangers and difficulties with their own unaided efforts, and by days and weeks of hard physical labour succeed in solving some problem of the great unknown. Surely in this case the conquest is more nobly and splendidly won.'

Many modern explorers agree with him, and so did an Edwardian one. Bowers, the most unquestioning of acolytes in the party of 12 who waved goodbye to Meares, Gerof and dogs at the bottom of the glacier, had been champing to face hardships with his own unaided efforts ever since Scott announced that man-haul would be pivotal to his plans. 'I for one am delighted at the decision. After all, it will be a fine thing to do that plateau with man-haulage in these days of the supposed decadence of the British race.' Halfway up the Beardmore he may have felt more ambivalent about 'the most back-breaking work I have ever come up against'. And apart from Scott himself, Bowers had the greatest appetite for back-breaking work. Did a show of British mettle require quite so much expenditure, and all for such snail-like gains?

By Christmas, as the deep slush thinned out and a harder surface gave them better traction, Bowers was sounding more chipper: 'Our routine,' he wrote on 23 December, 'is to actually haul our sledges for nine hours a day; five in the morning, 7.15 a.m. 'til 1 p.m.; and four in the afternoon, 2.30 p.m. – 6.30 p.m. We turn out at 5.45 a.m. just now. The loads are still pretty heavy, but the surface is remarkably good considering all things. One gets pretty weary towards the end of the day; all my muscles have had their turn at being [stiffened] up. These hills are giving my back ones a reminder, but they will ache less tomorrow and finally cease to do so, as is the case with legs, etc., which had their turn first.'

It was at the end of one of these days that Cherry-Garrard's diary entry even makes reference to 'a most pleasant pull'. One good thing about the work was that it kept you warm. 'When man-hauling, we used to start pulling immediately. We had the tent down, the sledge packed and our harness over our bodies and the skis on our feet. After about a quarter of an hour the effects of the marching would be felt in the warming of hands and feet and the consequent thawing of our mitts and finnesko.'

* * * * * * * * * * * *

On Day 40, Bruce doesn't know that the Norwegian team is less than a week away from the pole. The injury to Dave Pearce has further reduced his hauling party from what would originally have been eight to six. They have to drag less food, but they have to bring all the paraphernalia for two tents. Briefly, Bruce contemplates the option of sending back a second man with Dave and the dogs. The advantage is that a party of five men would have to pull only one sledge because only one tent would be needed. The disadvantage is that the remaining tent would be very crowded. Scott, of course, was to discover this for himself later.

Some of the British team, Bowers for example, have been waiting for this day. This anticipation is fuelled partly by a disenchantment with the dogs. Chris van Tulleken says he is 'looking forward to the simplicity of man-hauling'. They said virtually the same thing in December 1911 as they struggled with the ponies in deep drift. '"Oh for the simple man-hauling life!" was our thought,' reported Cherry-Garrard.

As usual, Bruce is ready with a Churchillian pep talk. 'This is it,' he tells his team as the six of them prepare for their first long, hard plug. 'This is the expedition start for real. This is where it's going to get really tough. You know my philosophy about the whole of the expedition – that we get on. Until now we've had dogs to vent our frustrations. We will get very tired in this next phase and we will want areas to release some of these frustrations. I implore us as teams to communicate, stay cool, stay friends. If you feel there's angst, chat away, get it out. If anyone wants to stop, they stop. If one team gets ahead, there's no them and us, ever. It's "Can I do anything to help?" That's what I'm looking for, rather than taking the piss out of the other team for being a bit behind. This is a BIG BIG moment.'

Bruce is evidently conscious that now is the time they can all truly begin to measure themselves against Scott and his team. Aside from the numerical disadvantage, the speech hints at a further infidelity to the original journey. He will not entertain the idea that the two sledges can go faster by competing with each other. In other words, the team is the priority, the race a distant second.

Scott's style of leadership was not underpinned by the touchy-feely ethos of bonding and togetherness, and this became more apparent when man-hauling began. By the time Scott reached the top of the Beardmore, at any one time he was involved in four different races at once. The most literal race was with Amundsen, but there was no way of knowing how they were doing in that. Then there was the race against time: they needed to be back before the enfeebling cold of the autumn descended. They were also racing against Shackleton's old journey in 1908–9. But up on the plateau there were also mini-races going on every hour. For Scott, these were the best motivational tool to hand.

It started one day on the glacier. 'There was a great deal of competition between the teams, which was perhaps unavoidable but probably a pity,' wrote Cherry-Garrard. Bowers boasts of 'leaving Scott in the lurch, and eventually overhauling the party which had left some time before us'. Somebody cannot have been telling the truth because Scott on the same day wrote, 'Evans's is now decidedly the slowest unit, though Bowers's is not much faster. We keep up and over either without difficulty.' Cherry-Garrard confirms that Scott's was the strongest team, but then it had the strongest men: the prodigious Scott himself, Oates, Wilson and the man-mountain Taff Evans.

There was a reason for Teddy Evans's sluggishness. His team consisted of two men who, of the dozen man-haulers, were among

Top: Oates, a cavalry officer, was privately unimpressed by the horses he nursed through the voyage on the *Terra Nova*.
Above: Wilson training his pony, Nobby, at Cape Evans. Each man worked with a particular horse to get them used to dragging the sledges.

Above: Bruce Parry's team hunker down in the polar night. They encounter their worst weather early in the journey, and are tent-bound for two days.

Left: Huskies are perfectly adapted to polar conditions. Their thick fur provides insulation, and they dig snow holes for further protection.

Opposite, top: 'The most back-breaking work I have ever come up against,' said Bowers of manhauling. Parry's two teams of three march across the Greenland ice cap.

Opposite, bottom: In a team of three, the frontrunner is condemned to a prolonged day without conversation. At the rear, the sledgemeter keeps count of the mileage.

Right: The mountains provide a spectacular alternative to the monotony of endless ice. Dragged by dogs, Rune Gjeldnes's team have time to admire the view.
Below: With fewer dogs to tackle the gradient, Bruce Parry's team have less opportunity to take in their surroundings.

Previous pages, main picture: Rune Gjeldnes (far right) and his team pay homage to the famous photograph of the Norwegians at Polheim. Previous pages, inset: Amundsen (far left) stands behind Hanssen, Hassel and Wisting. The photograph was taken by Bjaaland.

Above: With their camera on a timer (there was no fifth man to take the picture), Bruce Parry's team pose at their pole in the iconic style of their predecessors.

Left: Scott was knighted post-humously and, among many memorials, a statue made by his widow, Kathleen, was unveiled in Waterloo Place, London, in 1915.

the least likely to go to the pole: the surgeon Atkinson and the Canadian physicist Charles 'Silas' Wright, who 'like Bowers has taken to sledging like a duck to water', noted Scott approvingly, but who was drawing on dwindling reserves. As for Evans himself, he was a rapidly diminishing asset. By the time the rest of them started man-hauling, he and Lashly had already been at it for hundreds of miles. They were in the team of men who set out with the motorized sledges, only to see the machines falter in the inhospitable conditions. In his diary Lashly watched their stuttering progress with trepidation. 'We see dawning on us the harness before long,' he shivered one day. Then a few days later, once reality has dawned: 'Man-hauling is no doubt the hardest work one can do, no wonder the motor sledges could not stand it.'

'They had man-hauled four hundred statute miles farther than the rest,' wrote Cherry-Garrard. 'Indeed Lashly's man-hauling journey from Corner Camp to beyond 87 degrees 32 minutes S, and back, is one of the great feats of polar travelling.' If he exempted Evans from that accolade, it was because after One Ton Camp he himself had to be dragged on the sledge for six days.

Sub-Lieutenant Evans was 14 years Captain Scott's junior, and no doubt conscious of his subordinate position. As second-in-command, he seems to have been especially keen to prove that he deserved his position on physical prowess as well as naval rank. Returning from a spring journey to check on the depots, he route-marched his party through 35 miles and 24 hours, tail presumably wagging as he reported back to his leader. Having sacrificed his own vague plans to lead an expedition to Antarctica in order to fall in with Scott's, he was desperate to be selected for the final polar party. Once out on the southern journey, he became acutely aware that he was operating at a physical disadvantage. When there was a debate about either killing the last exhausted ponies short of their final depot point, or forcing them on for a dozen miles, Evans was all for putting them out of their misery, and no doubt apportioning out some of his own. 'We could now, pulling 200 pound per man, start off with the proper man-hauling parties ... Why, *our* party have never been out of harness for nearly 400 miles, so why should not the other eight men buckle to and do some dragging?'

Of course, such grumbles went no further than his diary. To moan would be unmanly, not to mention counterproductive. If qualification meant pushing himself to exhaustion, he was prepared. Then one day on the glacier Scott summoned Evans to his tent to discuss the sluggish performance of his team. Evans's canny response was to draw attention to scientific facts: he didn't complain about the extra miles he had man-hauled, but pointed out that he and Lashly had done them without the extra rations the expenditure of energy required. They'd been eating what everyone else had. It was simply a question of fuel.

Sadly for Evans, Scott had his own trump card: he offered to take some of the weight off Evans's sledge and distribute it between the other two. It would have been an admission of weakness to accept.

* * * * * * * * * * * *

'The first week is going to be hell,' says Rory O'Connor. 'A whole new set of muscles, and hard work. We should get fitter and stronger. By this time next week we should be in better shape.' At this point in the journey, Rory is the only one to have actually *gained* weight. His higher tolerance threshold with, specifically, the pemmican and, more generally, the cold conditions has translated physically into an extra 2 pounds around his midriff.

Whether consciously or not, the sledging teams are arranged much like Scott's. All the big, tall men in their twenties – Chris van Tulleken, Rupert Elderkin and Arthur Jeffes – are on one sledge. The slighter men in their thirties – much slighter in the case of the alarmingly scrawny Mark Anstice – are on the other sledge. Everything is set for a repetition of history. But it doesn't turn out that way.

For the first few days in hell, the smaller team finds itself consistently outstripping the other sledge. This despite the fact that Mark wonders whether he's the only one of the three doing any pulling. 'It's funny,' he says. 'I don't suppose there's any way of working it out, but there are times when I feel I'm pulling the whole thing and sometimes feel like they're catching me up. It's one of those things you've got to get used to: the constant jerking against the stomach.'

One afternoon they sit on their sledge and wait for nearly an hour for the others to catch up. Chris, the one who was most looking forward to man-hauling, is particularly apologetic for forcing the other three to sit still in the cold. Rupert and Arthur are less put out. It seems that there is a problem with the sledge. Through no fault of their own, it keeps on veering off to the right. This makes navigation, which is already hard, even more difficult.

The other problem they have is with ice sticking to their skis, so one day they decide to travel in the tracks of the front sledge, where the broken snow won't be so adhesive. 'We've been finding it easier today,' Chris reports, 'easy being a very relative word in this case. But we've been on their tracks, which is psychologically easier, easier to navigate and perhaps makes the surface slightly easier.'

Bruce is more understanding than Scott. When the sledge of Teddy Evans's exhausted team began to run badly, Scott 'told them plainly that they must wrestle with the trouble and get it right for themselves'.

In these early days of man-hauling, Bruce's plan is to pull at a rate of 1 nautical mile an hour for ten hours. The sledges are lighter until they reach the next depot. After a few days they take stock. In their last few days with the dogs (before Day 40), they travel up to 15 miles. Until the depot on Day 48, they manage up to 14. 'But it's so early,' says Bruce: 'good weather, good going and very light sledges.' On the physical side, Rory notes that there has been 'a lot more stress and strain on all the major joints. The hips and back are really taking the brunt of it. The quads are working hard today. Feet get hot and sweaty, which makes it more likely to get rubs and blisters.' But joints and sores can be attended to. The real worry is the weight. 'We hope input will match calorific output or the weight will just drop off.' Mark seems to be disappearing before everyone's eyes. The thinner they are, the harder it is to guard against the cold. And as they travel north, it is going to get colder.

'We're going to degrade,' says Bruce cheerfully. 'We are all lean and fit, and eating all the food. Soon it's not going to be enough.

How can we keep going as we start to degrade? Scott was OK at Day 99. It was his last 50 days where he started to degrade.'

The next key day is Day 49. That is when, according to the road map, Bruce must reduce his party to four men and one tent. Two men must be jettisoned.

His decision is partly made for him by an injury. Man-hauling is not good news for Arthur's shoulder. He has been complaining of it since Day 29. By Day 31 he is on aspirin, and periodically he refers to it. Falling over every now and again doesn't help. The odd back rub from Chris dams the flow of pain. 'From the way Art is describing it, there is a palpable knot in the muscle. It is not doing a huge amount of damage, but straining it for ten hours a day is not the right thing to do.'

'For a hurt muscle,' suggests Arthur, 'it does seem to hurt rather a lot.' One day the snow is sticky and the two of them take their skis off, only for walking to cause deeper pain to Arthur, so they put them back on again. Another day Chris suggests that man-hauling is 'no worse than the fifth circle of hell'. By now Arthur's shoulder is 'quite sore and I'm on lots of painkillers. I dread to think what it'd be like if I wasn't on lots of painkillers.' Chris prescribes long baths, rest and physio, though none of these is available on the Greenland ice cap. The best he can offer is codeine. For the first time Arthur admits that he wouldn't say no to going home.

But when? The original road map puts Day 49 as the day of selection, but owing to Dave Pearce's injury, there is an option to stave it off until Day 61. Arthur's preference is for the earlier date. Bruce's task is to persuade him to put the team before himself. With Rory he discusses pain thresholds – how much, out of ten, Arthur can put up with. 'Nick is one,' Bruce suggests. 'Arthur's eight.'

It is one of the oddities of the expedition that Scott's step-great-grandson is easily the least experienced member of the team. 'This is so new to him,' says Bruce. 'I'm more impressed with him than probably anyone else on this whole trip because he's never done anything like it. Never complained once, just got stuck in. It must have been a baptism of fire that first week, poor guy. Talk about the deep end, and yet there he was, as if he'd been doing it all his life like the rest of us.'

Bruce then repeats all of this to Arthur, with knobs on. But it turns out he is not complimenting him just for fun. 'What I really need to know is how much am I going to piss you off for ever if I ask you to stay? Because the truth is it will be better for the team if we can all stay, just for the next ten days.'

This is an unusual situation in polar travel: the leader more or less begging a member of the team not to leave. Bruce is worried about the weights on the sledges increasing as soon as they reach their next depot. If one man goes, they will not be able to have two sledges. So he will have to send back another. At this point he'd rather keep the group of six until Day 61 and drag supplies closer to the pole. He continues: 'I want to know if I do make that decision to ask you to stay, how much that is going to play with you and your morale? Because if it does piss you off, the morale of the team could be affected if we have to look after you on a daily basis. I'm just trying to be honest with you.'

Initially, Bruce's powers of persuasion appear to be deficient. Arthur says he wants to go home on Day 49. Bruce counters that 'It's the sort of thing that you might suddenly regret when you get in the aircraft on the way home. I'm sure you've had that go through your mind.' He also mentions the issue of self-esteem. 'You've got ten days to put in some pain. We all know how hard that is, or maybe we don't. Maybe you're going through something so extreme I've never experienced it before. It's a massive sacrifice, but is it a sacrifice that in the long term you might wish you'd taken?' Bruce insists that he is not putting pressure on Arthur. Of course, that is precisely what he is doing. Arthur duly concedes that he is happy for Bruce to make the decision.

This is where Bruce appears to be in his element: even in an essentially artificial reconstruction, he, as the leader, has the fate of another man in his hands. 'What I have to weigh up then – and it's pretty awful – is am I happy as a human being to sacrifice the pain of another human being for the greater good of the project that we've set ourselves as a team? You were part of that project from the beginning.'

'Yeah, no, I signed up, absolutely,' concedes Arthur. 'You won't hear a grumble out of me.'

Bruce now has to decide whether he can afford to let his injured man go. 'I am quite used to making decisions,' he says. 'I don't have any problem with it at all.' Except that it turns out he does have a problem. His decision is to let Arthur make the decision. The next day Bruce takes him aside. 'I think we have all signed up for pain here,' he tells him. 'I'm going to ask you to stay, but not tell you to stay, so it's kind of back to you.' In other words, Bruce is confident he has done enough work on Arthur's conscience. Arthur says he'll let him know his decision by the end of the day, which happens to be Day 47.

Chris advises his tentmate to extract some tobacco from Bruce in return for agreeing to stay. In the end, it seems to be an easy choice. Faced with the possibility of condemning someone else to leave 12 days earlier than they want to, Arthur concludes that there is 'not much of a choice really. There is one right choice, which is to stay until Day 61, and one wrong choice, which is to go the day after tomorrow, and much as it grieves me, I reckon that is the case. It's almost always the case in life, the short, easy answer is the wrong one and the long, hard, painful answer is the correct one. So I'm going to stick it out until Day 61, all things being equal, and get dinner out of whoever comes back with me on the grounds that I didn't pull them out two weeks earlier. I hope my girlfriend forgives me. I'll be able to look back and go, yeah I did a proper one. I don't know if I am completely convinced by that argument yet, but I'm sure I will be.'

Thus Arthur condemns himself to another fortnight of man-hauling. At the end of it, Bruce will not be able to duck a more difficult decision: who to send home with him.

* * * * * * * * * * * *

'This evening has been rather a shock … Scott came up to me, and said he was afraid he had rather a blow for me. Of course I knew what he was going to say, but could hardly grasp that I was going back – tomorrow night … Scott was very put about, said that he had been thinking a lot about it but had come to the conclusion that the seamen with their special knowledge, would be needed.'

Thus wrote Cherry-Garrard on 20 December at the top of the Beardmore Glacier. Scott brooded and brooded on who to send home, but in the end they learnt only the day before. 'There is a mournful air tonight,' wrote Cherry-Garrard a day later as he distributed spare gear, including a bag of tobacco for Wilson to give to Scott on Christmas Day. The other men to turn back were Atkinson, Wright and Keohane. Wright was privately angry that the visibly weaker Teddy Evans had been preferred. Scott explained that he needed a navigator on the return journey. Wright cheered up enough to note that the pole looked increasingly likely to be Scott's, as they had seen no Norwegian tracks on the glacier.

To those leaving, it felt as if the executioner's axe had fallen. Little did anyone know that Scott was sparing them a death sentence.

The leader received his tobacco on Christmas Day, but it was nothing to the present his men gave him. 'Scott got fairly wound up and went on and on,' wrote Bowers. 'My breath kept fogging my glasses, and our windproofs got oppressively warm and altogether things were pretty rotten. At last he stopped and we found we had done 14½ miles. He said, "What about fifteen miles for Christmas Day?" So we gladly went on – anything definite is better than indefinite trudging.'

Two weeks later, with the plateau attained, Shackleton's journey finally overhauled, and their goal less than 150 miles away, Scott prepared to send home four more men, leaving a final group of four to head on to the pole. Controversy continues to dog his final choice. Up until the last day of 1911 he seemed to be adhering to the original plan, based on the organization of sledges, tents, ration-boxes and cookers around four-man units. On 31 December Scott ordered the men on the second sledge to depot their skis. To this day his intention remains unclear. The record of Shackleton's journey indicated that there were huge sastrugi ahead. But whatever the reason, surrendering his skis did for Teddy Evans (and the debunkers would argue that that was Scott's intention). Scott noted that progress became 'a plod for the foot people and pretty easy going for us'.

Nobody felt his own place in the final party was certain. Wilson was convinced he would not make the cut, as he thought Scott wanted only seamen for the four-man polar team. Bowers may have hoped, but he was one of the four who had deposited his skis. Then there was Oates. According to Cherry-Garrard, Atkinson 'did not think Titus wanted to go on, though he (T.) did not actually say so. He thinks Titus knew he was done.' Within the privacy of his diary, Oates confessed that his feet, wet since Cape Evans, were a mess. Nor was Taff Evans in the best shape for another 900 miles of man-hauling.

Scott wanted a non-officer at the pole, and he had three to choose from, all of them veterans of the *Discovery* expedition. To assist in the decision, he sought medical advice. Both doctors reckoned that, of the three petty officers, Lashly was the one most up to the task of continuing on. Teddy Evans thought otherwise. 'Lashly and I,' he wrote, 'knew we could never hope to be in the polar party after our long drag out from the Cape Evans.' But this comment cannot necessarily be taken at face value: Evans no doubt wished to believe that Lashly was as all played out as he was. It appears that Scott agreed with him.

According to the doctors, Crean was the next best choice, and only then his fellow petty officer Taff Evans. They came to this conclusion even though they had no idea he had cut his hand shortening the sledges. But Scott was loyal to the petty officer who, more than Crean and Lashly, had impressed him in Antarctica a decade ago. He overlooked the fact that Evans was fond of a tipple and twice had to be forgiven for drinking himself into a stupor. In the end, Scott was impressed by his sheer bulk.

Scott announced to the men in Teddy Evans's tent that he would be taking his own sledging team of himself, Wilson, Oates and Taff Evans. The choice seems partly to have been made out of loyalty to old comrades, but also on the available evidence. His quartet of man-haulers had so far proved the strongest by far. But Scott wanted it to be stronger still. In a decision that has bemused polar historians ever since, he asked his second-in-command if he could spare Bowers for the coming journey. Lieutenant Evans, Lashly and Crean were being asked to hand over their fourth man so that Scott could have a fifth.

It says much for Scott's singularity of purpose that he disregarded the life-endangering inconvenience this would cause the returning party, who were already without a sledge-meter and were now being asked to travel home without their navigator. They were left to haul their sledge through 750 miles on less than three-quarter strength, as Bowers was their most powerful man-hauler. And Scott was asking him to plough on without skis. Then there were the difficulties Scott created for his own party. If everything about polar travel was set up for four-man teams, the most significant inconvenience was the size of the tent. They could take more fuel and rations, and cook for the extra 30 minutes required to boil down the larger pan of snow. But there was no enlarging the tent.

However, his decision was made. Scott needed a navigator to find the pole 150 miles to the south, and he needed the strongest men to drag the sledge. Evans was desperate to make it to the pole, so he kept quiet about his injury. Oates was also big and strong and apparently fit.

The second returning party turned for home on 4 January 1912. As they waved the five men off into the white expanse, Crean wept, the usually imperturbable Lashly showed stirrings of emotion, and perhaps Lieutenant Evans cursed his luck under his breath. They would have a desperately hard journey home.

* * * * * * * * * * * *

There are two prevailing topics of conversation on the Greenland ice cap. In one tent the talk is all of how much Bruce and Mark are hating it, and how much they resent Rory for loving it. In the other tent the talk is all of who will be selected to go to the pole. In short, there is a tacit understanding in both teams that history is repeating itself. Like Scott, it is assumed that Bruce will select his own sledging partners, and he will cherry-pick the best man from the other tent. He too is guided partly by loyalty: where Scott took Wilson, Bruce takes Mark. And it is inconceivable that he could leave behind Rory, the one team-member who seems genuinely happy with the simple man-hauling life.

What Bruce doesn't know is that on Day 59 Anstice's heels start to cause him 'debilitating' pain. He privately asks Rory for painkillers in order to get through the day. Only much later will this come out. 'I didn't want Bruce to know. I thought if he knew, he'd send me home, and I was sure I wasn't on his list to go. There were a couple of hours where I was in a dark place, cursing my heels and thinking, forty days to go, can I do it?' He subsequently admits that 'every sensible part of me wanted to go, except that bit governed by pride and self-respect and wanting to be one of the last four. I can't understand anyone not wanting to be part of the last four. I wasn't facing long-term damage. It was just a bit of pain I had to get over each day.'

The parallel with Oates is compelling. When he made his selection for the pole, Scott was ignorant of any infirmity Oates may have been suffering. Before departure Oates was in two minds about whether he wanted to go all the way. 'I have half a mind to see Scott,' he wrote to his mother, 'and tell him I must go home in the ship but it would be a pity to spoil my chances of being in the final party especially as the regiment and perhaps the whole army would be pleased if I was at the pole.' By keeping quiet about his feet, he made sure that his chances went unspoilt.

As their time together appears to be drawing to a close, the modern sledge team discuss how well they all know each other, and how much they have enjoyed each other's company. One of the things that bonds them during the three weeks of man-hauling is the running joke about the weight of their sledge, and how they would be faster than the other team if they weren't the ones who have to stop off and build marker cairns. 'As long as each sledge is pulling and you're within 5 per cent speed of the other sledge, it's fine,' says Chris. 'I think we all agree that there are days when we've been quicker and days when they've been quicker. To tease out from that who are the quickest man-haulers – I couldn't do it.'

Chris discovers that the other team claims to be quicker. 'I don't think that's very professional, and I don't see how they can say that. If you go through it day by day, session by session, I don't think that's the conclusion we can reach. Right from the beginning Bruce said, "I'm not necessarily going to take the four strongest people." He's taking who he thinks will be strongest over the next 40 days. If it is between me and Rupe, I think it's a difficult position.'

Where the original plan was for Bruce to jettison four men, the three injuries mean that only one will actually be told to go home, rather than asked to. If he takes his own tentmates, it does indeed boil down to a straight choice between Rupert and Chris. Rupert admits he is on the trip because his friend Chris invited him at the last minute. 'We have been through the hardships and the laughs of the trip together, and I just think it would be quite odd, knowing that the other one wants to stay, to find either that I am going or I am staying. It's a tough call, but it would be the nicest thing of all if all of those that want to stay could stay and just push on to the end together as a bigger group, but that is something that is not going to happen.'

Bruce is not going to take five men to the pole. There seems to be no useful criterion for choosing, and at no point does Bruce offer one. Like Scott, he decides to make his announcement the day before, but brings it forward on request from the evening to lunchtime. And when he does, it's over very quickly.

'Rupes, bad news. You're going home. You know this is incredibly hard. You're so a part of this team. There's nothing you should take as negative. You've been 100 per cent with us the whole way, but two must go back. Anything you want to know or ... I could go into justifications but ... '

'Not unless you want to,' offers Rupert. 'I know you had to make a decision.'

'Not been an easy one.'

The next morning a plane arrives to take away Rupert and Arthur. Nobody emulates Crean by crying, though there are manly handshakes and regrets all round. In two days they will be washed, well fed, well rested and in London. For the remaining four of Bruce, Mark, Rory and Chris life will continue as drearily as before: man-hauling, pemmican, reindeer sleeping bags, cold. But in two days, they will be 20 nautical miles closer to the pole.

Bruce Parry's Diary

DAY 41

Silence filled the air when the plane was out of earshot, for the first time in about two months, and it was bliss of course. I'll miss the dogs: they were real characters and some of them had become real pet friends, but I'm also glad for their departure 'cos of all the chaos, uncertainty and frustration. Now it's just us and no one else to blame.

Stopped after just three hours having done about 3 nautical miles. Good result and perfect for my planning if we can keep it up for 10–12 hour days.

It's dawned on us how much more personal time we'll now have to rest and to recuperate, and I'm generally really pleased with our first day of the next phase.

DAY 42

Can't write a thing about earlier today until I express how I feel now. I'm knackered, tired and aching. Big day. Big day indeed. It's been our first full day's hauling and what an epic. A big learning curve for everyone. At first it was too hot and we all stripped to our first layer. Mark remarked that I was the smelliest. Then the sun went in and we were faced with near white-out and flat light conditions all day. I had a nightmare navigating and had to stop all the time at first, then I got the hang of it and started taking bearings on clouds and shadows or whatever lay in our path. It was relentless and mind-numbing and that was basically my whole day. The time just went so, so slowly that nine and a half hours seemed like a lifetime. In a bizarre kind of way I actually enjoyed some parts of the day, though. I enjoy the feeling of being knackered (to a degree) and I'm really looking forward to getting really fit again. I just wish we were doing this through somewhere a little more exciting, that's all.

Now just looking forward to a good night's sleep. Done blood sugar and piss test and I was very dehydrated – the end of the scale, so must drink and drink tonight.

DAY 43

Enjoying my time with Mark and Rory. Most days we have down to a tee now, it's just fine-tuning to optimize our down time. Even having a dump together with a pipe ready-filled so as to speed up fumigation while we sit and sort ourselves for the last 15 minutes makes a treat. Great stuff.

11 nautical miles today and everyone happy with that.

DAY 44

Today I said that I was enjoying myself five times, much to Mark's dismay. When it came to our first 3, 2, 1 go jump-start of the day, the sledge already shifted by number 2. The going was just superb and it glided most of the day. We set a ski pace about as fast as I could probably ski solo, and the momentum just kept the sledge moving.

Finally clocked up a good 14 nautical miles, which was fantastic. It could easily have been quite a lot more, but Chris and the others didn't have such a good day, with their sledge veering annoyingly off to one side all day. I hope they can sort out the issue tomorrow because there was a noticeable speed difference and at times we had to wait because they were getting out of sight and in danger of losing our tracks in the flat light. Being separated out there wouldn't be fun.

More thoughts today on the final four. I've basically decided on the team, and feel bad about giving the news to the poor fellow who will have to be going home against his will. Arthur has volunteered to go home and I am happy with that, although he will be miffed. A great guy who has one of the best qualities required for expeditions (especially with me): he's so mellow, he's horizontal. He's hardly ever done any real expeds before but he's come up trumps. Nick, for all his verbosity, couldn't hold a candle to him. I've got to send someone home who wants to be here, and I'm not letting Mark off that early because I need him for my sanity. I know who this person will be, but won't say so until the day before the decision is made to maintain morale and an even thrust forward. Yet should it be day 49 or 61? I've got more maths to do yet as we pick up eight more unit boxes at Upper Glacier and would four people carrying seven boxes and all the communal kit, including theodolite and toolkit, etc. be better than two lots of three carrying four boxes each and splitting the communal kit?

DAY 45

Today was tough. The morning wasn't too bad, but as the weather changed dramatically from warm and blustery to hot and humid, the snow conditions just turned into sticky mud and treacle. Our skis had about 6–8 inches of snow underneath and glide was almost impossible. The guys up front had an even harder time of it. Breaking track all day must have been really tough. All soaked and sleeping bags will be too now.

DAY 46

The big story of the day remained Arthur. I chatted to Rory and Chris about his injury, pain and morale. Then I chatted to him. In a nutshell, his injury seems to be muscular and not likely to cause him permanent damage and he is cool whatever, though he admitted to me that if given the choice, he'd go home on Day 49. I then chatted to his tent group and gauged that everyone is cool either way and happy with my decision. Not easy and I'm still as yet undecided.

I had more chats today about day or night routines. I'm dead against constant change and I feel that the grass will always be greener and we can never fully predict the weather. For me it's either day or night and no in-betweens.

Much talk about time and distance and we're nearly half way. What a f**king epic.

DAY 47

Trekked till 6.45 and did 15 nautical miles despite the shite conditions. Arthur announced that, due to his improved pain control, he was willing to slog on till Day 61, which was fantastic news for everyone. Good lad and the right decision for the whole team, and one he will be pleased with in the long run. Love him.

DAY 48

Upper Glacier Camp. At f**king last. So, this is the real turning point of the expedition and where things start for real in many ways. No more depots ahead. This is where Scott went down to eight men and we are the same (although obviously we've lost two already). From here we deposit food and mark the route for our return. 260 pounds per person for the next phase as opposed to the 175–200 or so this last week.

Mark has made a chocolate butter to go with our biscuits, which is divine and a great addition to our menu. Just cocoa and butter mixed and melted in water in an old butter pot. Glad we only just discovered it – it's such a treat to have something new.

DAY 49

The sledges looked bigger and bigger as we slowly packed them. The amazing thing was that it went OK, and although we could all tell its extra weight it actually didn't feel too bad. Admittedly the snow conditions were probably the best we'd had for a long time, so the glide was good, but it was still a pleasant surprise.

DAY 50

The further north we go, the greater the declination and the more sticky and erratic the needle and the more we go round in circles. Another thing Scott didn't have to contend with, but what the hell.

Did bioimpedance this morning. Lost 4½ pounds of fat. Happy with that, but how long can we stay healthy dragging a silly sleigh across the ice? It all depends on the weather I suppose (as with Scott).

DAY 51
Our hardest day so far. Sobering really. Mark magnanimously apologized for his repacking of the sledge to put the weight at the back. This could well have been an issue today, but his apology was unnecessary and very big of him. Anyway, Arthur cuts a very straight line and they got to the end of the day about an hour or more before us.

DAY 52
Nice hot, sunny day today and thankfully the sledge felt much better. What a relief after yesterday's effort.

DAY 53
Woke to a wind and stayed windy all day. Very overcast and grey and flat light. Poor Arthur had an epic navigating. Twists and meanders all day. God knows what bearing we're on now. Another plain grey day in hell.

Day 54
I hate navigating. I always get the shittiest weather. It's becoming a standing joke. Bruce on nav: white-out.

I tried navigating with a compass in my left hand as I found the waist plate wasn't working, and I did OK for a bit. Then it just got worse and I had to resort to the plate soon enough, but not before I'd totally knackered out my right arm by only using one ski pole. Twat.

The day went on and on. Arthur was in particular pain today and the others even told him to rest and ski alongside. Tough one for him and we took some weight off like the nav gear to help out. Arthur's dilemma caused some conversation. Mark was most outspoken and put it that his issue was now one of pride and being a man to overcome his pain and not make his friends do any extra work on his behalf. We'd all thought things similar, though I for one would never say it, especially as leader and in front of the others, and not knowing how to gauge another man's actual pain. But Arthur agreed to come on this extra ten days. He knew it would hurt, and we've all signed up for pain and his stated aim was to have a taste of what his indirect ancestor had gone through. Well, I might suggest that none of us will ever experience even 10 per cent of that sort of pain. So that was my answer and I pressed on. Nevertheless, at about 6 p.m. we stopped for the others to catch up and I asked their permission to continue. Arthur was the first to agree. Top man. Back in his harness and credibility topped up.

200 nautical miles to go. I confirmed that we'd have a party that night. The others were close behind and soon both tents were up and all the cooking gear was coming into our tent for a night's revelry. Great to see the others in our tent as it had been some time since we'd all been together socially. I said a few words about the guys not present and those about to leave, then we tucked in. I was glad to say a few words as I think they went down quite well and we all miss Dave especially. Nick deserved a mention too, and so did Arthur.

DAY 55
A day off, it's been decided.

Arthur was tasked with building a long cairn for our return and I asked him to personalize it so as for us to remember him when we get there. He's done a great job (though not as creative as I was expecting, considering his mum is a sculptress), but good job anyway. I hope the day off helps his arm, it was a deciding factor in awarding it (kind of).

Rory, diligent as ever, has helped me in doing some depot/cache markers and has spent the afternoon making flags, while Mark has, like me, done some personal repairs and maintenance jobs. I've sorted my finnesko, a long overdue job, and tried to dry them. I've taken the bold decision to go fur-side out on my sleeping bag – if the others can stand the awful stench. My bag really does smell the worst – farts mostly – so we'll see how that goes.

DAY 56
We struggled all day long. Really hard going and we felt every bump and ripple of the ground. The smallest sastrugi felt like a mountain, and often we came to a grinding halt when one of the three of us missed a step. Constant restarts, often false restarts, and no conversation all day long. I even got my first proper ache in my lower back, which troubled me for a while and worried me somewhat in case it deteriorated and became a problem. Luckily, I wished it away, but it was something of an omen maybe – I hope not.

Cairns were erected every hour or so at estimated intervals of 1.5–2 miles. Mark would note the distance, the cairn number and bearing back to the last one which I gave him. I'd then cut the blocks as big as possible – Rory would erect the obelisk. A flag placed on top would then hopefully provide our homeward salvation. We found on such a clear, sunny day that a good cairn was visible to the naked eye at about 1 mile, and a mile and a half with binos before it went over the horizon.

8 miles today. Not good enough really – hope it improves as we're in for a bigger slog than I want.

DAY 57
Windy, windy, windy. From our camp tonight we can see back five cairns through the binos. We came downhill today, else the curvature of the Earth would've hidden them.

DAY 58
More wind – what's going on with this place? Cold too.

DAY 59
Started great today. Sun was back and no wind to boot, so it was a thermal tops only day. Reminded us of the earlier high-pressure heatwave and brought some longing for it back. Of course it didn't last too long and soon we were back in cloud and a cold wind. Oh well. Good day nonetheless and the sledge definitely felt better, though Mark's feet are playing up today. He's mentioned them on a few occasions of late, and today he tried a new footwear arrangement, but he had to change that in the morning, then by late afternoon he was back on painkillers and not enjoying it at all. He's a tough guy, is our Mark, and it won't stop him at all, but he's got a history of bad heels. Back home he wears down his boot heels within months, and this type of posture puts almost the entire 285-pound pull through the heels. Poor bastard. I hope it improves. He plans to make a heel padded insert from felt tonight.

Decision day tomorrow, so I hope everyone gets a good night's sleep and doesn't worry too much.

DAY 60
Today I announced my decision on who was going to go to the pole. In essence it meant choosing one person to return with Arthur. In my head I was in fact happy to take any combination of the five guys I had to choose from, so it was not a question of singling out the worst, but more making a choice of the ones I wanted and needed most. So I chose Mark for his fixing skills, Rory for his organization and incentive, Chris for his conversation (as well as he and Rory being doctors and navigators), leaving poor old Rupert to go home. Rupert, of course, has many skills of his own, including being probably the best navigator, one of the strongest pullers and an absolute star team member. But on detailed analysis I deemed that the best team combination was the others, so that was that. Chris and Rupert were eager to know, so I agreed to break the news at lunchtime. It was one of the worst moments of the trip for me as I hated to let anyone go, but Rupert took it incredibly well

and everyone was cool. It reminded me how happy I am with every aspect of the entire team. I told Rupert in private first and then announced it to the others. It was a sensitive announcement but went ok I think, and instantly everyone expressed their condolences to poor old Rupes who was cool. I then let the three amigos go off to have time as a trio to chat and that was quite therapeutic for all of them I'm sure. In anticipation of delays the next day I asked if we could push out the distance for our last day together and we did a commendable 11.5 miles by the end of the day.

DAY 61
Woke at 7 a.m. (bliss) to a total white-out. No flight as yet and not looking likely. Can't really take apart the sledge to make our sail until we know the flight is confirmed. We took across all the extra unit boxes and nav gear and other extras and our sledge now looks simply massive. It will easily be the largest and heaviest sledge of the entire trip and is somewhat daunting in its scale. Mark gave up on the sail due to cold, shitty conditions, and the necessity for bare-hand fiddly work seemed unnecessarily painful. So tomorrow we shall definitely set off with four guys, one enormous sledge and a half-built sail. Who knows what will happen?

CHAPTER NINE

The Inner Life

THERE IS A RICH VARIETY OF THINGS TO THINK ABOUT. SOMETIMES YOU
THINK OF NOTHING AT ALL. THERE IS A FAMOUS STORY THAT CHRIS KEEPS
RECOUNTING. THEY WERE PLODDING ALONG IN THEIR GROUP OF THREE
FOR A WHILE WHEN CHRIS PIPES UP AND SAYS, 'WHAT HAVE YOU BEEN
THINKING ABOUT?' AND ARTHUR SAYS, 'NOTHING.' THEN RUPERT, WITH
A BRAIN THE SIZE OF A PLANET, SAYS, 'I'VE BEEN COUNTING IN
MY HEAD.' WHICH IS UTTERLY FANTASTIC. SOME MOMENTS YOU HAVE
FLASHES OF INSPIRATION, AND OTHER MOMENTS YOU HAVE NOTHING.
Rory O'Connor

Polar travel takes its toll on the body. For this – the physical
challenge – it is possible to prepare. You can put on weight, do
fitness training, get your Telemark skiing up to scratch, but polar
travel also puts immense strain on the mind. No regime has yet been
devised to get your head ready for the epic monotony of the ice cap.

One aspect of the race for the South Pole that is almost always
overlooked is the silence. Scott and Amundsen and the men with
them committed huge numbers of words to the pages of letters and
diaries. Their achievements have come down to us in the form of
literature. For all this daily outpouring of words, however, of
conversation there was disproportionately little. For many hours

each day, the pulling, the navigating and the dog-driving was done as if by Trappists. Perhaps Scott's men coaxed or berated their ponies, Amundsen's now and then shouted right or left commands to their dogs. But the actual work itself consigned each man to his own world of private thoughts. It is entirely possible that for large swathes of their heroic Antarctic journey, the men who travelled with the two leaders were *incredibly* bored. When they did talk, they tended to talk to the men in their own tent: it was too cold to stand around chatting to the man in the neighbouring tent.

It is the same in the modern British team. After they leave, Rory O'Connor regrets that he has hardly spoken to Arthur Jeffes and Rupert Elderkin. Chris van Tulleken, on moving into the other tent, notes that he hasn't spent more than five minutes a day in the past two months with his new tentmates. Stimulating conversation in his own tent had more or less dried up. 'Art and Rupert and I had slightly run out of things to say to each other.'

And even once they were under canvas for the night, how much did they really talk? As soon as man-hauling began, Scott made sure they were always exhausted by the end of the march. When they made camp, he and Cherry-Garrard were usually writing. Up until they abandoned their diaries, so were Wilson and Bowers. Of the petty officers, only Lashly kept a diary, but it was a full one. The others no doubt puffed ruminatively on their pipes. (The Norwegians had a no-smoking tent until they got to the pole, whereupon Bjaaland ceremonially presented cigars, and Wisting produced enough tobacco for Amundsen to have two smokes a day on the journey home.) Among the five men of the polar party, Oates was always a taciturn fellow. 'You've quite opened up,' Scott remarked on a rare occasion when he did become chatty. Taff Evans was full of anecdotes, even among all those officers and gentlemen, though after his injury he disappeared increasingly inside himself. Only when his mind started to go on the long journey home was it noted that he had taken to complaining vociferously.

When they weren't writing they were as often reading as talking. Wilson had *In Memoriam* (1850), Tennyson's monumental lament for a lost friend, to wade through. '[I] have been realizing what a perfect piece of faith and hope and religion it is, makes me feel that if the end comes to me here or hereabout … All will be as it is meant to be.' His copy was lent to him by Cherry-Garrard, and found about his person when their bodies were discovered. A devout Christian's choice of reading was preparing him for the worst eventuality. There was little apart from heavyweight literature in Antarctica that summer, but there was occasional light relief. In one diary entry Cherry-Garrard talks about the horrific struggles of the ponies, and turns on a sixpence to make a note about what he's reading. 'It is a terrible end – driven to death on no more food, to be then cut up, poor devils. I have swopped [sic] the *Little Minister* with Silas Wright for Dante's *Inferno*!' Did that exclamation mark acknowledge the absurdity of following a light confection from the author of *Peter Pan* with one of the great works of world literature? Or was he joking about the appropriateness, given the location, of reading up on hell?

Those days of bad weather when the Norwegians were cooped up in their tent were 'never very amusing,' recalled Amundsen. 'You soon get tired of talking, and you can't write all day long, either. Eating is a good way of passing the time, if you can afford it, and so is reading, if you have anything to read; but as the menu is limited, and the library as a rule somewhat deficient on a sledging trip, these two expedients fall to the ground.' Mostly they slept. 'Happy the man who can sleep round the clock on days like these; but that is a gift that is not vouchsafed to all.' One night after he had sent his men off to reconnoitre a route through the glacier, Amundsen 'dreamed of mountains and precipices all night, and woke up with Bjaaland whizzing down from the sky'. The advent of scenery was clearly stimulating.

Of the modern Norwegians, Ketil Reitan is singled out as an 'extreme' sleeper who is out the second he lies down. 'There's about 45 minutes every day after Ketil goes to sleep,' says John Huston, 'he'll go "Interesting" or "I don't know where that place is".' Rune Gjeldnes tells Harald Kippenes that he is sleep-talking about navigation in English. They all seem to snore, but lightly. Bowers was much the most disruptive snorer in Scott's polar party. Amundsen, mentioning no names, recalls how one of the party 'very nearly snored us all out of the tent'.

Bruce's men have taken books too. Rory is reading Scott's journal as he re-creates the journey. As the journey continues, he starts to read it out loud. 'It focuses the mind,' he says. 'And it makes you realize how tough these guys were. Their temperatures were a lot lower than what we've experienced so far. Compelling reading.' Mark plays a psychological trick on himself by bringing along a book about Stalin: if, after the end of a gruelling day, he can be reminded that he is not living through the Great Terror in the Soviet Union, there is something to be thankful for. On his birthday he is given one of the Flashman novels. Scott's men would have been familiar with the character from Tom Hughes' *Tom Brown's Schooldays* (1857). When the dogs are still there to do the pulling, he has a fantasy of being able to sit back and relax on the sledge, smoke his pipe and read. Rupert has the same idea, but as he is on a two-man sledge, is rather luckier when it comes to implementing it. This is the cause of some light-hearted resentment. 'We're holding on for dear life and Rupert's reading Graham Greene,' says Rory.

And then there is poetry. In one of the tents there is even the odd recital. One of the poems is Robert Browning's brooding 'Childe Roland to the Dark Tower Came', which was a favourite of both Shackleton and Wilson. 'They became friends through a mutual love of Browning,' explains Chris. 'It's something they probably would have read on their trip.' Among the classic poets they also have Rudyard Kipling, John Keats and G.K. Chesterton, but there is a collection of poetry on an Arctic theme too, mostly from the early twentieth century. One day in the tent Chris reads out 'The Cremation of Sam Magee' by the Canadian poet Robert Service, which he and Rupert memorize. 'Service describes the landscape in an evocative way. It's nice knowing when you're miserable that some people have felt a similar way and expressed it very articulately.' When they build the first cairn, Arthur and Chris are forcibly reminded of the crumbling monument in the desert described by Percy Bysshe Shelley in 'Ozymandias'. Bruce Parry also has a poem by one of the Romantics on the go in his head: Samuel Taylor Coleridge's 'Kubla Khan'.

The rhythm of language helped some of Scott's men. On the appalling winter journey to fetch emperor penguin eggs, Cherry-Garrard recalls one rhythmic phrase that rolled around in their heads as he, Wilson and Bowers yanked the sledge in the unbearable cold back towards Cape Evans. 'You've got it in the neck, stick it, you've got it in the neck.'

And if they didn't read, they might talk about reading. 'There were meals when we had interesting little talks,' says Cherry-Garrard, 'as when I find in my diary that "we had a jolly lunch meal, discussing authors. Barrie, Goldsworthy and others are personal friends of Scott. Someone told Max Beerbohm that he was like Captain Scott, and immediately, so Scott assured us, he grew a beard."

'But about three weeks out the topics of conversation became threadbare. From then onwards it was often that whole days passed without conversation beyond the routine "Camp ho! All ready? Pack up. Spell ho." The latter after some two hours' pulling.'

Polar travel exhausted the body, and it exhausted conversation, leaving the imagination to its own devices. No one discovers this more forcefully than Inge Solheim. An ice cap is a lonely place, but it is loneliest of all for the man who volunteers to break a trail on skis out in front. For hours every day, he is on his own, ploughing a solitary furrow through virgin snow. He has volunteered for this. Some way into the journey he admits that he doesn't much like dogs, and is happy not to be in charge of one of the four sledges. He kills the hours in a variety of ways. One is to sing to himself. One day, while covering 21 miles, he works his way through a tenth of Elvis Presley's entire songbook. The next day he promises he'll do some more contemporary hits. The snatch of a familiar song is a friend in the wilderness. On the winter journey Wilson, Bowers and Cherry-Garrard sang 'songs we remembered off the gramophone'. Inge notes that it has a practical application too: 'When I lose my rhythm skiing, I just find a song that fits.' One day he has two songs running through his head: the theme from Forrest Gump (1994), and a song by Garth Brooks. Once a song gets stuck, it takes more than a toothpick to dislodge it. Scott's men sang hymns on the plateau. (Months later, as they lowered the tent over the bodies of

Scott, Bowers and Wilson, they sang Scott's favourite hymn, 'Onward, Christian Soldiers'.)

With nothing to talk about and no one to talk to, music runs through every head. 'That's a very big feature of this environment,' says Arthur. 'You get a line of song going round and round in your head and it stays there. If you're lucky, it's a good one.' There are also communal stabs at music-making in the tent. Arthur, who is a music producer by profession, plays on a penny whistle, though his tentmates worry that the other tent think this is pretentious. Inge plays 'Hey Jude' on a mouth organ, and the whole team joins in. One morning Harald plays 'Sailing' and 'Abide with Me' while sitting on the sledge. When the dogs pull off, he carries on playing. John picks a song a day and toys with the lyrics, but quietly: 'I'm not a very good singer,' he says. One morning Inge starts singing U2's 'One', and it lodges in his mind for the rest of the day.

But when the music stops, what else can they do to while away the empty time in that infinity of ice? Some are better equipped for it than others. When he's not singing, John picks a couple of topics a day to think about and works through them. Inge goes through 'the whole range of emotions from happiness to homesickness. Sometimes I want to go home because I'm really tired and my feet are aching but most of the time it's happy thoughts, thoughts about my family and my friends and things I want to do when I get home. During one day I could have every feeling possible, but I know about them and I'm prepared for them. Before this expedition I tried to prepare for these emotions so that I could recognize them when they came and deal with them. It's almost like an emotional rollercoaster.'

Inge likes it out in front because, in the mountains at least, he is the first to see all the sights, and he has all the thinking time in the world. He spends the hours thinking methodically through his entire childhood, his friends and family, and he claims to be constantly thinking about how he feels within himself while working through his repertoire of songs. 'Even if expedition life is monotonous and repetitive, it's mentally a colourful world with lots of changes every day. Even if the surroundings are white, it's amazing how many interesting thoughts you can have during the day. It's like a cleansing process.'

Rune tells him he is envious. Implausible though it sounds, for him the business of travelling with four companions and 48 dogs through a completely empty landscape, when he is used to travelling with one, gives him a feeling of what sounds like claustrophobia. 'You never really relax,' he says. 'I try to think for the whole team, and then I try to think in front of us, what to do. So what I miss most up here is maybe that nice, easy-going evening. I would like to get more silence maybe.' In other words, the Greenland ice cap is not boring *enough*. Generally, they find coping with the monotony easier in the Norwegian team.

Dave Pearce, a mountaineer who has been up Everest, is not so robust on the flat: he finds the landscape dispiriting. 'There's nothing here to look at,' he complains. 'No geology, flora or fauna. No different cultures. To look at nothing day in, day out is pretty challenging mentally.' It is possible that an inability to cope with the tedium contributes as much to his premature departure from the expedition as the frostbite in his finger. He is the antithesis of Rune, a seasoned Arctic veteran, who likes the interiority of polar travel. 'In the jungle you get more experiences. You are bombarded with sensations. In polar areas it's much more of a mental experience. You are living inside, not outside. I do prefer ice.' On another occasion he talks about 'the spiritual element' of being there. 'It feels good inside. It is special to be in a place like this. Cold, inhospitable, no life. Not many things apart from thoughts.' It's not all serious. They are conscious that the business of looking within is ripe for satire. One day, when they are doing the navigation, they joke about finding out 'who we are' instead of 'where we are'. 'I definitely have a spiritual experience up here,' says Harald. 'We are in a very desolate place and you don't have the distractions that you have back home that take your attention away from personal reflections. I've actually been thinking when God created this planet, why would he leave this huge space covered in ice? Was it to conserve a lot of water for future generations? Or maybe it was to leave a nice place for a few guys to go for long skiing trips. In that case, it was nice of Him.'

The outside world is never far away. Rune often counts aeroplanes overhead. His record is 13 in a day. Once he is convinced he has seen Air Force One (the US president's plane). Chris imagines his mother, a frequent transatlantic flyer, sitting in one of the planes crossing Greenland, and therefore being only 10 miles away as she passes. Of course, this option wasn't open to the men of 1911, but it cheered them up whenever they saw a bird in flight. On 2 January Wilson wrote, 'We were surprised today seeing a Skua gull flying over us – evidently hungry but not weak. Its droppings, however, were clear mucus, nothing in them at all. It appeared in the afternoon and disappeared again about half an hour after.' How golden that half-hour must have seemed to them. It was a fleeting reminder that here was life, not just ice. (On their way back across the Barrier, Amundsen and his men greeted the sight of two skuas with paroxysms of delight; Bjaaland even fired a shot into the air.)

They valued their time on dry land too. Upon reaching the Transantarctic Mountains, Amundsen skied over with Bjaaland to a small peak he'd named after his childhood nanny 'for the sake of having real bare ground under our feet; we had not felt it since Madeira in September 1910, and now we were in November 1911 … it was a pleasure to set one's foot on bare ground again, and we sat down on the rocks to enjoy the scene'. They photographed themselves in what Amundsen referred to in inverted commas as 'picturesque attitudes': to him, larking about did not come naturally. The geologizing performed by Wilson on the way back through the Beardmore had a similarly life-affirming side-effect. 'It has been extremely interesting,' wrote Scott, deputed like the others to scour for samples. 'Wilson, with his sharp eyes, has picked several plant impressions, the last a piece of coal with beautifully traced leaves in layers, also some excellently preserved impressions of thick stems, showing cellular structure.' As a relief from boredom, this was invaluable. And the evidence of botanical life, albeit millions of years old, must have been cheering too.

Wilson was the most fortunate of them: he had his painting. That he managed to sit on the sledge in his sleeping bag and sketch in the cold temperatures is testimony to his extraordinary, faith-fuelled capacity for enduring discomfort. At a moment of supreme misery, he even sketched the Norwegian flag, perched on a ski, at the pole. As they fell in among the mountains on the way home, he drank in the colours of the rock as if sating a thirst for visual stimulus: 'The Dominion range rock is in the main all brown madder or dark reddish chocolate, but there are numerous bands of yellow rock scattered amongst it'. On the face of it these were scientific observations. But, according to Cherry-Garrard, his was the diary 'of an artist watching the clouds and mountains, of a scientist observing ice and rock and snow, of a doctor, and above all of a man with good judgement. You will understand that the thing which really interested him in this journey was the acquisition of knowledge. It is a restrained and for the most part simple record of facts. There is seldom any comment, and when there is you feel that, for this very reason, it carries more weight.'

* * * * * * * * * * * *

When they get under way each day, what do they think about? Unlike his forerunner, the one thing Rune doesn't think about is the opposition. 'It is our expedition going on here and I don't want to focus on them. Whether they are in front of us or a long way behind us, it doesn't matter for me. It is here that counts, my team and what's going on here, our progress, not the other team. That is up to them.'

Of course, it was easier to have concrete thoughts about the future in 1911. Scott hoped for a glorious return, naval promotion and a knighthood to match Shackleton's. Oates planned to get home and sit his exams to become a major. Taff Evans had the dream of nest-egg and perhaps a pub in Swansea dragging him ever onwards. For the modern travellers, who are much less used to the pemmican, the overwhelming majority of their thoughts are taken up with food – 80 per cent, according to Chris, who also dreams about food (and sex, which must be inconvenient, though it's worse for Mark, who confesses to having 'sordid sexual fantasies'). Inge thinks about good food at least once an hour, specifically about the chicken tikka he is going to eat twice a week when he gets off the ice. At least he eats the pemmican. Ketil prefers to eat the dog pemmican.

Amundsen had a comparable memory of the cuisine back home when 24 dogs were slaughtered at Butcher's Camp and portioned out to dog and man alike. He got quite carried away as he watched Wisting slicing up dog chops with an axe. 'I could not take my eyes off his work; the delicate little cutlets had an absolutely hypnotizing effect as they were spread out one by one over the snow. They recalled memories of old days, when no doubt a dog cutlet would have been less tempting than now – memories of dishes on which the cutlets were elegantly arranged side by side, with paper frills on the bones, and a neat pile of *petit pois* in the middle. And my thoughts wandered still farther afield – but that does not concern us now, nor has it anything to do with the South Pole.'

It is amusing to see the polar memoirist rapping himself on the knuckles. How dare his imagination get in the way? But as with any less seasoned polar travellers, there is no choice, and food is all they can talk about. In one tent Rupert starts up a recipe book in the back of his diary. On a typical page is Arthur's steak recipe and Chris's spare ribs. There are recipes for Greek lamb, roast chicken, even scrambled eggs. Sometimes he reads it before he goes to sleep. But other times it is less cheering. 'I can't actually start to read this,' says Rupert when he produces it. 'I'm going to start to feel miserable.' When he knows he is going to leave on Day 61, Arthur has a very concrete fantasy about sitting 'in a very nice restaurant and having chicken and goat's cheese mousse followed by this kind of *foie gras* thing on a sweetcorn bread thing with my mum and my girlfriend, so I am perfectly happy just to get about as thin as possible'.

Before the journey begins, Chris professes a clinical fascination for the physical deterioration that is bound to occur. He rather loses interest as he discovers just how unpalatable pemmican is, but his interest revives as he notices some unlooked-for psychological side-effects of extreme weight loss. It is even possible that they are beginning to suffer from delusions about their body image normally associated with anorexia. Rupert and Arthur 'have talked a lot about how fat they are and how they want to get thin before they go home, and I feel a bit the same myself,' says Chris, 'and part of that was being overweight before. There has been a slight alteration in the normal pattern of food psychology and what you crave and what you're comfortable with and how you see your body. I'm now under my normal weight, but I'd quite like to be a little bit thinner before I go home.' He will certainly have his wish.

* * * * * * * * * * *

So long as the going was good and hope still fuelled his progress, Scott had his defence against boredom in place. 'What a lot of things we think of on these monotonous marches, what castles one builds, and now hopefully that the pole is ours.' It was Cherry-Garrard's belief that Scott's manifest anxiety 'served as a stimulus against mental monotony rather than as a drain upon his energy'. Meanwhile, in the modern team, Mark deals with the boredom by embarking on an almost ritualized routine of moaning and groaning. It is as if the only way he can make sure this isn't going to be remembered as the worst time of his life is by constantly asserting that it is. He constructs huge parabolas of complaint, great arcs of anger and frustration. It is very funny, and that is the point of it: it is gallows humour, designed to alleviate. 'Last night Rory found a lump of honey in the pemmican, so we carefully excavated it from the surrounding fat and served it up on three biscuits. It was highlight of the week really, wasn't it?' Bruce's relationship with the expedition is slightly different. He is just as unhappy, but is less inclined to lace his misery with humour. Strangely for a leader, he is perfectly happy to admit that he is hating more or less every minute. As early as One Ton Camp he is saying, 'I've set myself a challenge and I'll get on with it, but it isn't half dull.' Much later he says, 'I just crave for it to be over. If I could get whisked away for a lovely meal and be brought back, I wouldn't go. Let's just get this thing over with and get home.'

Thankfully, they have in the tent a butt for their jokes, someone at whom they can harmlessly vent their frustration. Rory's appetite is so whetted by this trip that he is planning to go the South Pole.

'Just walking for 50 days to get to a pole,' Bruce tells him, 'unless I'm the very first person and it's a big event, has no appeal to me whatsoever. I'm not slagging off people who want to do it, especially you, Rory – good for you, mate, absolutely good for you. Please don't think I'm being rude. It's just the furthest thing from my mind. I have no aversion to the cold as such; it's just this unending nothingness and days that are all the same. It's too much really. I need more excitement in life.'

Mark then feels the need to remind Bruce that this trip is all his fault. 'I just very much hope that I do not forget how grim this really is, and if anyone ever phones me up, as Bruce did, and says "Do you want to cross Antarctica, or go to the South Pole?" or something like that I'll tell them where to get off. Politely of course, but no thanks.'

Rory is just as good at teasing them back. 'Lovely view today, don't you think?' he says.

'Yeah,' says Mark, 'these clouds that have been gripping everyone's attention for days and days ... they're great.'

'We had some interesting fog this morning,' says Rory.

'And some great hoar frost on the guy ropes grabbed *my* attention,' says Mark. 'God, it's dull here.'

But some days even Rory has to take himself away somewhere else to fend off the tedium. One day he kills three hours of the march by pretending he is on a walk in the Yorkshire Dales. His sledge-mates no doubt wish they were there with him.

Compare and contrast with the attitude of the Norwegian team. As a rule they are more accepting of their environment, and happier with the challenge that has been set them. It is, concedes Ketil, 'probably the most boring landscape on Earth. Even on the ocean you can see some wildlife once in a while, but here there's hardly anything. We have seen a few birds, but with many days in between.' And yet he speaks for them all when he says 'we don't have time to get bored'. For him in particular the constant checking of the compass against Inge's front-running yields 'no spare time: I have to keep concentrating. I cannot relax for one minute.' For those coming up behind, the dogs 'help quite a bit,' says John. 'They have a lot of personality and they work hard and there's something to look at all day and there's little nuances that are different each day with the dogs that are fun to pick out.' Harald says that thanks to the dogs he finds it difficult to follow his own thoughts for more than half an hour.

But then the Norwegians have less cause for boredom or complaint. Their work is much lighter, their rate of progress much greater, and they also have the incalculable advantage of five to a tent, which provides more conversational variety than four or three. Their rate of weight loss is much lower. 'I think there is some potential for monotony on the plateau,' says John, 'but it's also a true wilderness environment. There's very few people who have the privilege of travelling up here, and I don't take that privilege lightly. I really enjoy sitting on the sledge and daydreaming the day away, or focusing on my dogs as they have their little subtleties that come and go each day. And the snow is a little different, the sky's always different. I'm pretty happy at the end of the day most days.' He adds that 'doing Amundsen's trip is really the chance of a lifetime. Each member of the group considers himself to be very privileged to be out here.'

Ketil is heard to say that he doesn't like rest days because he finds them boring, but he and the others are happy to make an exception for Day 19, which happens to be Norway's Constitution Day. This is not without significance to polar exploration. It was through the achievements of Nansen and then Amundsen that a newly independent Norway found international recognition. To celebrate, Rune declares a day off and organizes festivities.

They begin with a parade holding the flags of Norway and Greenland. They sing the national anthem as they march three times around the camp. Inge accompanies them on the mouth organ, while John, who is American, reads from a phonetic transcription of the words. At the end of the parade, Harald stands on a sledge and makes a speech. After much cheering, the national anthem is sung once again, before they move on to the next phase of the entertainment: the games. Back at Cape Evans, Scott's men played a huge amount of football in the snow, but out here the options are limited, improvisation essential. There are three events, and each of them involves pemmican. A bamboo cane is erected and turns are taken throwing a piece of pemmican at it. The closest wins. In the second game they each hurl a piece of pemmican as far as they can. In the third the bamboo is now used as a javelin: whoever throws it closest to the furthest piece of pemmican wins. By the end of the festivities, morale is high, and that is the best a leader can hope for on the ice.

Rune Gjeldnes's Diary

DAY 19

Congratulations! To us and to Norway! '17 May, how we love you', and according to tradition we're making it a resting day. My fourth 17 May on an expedition. Know we've got a lot to do in terms of repairs and maintenance. Have to look over the sledges to see if all is OK with them. John is going to put brakes on my sledge. As team leader I've had a great time. But the team basically leads itself. Everyone has a lot of initiative and capacities. The motivation is at the top level almost all the time. Can feel some negative vibes, but they're outweighed by good work in other areas. Yes, it's all very good. I think the worst thing is if we don't keep to schedule. We ought to be at the pole in 23 working days – 413 nautical miles to go. We have to do 20 nautical miles per day at least if we're going to make it. That's not impossible. But time will tell. We're marking the route with bamboo sticks. We should have had 140, but we only have 80, which means one every 6.5 km from Depot 82 to the pole. Otherwise Ketil and I have been working on the dog food for the rest of the trip. Not a lot of dry dog food left. Have to cut down on that.

Have celebrated 17 May outside, with parade and singing. Harald gave a great speech. Afterwards there was a pemmican competition. John won at javelin, Ketil won the rest.

CHAPTER TEN

Efficiency

ALL WE HAVE OUT HERE IS OURSELVES, SO WE HAVE TO BELIEVE IN
OURSELVES. WE DO. COMPLETELY.
John Huston

An irony dogs the triumph of Amundsen. They often say that nobody
remembers the runner-up. Doubtless the visceral fear of coming in
second is one of the things that all winners have in common. The
irony, therefore, is that in the race to be first to plant a national flag
at the South Pole, the explorer who found the Norwegian emblem
already flapping there is the one whose memory resonates down the
century. Outside his native country, the victor has been reduced to
the status of an also-ran.

Why has this happened? The most obvious answer is that Scott
wrote himself into the wider consciousness in the style of his
death. But other clues are to be found in the journey reconstructed
in his honour by the Norwegian party led by Rune Gjeldnes. They
have been given the same equipment, the same number of sledges
and dogs, the same food. They also seem to have inherited from
their predecessors the same quiet fixity of purpose, the same
undemonstrative resolve, the same grinding, machine-tooled
efficiency.

Take the diary entries for Day 21. Thus Harald Kippenes: 'Compared to the expectations that I had, it seems to be fairly easy. We are making big distances.' 'Things are getting better every day,' says Ketil Reitan on the same day. 'We had the best day so far yesterday. We made more than 50 km and everybody is happy and we feel that we are going to achieve the goals that we have set.' Rune: 'In three weeks' time we should be at the pole. That's the same amount of days we have been out, exactly on schedule, which is also very satisfying.'

Much closer to the pole, John Huston, sitting on his sledge on Day 32: 'The group dynamic is extremely positive and easygoing. Every morning Rune says, "It's gonna be a good day", and I think he truly believes it. That optimism is infectious. I can't think of one time I've heard something along the lines of "I can't" or "This is too hard". Everything is always solution-oriented and positive.'

At no point is there an impression from any of Rune's men that they would rather be somewhere (or even anywhere) else. They think of the people they have left behind – girlfriends or wives and, in the case of Ketil and Inge Solheim, children. (It is a standing joke among the rest of them that Harald is temporarily single.) But the sense of mission is palpable. Over in the British camp the relentlessly sunny mask of the leader occasionally slips as reality starts to bite and the physical grind takes its toll. Sometimes the men under him are left to find motivation where they can. By contrast, Rune often talks about the happiness of his team, less because he needs to buoy them up than because their daily performances are, as it were, self-buoying. Either they put in a big distance, or they drag an extra load taken on from the depot further than they dared hope, or they have a successful day of navigating by dead reckoning. Every day they stop at regular intervals to build cairns to guide them back to their depots on the journey home. Rune in particular enjoys the work. At the end of each day, they know their routines: they feed the dogs, dig out a patch of snow for the tent, and then all five of them climb into the tent, where they cook, eat, talk and sleep.

The miles are swallowed up, and every day they stride – or

rather their dogs stride – unimpeded towards their goal. If anything, they are even more efficient than Amundsen. This is not simply because they travel secure in the knowledge that any form of injury will result in an airlift. All knowledge is power, and just as Amundsen knew more than Scott about dog travel, diet and clothing, they know more than Amundsen.

The dogs, for example, are fed almost twice as much of their daily diet of pemmican and seal blubber as Amundsen's men fed theirs. It might be historically accurate to do it the 1911 way, but the dog experts prefer to use their own method. 'He fed them 16 ounces and we are supposed to be feeding them 28 ounces,' says Rune. 'We are also giving the dogs water because that's how good dog-handlers do it today. They get about 2 pints every day.' Amundsen's dogs ate snow. Having stronger dogs, Rune can plan the journey in terms of hours travelled per day rather than distances. 'Amundsen was thinking mainly distances – 15 miles per day up to the 82 or 83 degrees depot – and then they were trying to do 22 miles per day after that. But we've tried to do eight or nine hours per day, and if we can go longer than the average distance per day, it will be very nice, and if we can do that for half of the trek, that will make many days' work shorter. Just one hour per day or 2 miles, and in ten days we have 18 miles. That's one day, and it can be much more than that.'

The shorter distances did not stop Amundsen's dogs from entering a state bordering on starvation. On this trip Ketil realizes why each of Amundsen's sledges had a heavy wooden box. 'Amundsen wrote that they have the wooden boxes because it should be faster to unpack everything,' he says, 'but I think the reason is because they didn't have any chains to tie up their dogs at night, so they had to find a way to protect the dog food.' Even early in the journey, they kept their ski bindings out of reach, either hung at the top of upright skis, or in provision cases. Otherwise the dogs would have eaten them. 'The dogs have become quite dangerous,' wrote Amundsen as they neared the pole, 'and must be considered as enemies when one leaves the sledges.' Without chains, John wonders how they caught the dogs each morning.

Their other advantage is that Greenland is not *terra incognita*. They know what awaits them. When Amundsen and his men clambered to the top of the glacier on 21 November they may have assumed the worst was behind them. It wasn't.

* * * * * * * * * * * *

They made camp on their first night at altitude with heavy hearts. In the tent Amundsen got the Primus stove going quickly. 'I was hoping thereby to produce enough noise to deaden the shots that I knew would soon be heard – twenty-four of our brave companions and faithful helpers were marked out for death. It was hard – but it had to be so. We had agreed to shrink from nothing in order to reach our goal ... There went the first shot. I am not a nervous man, but I must admit that I gave a start. Shot now followed upon shot – they had an uncanny sound over the great plain.' Some slaughtered dogs were disembowelled and fed to their companions, most of who fell ravenously on this appetizing variation to their regular diet. Their masters had the decency to wait till the next day before they feasted on boiled Greenland husky. They named this place the Butcher's Shop. Wisting was butcher and cook. 'Wonderful dinners we have enjoyed from our good Greenlanders,' wrote Bjaaland, 'and I'll say they tasted good.' His leader agreed, up to a point: 'One cutlet after another disappeared with lightning-like rapidity. I must admit that they would have lost nothing by being a little more tender, but one must not expect too much of a dog.'

The plan had been to rest and acclimatize here for two days. In the event, the weather immobilized them for four, during which they meticulously reorganized their provisions as they discarded Hassel's sledge. It was cold work counting thousands of individual biscuits and pieces of chocolate in a gale. On the fifth day the storm was worse than ever, but all five men contemplated the prospect of yet another day of incarceration with such horror that they unanimously voted to head on out. At the recollection of it, Amundsen's chest swelled with pride. 'When I think of my four friends of the southern journey, it is the memory of that morning that comes first to my mind. All the qualities that I most admire in a man were clearly shown at that juncture: courage and dauntlessness, without boasting or big words. Amid joking and chaff, everything was packed, and then – out into the blizzard.'

The next few days were the most difficult of the entire expedition. With visibility virtually nil, they found themselves losing altitude when they expected to be emerging up on to the plateau. Before the surviving dogs careered any further downhill, they had no choice but to stop and camp after only a few miles and wait for the sun to peer out from behind the clouds. In the middle of the night it did, and they leapt out of their bags to view their surroundings. The next morning they set off with more confidence, only to be impeded by terrible surface conditions. 'A sledge journey through the Sahara could not have offered a worse surface to move over,' wrote Amundsen. Then the next day: 'Fog, fog – and again fog. Also fine falling snow, which makes the going impossible.' And still they were losing altitude. The clouds drifted briefly apart to reveal four mountains, which Amundsen promptly named after his companions, as well as a fifth mountain, the size of which took their breath away. These peaks were like icebergs: mostly submerged, but hinting at an overwhelming vastness below.

And then, on 28 November, they saw what Amundsen described as a huge glacier lying athwart their route to the south. They stopped to build a depot in order to lighten the sledges for the climb ahead. 'The snow was excellent for this purpose – as hard as glass.' As they edged into the maze of crevasses and ice falls, Wisting was the first to be nearly claimed as they 'came upon such a labyrinth of yawning chasms and open abysses that we could not move'. They camped. Amundsen roped up to Hanssen and set out to reconnoitre a route. The pair of them soon came upon terrain so disturbed that Amundsen imagined a battle had taken place in which 'the ammunition had been great blocks of ice. They lay pell-mell, one on top of another, in all directions, and evoked a picture of violent confusion. Thank God we were not here while this was going on … it must have been a spectacle like doomsday.' Who says Amundsen doesn't have a way with words? Even in these desperate straits, with the entire edifice of his long-planned expedition under threat, the sardonic poet in him found time to appreciate his surroundings, although at his most enraptured, words often failed him: 'it was a fairy landscape in blue and white, red and black, a play of colours that defies description … Mount Nilsen – ah! Anything more beautiful, taking it altogether, I have never seen.'

'No artist could achieve anything so magical,' agreed Bjaaland.

Looking for a barely navigable route through this death trap, the two of them decided to name it the Devil's Glacier. Breaking the news to their tentmates, they met with hearty approval. With so many opportunities to be swallowed whole by the force of gravity, no wonder their thoughts turned to the infernal basement. Some of the crevasses were 'hundreds of feet wide and possibly thousands of feet deep'. One conduit flanked intimidatingly on either side by crevasses they called the Gates of Hell. For one of their four terrible days on the Devil's Glacier Bjaaland reserved the special label in his diary: the Devil's Name Day.

In his diary that night, Amundsen wrote, 'What will the next surprise be, I wonder?' The surprise element lay partly in the fact that they could hardly see where they were going. In such foul weather they were effectively travelling in the style of Scott's men who went on the winter journey, or of the extremely short-sighted Cherry-Garrard on any journey. For the dog-drivers, extreme caution was essential: 'a slight mistake might be enough to send both sledge and dogs with lightning rapidity into the next world.' In his account Amundsen claims that every 2 miles covered brought only 1 mile of gain. Elsewhere he rounds the ratio down to ten to one.

As they crossed snow bridges, they gave thanks for the long Telemark skis that distributed their weight. Self-congratulation soon turned to self-recrimination when the next morning they woke up to find a storm had blown away the top dusting of snow to lay bare a substratum of hard ice. Skis were now of no use, and they had left their crampons at the previous depot, assuming they would not need them on the plateau. 'Without them, climbing on sheer ice is supposed to be practically an impossibility. A thousand thoughts raced through my brain. The pole lost, perhaps, because of such an idiotic blunder?' Amundsen was capable of making mistakes after all.

The ice was so hard that they found it difficult to pitch their tent. Armed with an axe, Hassel went out to find an ice block to melt in the cooker, and was delighted to find a small conical mound of ice outside the tent door. He smashed it, only to discover it was hollow. As the axe was pulled out the surrounding part gave way, and shards could be heard falling down through the freshly opened hole. 'It appeared, then, that two feet from our door we had a most convenient way down into the cellar. Hassel looked as if he enjoyed the situation. "Black as a sack," he smiled; "couldn't see any bottom." Hanssen was beaming; no doubt he would have liked the tent a little nearer.' Their nonchalance in the face of danger was a running joke.

The ice affected the dogs too: they could not grip with their claws. Every dip they entered they were unable to pull the sledge out, so their driver had to do it for them. Most dips turned out to be snowed-in crevasses, and as they tugged and heaved to pull the sledge up the slope, they didn't always take care to hold fast to the safety strap or lashing: 'Familiarity breeds contempt,' wrote Amundsen, 'even with the most cautious, and some of the drivers were often within an ace of going down into "the cellar".'

The weather, meanwhile, was 'vile', frostbite a constant danger. It was the wind rather than the cold that caused the problem. When they camped one night, they left behind their reindeer-skin clothing because it was too warm. Their mileages varied: 18.5, 9.25, 15.5, then 2.5.

On the fourth day on the Devil's Glacier 'we came to the formation in the glacier that we called the Devil's Ballroom'. The first sign of trouble ahead was when Wisting's sledge-runner went into a crevasse. He and Hassel set about pulling it out, while Bjaaland produced his camera to take a picture. Amundsen, watching from a distance, eventually asked them what the crevasse looked like, assuming from the leisurely way in which the other three went about their business that it was full to the brim with snow. 'Oh, as usual,' they replied; 'no bottom.' Amundsen presented this as evidence that 'one can grow accustomed to anything in this world. There were these two – Wisting and Hassel – lying over a yawning, bottomless abyss, and having their photograph taken; neither of them gave a thought to the serious side of the situation.' Soon afterwards, Hanssen's leading dogs fell through a thin crust of ice, only to reveal a lower layer of ice underneath. Then Bjaaland fell through the lower layer and grabbed a loop of rope on his sledge just in time. 'Time after time the dogs now fell through, and time after time the men went in. The effect of the open space between the two crusts was that the ground under our feet sounded unpleasantly hollow as we went over it. The drivers whipped up their dogs as much as they could, and with shouts and brisk encouragement they went rapidly over the treacherous floor. Fortunately, this curious formation was not of great extent, and we soon began to observe a change for the better as we came up the ridge. It soon appeared that the Ballroom was the glacier's last farewell to us.'

The plateau beckoned. They did not know it, but the worst was over.

* * * * * * * * * * * *

Their successors have nothing so dramatic to cope with on the Greenland ice cap, and they do know it. They have read the literature. 'Compared to Amundsen,' says Rune, 'we know our route, we know what we will meet up here, we know there are no mountains in front of us. Amundsen didn't know anything about that, so he also had to be very careful with how he planned and acted when he was moving forward.' Their diaries reveal that they are always expecting some problem or other to rear up in front of them and present them with some insuperable challenge. But nothing seems to happen. On Day 22 the bridges that support the load on Harald's sledge buckle and break. Ketil fixes them, and pledges to keep on checking. They have to alter the length of their ski poles when they have to do more skiing after the Butcher's Shop depot. And a sledge-meter breaks. Inge keeps a book in which to note down anything of medical interest. The pages remain for the most part defiantly blank. 'We have fewer injuries and physical problems than an average working place.'

The only concern is keeping the right body temperature and avoiding frostbite. Amundsen's men all succumbed to frostbite on the plateau as they headed south. 'We looked like the worst type of tramps and ruffians, and would probably not have been recognized by our nearest relations.' And they didn't just look bad. The merest puff of wind 'produced a sensation as if one's face were being cut backwards and forwards with a blunt knife'. No wonder the modern Norwegian team do their best to make sure they don't suffer the same fate. 'If you get frostbite,' says Ketil, 'you're going to have a hard time protecting your face the rest of the trip. The frost sores can very easily come back, so you have to try to feel your face all the time. If I feel I am getting cold on my chin or my nose, I just take off my mitten and press on the skin so I get some air circulation.'

Once they come through the mental and physical challenge of the glacier, says John, they have the luxury of being able to 'sit on the sledge and think. The dogs have a very low stress level and are happy just to run over the flat terrain in cooler temperatures. It makes our days much more enjoyable when we don't have to untangle fighting dogs or push our dogs up hills. Amundsen had a few easy times too. He sat on his sledge quite a bit, and the fact that we don't have to sweat our way through every day is really nice.' It is here that they start to put in some astonishing distances. To reach 82 depot they do 30 miles: 'An amazing distance,' says Rune, 'so we are just cruising over here ... the best day so far on the expedition.' They go so fast that Inge cannot possibly ski out in front, so Ketil navigates from the front sledge.

They even do their route-marking at speed. On Day 24 Rune proudly announces that they have built a cairn in record time: 'Twelve minutes,' he says, 'and Inge is on the move again. We were discussing it yesterday – that we might be using too much time to build the cairn, and also resting and talking during the long breaks. So 12 minutes is very good.'

As they speed across the ice cap, they start to sound almost guilty that they are outstripping their famous compatriot, even though this is the plan – to cover the same mileage as Amundsen in

80 days as opposed to 99. 'We are very humble towards what he did,' says Rune, 'but I think the experience we have today, and the knowledge on our route, we should be able to do it in 80.' He even fantasizes about doing it in 70. But they continue to surprise themselves. Even when they have taken on huge extra weight at their final depot, they make 24 miles after starting late. 'I think today is the heaviest load we will have on the entire trip,' says Ketil. 'I thought we didn't make that much today because it had been kind of slow conditions and it's the heaviest load. I would think each sledge is about 650 pounds and in this snow it's hard work to pull the sledges, but the dogs kept their spirits up all day.'

With two dog experts in the team (as opposed to none in the British team from Day 6 onwards), the Norwegian team have applied themselves methodically to the business of getting the best out of their huskies. The dogs have been in Greenland 'for thousands of years', says Ketil, 'and they are very well adapted to the use they have been bred for, but they are not always the easiest dogs to handle.' The handling almost always involves internal politics. In a team of 12 there can be only one leader. In order to establish the hierarchy, they have to fight. But it turns out that the leader is not necessarily the lead dog. Ketil's team had two lead dogs, Bonza and Pamda – brothers who are both four years old. 'Bonza', he explains, 'always had to keep control of other dogs behind him, so he tended to walk back and check out the team, or he wanted to fight with another dog behind him. Every time we made a stop he would turn back and start to make a big mess in the team. After a while I tried out different lead dogs to put beside Pamda – he's the one that started to listen to commands during the first week. So I had to try and find a dog that could run beside him, and I thought it would be best to find a dog that would not be a challenger, so it had to be a younger dog. I tried a small male, Tutu, who is a bit younger than Pamda. He's about three years old and a very social dog, so that makes it easier for me to work with him. Right now Tutu is the one most eager when we take off – he's probably the hardest-working dog on the team – but it's very nice to have him beside Pamda. He doesn't try to challenge Pamda's position: he knows he's a smaller and younger dog, so he's not trying to fight with him. He always shows Pamda that he is below him in rank.'

The day comes for them to release some dogs. In the early part of the journey they had problems with some of the dogs, but these have long since been ironed out and now the business of picking out the weaker ones tugs on Norwegian heartstrings. Their operation is so efficient that, unlike in the British team, there are scarcely any malingerers: the alpha dogs have been separated and the entire team firmly advised who is in charge. 'We spend so much time with these dogs,' says Ketil, 'and all day they keep us company, so it's going to be hard to send them back.' They have a glimmer of insight into how Amundsen's men must have felt at the Butcher's Shop, feasting hungrily on husky cutlet.

There are twelve dogs per sledge. Three each go from the sledges of Rune and John, and four from Harald's, and the shortfall is made up from Ketil's team. Unlike Amundsen, who at the Butcher's Shop got rid of the fourth sledge, the modern Norwegian team will persevere with four 'and see how that works', says Harald. 'Later on we are planning on leaving one sledge and going with three dog teams.' Although there is a loss of pulling power, in a way it is a relief. For most of the trip they have been sitting on their sledges for hours at a time. Now they can get off and ski behind on a tow rope. 'Sitting on a sledge all day is boring,' says John. 'There is not much to do except look at your dogs. Skiing behind gives you more exercise. The challenge has been to keep from sweating too much. If you do, you need more water and you use more energy, and when you get cold, you cool down quickly.'

Ten days later, ten more dogs have to go, and the Norwegians take up the configuration that they will maintain until they cross the finishing line. And so the days pass, as the dogs drag them across the ice cap towards their goal. They remain blessedly free of alarms, incidents and injuries. 'The trip has gone into a phase now where all the days seem to be more or less the same,' says Rune. 'We're well into all the routines: we get up, harness the dogs, three hours, half-hour break for cairn, three hours do the same and another three hours before we put up camp.' Their very efficiency means they have far more reason to be bored than Bruce Parry's team. But it is a function of their efficiency that they are never bored, and more than once they say that the hours and days simply race by. And as they home in on their goal, they become a living, breathing embodiment of the reason why Amundsen's victory failed to capture the imagination in the way that Scott's defeat did. They may not get bored, but to those not looking closely enough their journey could be perceived as boring.

* * * * * * * * * * * *

It was at 87 degrees south that Amundsen and his men counted themselves unequivocally on the plateau. The mountains behind them had sunk below the horizon to the northeast, the pole was 180 miles in front, and they were over 10,000 feet above sea level. Bad weather moved in, in the form of blinding drift, 'but a feeling of security had come over us and helped us to advance rapidly and without hesitation, although we could see nothing'. Their patience was now tested by a new form of obstacle: not holes in the ground, but huge sastrugi – wave-shaped hurdles that, casting no shadow in the bad light, rose up unannounced. 'If one came on them unexpectedly, one required to be more than an acrobat to keep one's feet.' They fell over frequently and, thanks to the altitude, struggled for breath every time they hauled themselves up. Hanssen and his dogs went first, and the others watched his struggles and noted where the next hump lay.

By the following day, 6 December, as they rose above 11,000 feet, the sastrugi disappeared and they proceeded as if across a pane of glass. Amundsen was thrown to discover that the water was boiling at the same temperature as the day before. They had reached the summit of the polar plateau earlier than expected. By now, as they covered huge daily distances, they had to bury the sledges in snow at each camp to stop the hungry dogs from devouring anything and everything they could sink their teeth into. The low cloud lifted a touch and they were dazzled by the glare, although there was no sign of the sun, the appearance of which now became a pressing concern: they needed to find out exactly where they were. 'I don't know that I have ever stood and absolutely pulled at the sun to get it out as I did that time,' wrote Amundsen. Eventually, it burst through the clouds and, in the middle of a sea of snow at the bottom of the world, they sat on the sledges and laboriously worked out exactly where they were. They had travelled on dead reckoning for nearly 100 nautical miles. But despite the ceaseless jerks and jolts that made navigation by compass a near impossibility, 'it turned out Hanssen had steered to a hair,' marvelled Amundsen, 'for the observations and dead reckoning agreed to a mile'. They were exactly where they thought they were: only 7 miles short of Shackleton's record for the furthest south, set three years previously.

Amundsen happened to be skiing in front that day, and recalled falling into a reverie as he ploughed forwards, only to be brought back from his daze by cheers. He was overcome as the silk Norwegian flag was hoisted on Hanssen's sledge and the sun broke through. '88° 23' was past; we were farther south than any human being had been. No other moment of the whole trip affected me like this. The tears forced their way to my eyes; by no effort of will could I keep them back. It was the flag yonder that conquered me and my will. Luckily I was some way in advance of the others, so that I had time to pull myself together and master my feelings before reaching my comrades. We all shook hands, with mutual congratulations; we had won our way so far by holding together, and we would go farther yet – to the end.' Bjaaland was coming up a mile behind and found the captain 'in a shining humour'. They awarded themselves extra chocolate as they paid their respects to Shackleton and his men. The English explorers had hauled their own sledges this far before turning back in the certain knowledge that, with barely enough provisions to get home, to press on to the pole would have been suicidal. 'Pluck and grit can work wonders,' noted Amundsen.

There was more good news the next day as they rested themselves and the dogs. The sun now returned for a longer visit, and the water in their cooker now boiled at a higher temperature. They would have a downward run to the pole. A final depot was marked with 'quite a respectable monument'. They took on enough food for a whole month in case they somehow contrived to miss this stash of dog pemmican and biscuits on the way back, but that would indeed be hard: the depot was marked with 60 splinters of packing-case planted either side, 100 paces apart. In total the landmark stretched across 6 miles. For ease of orientation, the ones to the east were marked, while those to the west were unmarked. And when they set off, the cairn-building intensified to a new pitch, though Amundsen noted that the powdery snow was not best suited to this work. It was so feathery that they could insert the tent pole 6 feet down.

Their advance met with equal lack of resistance, but to preserve the strength of the dogs – particularly Bjaaland's – for the return journey, they once again limited their mileage to a quarter of a degree of latitude a day: 15 miles. Thus the first men to bear down on 90 degrees south eased up as they approached the tape. There was to be no risk. On 10 December they reached 89 degrees south; on the 11th, 89 degrees 15 minutes; on the 12th, 89 degrees 30 minutes. And then, on the 13th they camped at 89 degrees 45 minutes. 'It was like the eve of some great festival that night in the tent. One could feel that a great event was at hand.' Amundsen compared it to the night before Christmas. 'The excitement is great,' wrote Bjaaland in his diary that night. 'Shall we see the English flag – God have mercy, I don't believe it.'

Rune Gjeldnes's Diary

DAY 31

Well, didn't we have another good day! With a new record. Thanks to everyone, but especially Inge and the dogs. Rather fantastic! I like it. We race towards the pole! A big dogfight at the end of the day. John lost his skis and the bucket with the dog food, and they were after mine. John was shouting and screaming, but it's nothing unusual for him. But when I turned around they were only 60 feet behind me.

DAY 37

Evening again, and it has been a hard day for everyone. The snow has been sticking like glue under our skis. It's the wind's fault. The snow is blowing along the ground. Despite it being cold, the snow is sticking to the skis. But we managed to do a good 24 miles. That's great. Inge has done a great job going in front, even though the visibility has been quite poor. Hoping the wind will calm down by tomorrow so the snow can settle and the sun can work on it a bit. There must be low pressure to our east, causing the bad weather the last few days. But the distance has cheered me and us up, even with these conditions, we were able to manage the average distance we have to do to get to the pole. Eight beacons were built – two large ones and the rest small. Hope to be at the pole in six days.

DAY 39

New day. Some wind today as well, and I'm wondering what the going will be like. The last hour yesterday was not so fun, but let's hope today will be better. Need a good day now. And that's what we'll get – whatever! It's basically speed that counts at the moment. Schedule to be kept, food and dogs that are going out various days. Will build more beacons than yesterday. The small beacons will be good to have on the way back. We can't miss a single depot or we'll be in trouble. BIG TROUBLE. Hoping for a good dreaming-day today or for the thoughts to flow easily. Most of us are thinking a lot about food at the moment, considering the dull food we've got. Yes, food fantasies!

The morning routine was done in two hours and 15 minutes. New record! I overslept half an hour, but managed to make up the time. GOOD. Have done a good day, and the going is better.

DAY 41

Evening again, and a good day for me, but Harald has been struggling with Fjumse, who's scared of the sound of snow cracking. The leading dog runs behind the sledge for every cracking noise, and there are a lot of them. The noise is like thunder. Guess we've waited about an hour in total for him and John. Changing the dogs around didn't help, but will try with a couple of Ketil's dogs tomorrow.

CHAPTER ELEVEN

Deficiency

WE ... APPEAR TO BE ON A VERY GRADUAL DOWN GRADIENT.
Dr Edward Wilson

When Teddy Evans, Lashly and Crean returned to the base at Cape Evans, they carried glad tidings. 'Scott must reach the Pole with the greatest ease,' wrote Cherry-Garrard. 'This seemed almost a certainty: and yet it was, as we know now, a false impression.' Perhaps their optimism was fired by the assumption that the polar party could not possibly have as grim a time as they had themselves endured on the return journey, without a sledge-meter, with only three to pull the sledge and warm the tent, and Evans nearly dead from scurvy by the end.

On 4 January 1912, the sixty-sixth day of Scott's epic journey, there were five men left: Scott, Wilson, Oates, Bowers and Taff Evans. They were 148 miles from the South Pole. On Day 61 of the modern re-enactment, there are four men left: Bruce Parry, Rory O'Connor, Mark Anstice and Chris van Tulleken. They are 147 miles from their own pole.

It may appear to be an inaccuracy in the reconstruction that Bruce is a man down on Scott at the equivalent stage. But their situations are in fact reasonably parallel. The remaining tent has had only three men in it since Day 7. Bruce and Mark have both done stints in the other tent, but Rory has not slept in a four-man tent for 54 days. Scott's tent was certainly more crowded, but just as Scott had to find room for Bowers, three tent-mates now have to budge up and find a space for Chris. And Bowers was very nearly a foot shorter than Chris is.

On balance, it was still worse for Scott. An inner lining further reduced the space inside. Cherry-Garrard shuddered at the thought: 'When stretched out for the night the sleeping-bags of the two outside men must have been partly off the floor-cloth, and probably on the snow; their base must have been touching the inner tent and collecting the rime which was formed there.' They also noticed at once that it took half an hour longer to cook for five than four, simply because it takes longer to boil a larger lump of snow. 'Half an hour off your sleep, or half an hour off your march?' The modern tent finds the same thing.

There were, and still are, advantages and disadvantages in the extra man. With the fifth reindeer sleeping bag, Scott's sledge became top-heavy and vulnerable to capsizing whenever the terrain delivered wave upon wave of sastrugi. On the plus side, the pulling power was increased out of proportion to the amount of extra food they had to bring. So it is for their successors. Although the sledge on Day 61 is much the heaviest they have experienced thus far, the weight distributed between four men makes for lighter pulling. So long as there is a following wind, it helps that they have a sort of fifth man of their own, in the form of a square-rig sail that Anstice customizes using the remains of the discarded sledge as a mast. Anstice's knowledge of sailing is confined to light dinghies. 'I am not hoping to be towed along by a fast-moving sledge. All we hope is that it provides the power of an extra man. This sledge is going to be half a ton.'

Scott's fifth man travelled with a significant handicap, as Scott had mystifyingly ordered the second sledge team to depot their skis several days earlier. 'Our party were on ski with the exception of myself,' wrote Bowers in his diary. 'I first made fast to the central span, but afterwards connected up to the toggle of the sledge, pulling in the centre between the inner ends of Captain Scott's and

Dr Wilson's traces. This was found to be the best place, as I had to go my own step.' Bowers was by four years the youngest of the party (though 'exceptionally old for his age', noted Cherry-Garrard.) He was 15 years Scott's junior. He also had the shortest legs, but in compensation he could draw on the deepest reserves of energy, enthusiasm and, probably, sheer belief. Scott was aglow with admiration: 'Nothing comes amiss to him, and no work is too hard. It is a difficulty to get him into the tent; he seems quite oblivious of the cold, and he lies coiled in his bag writing and working out sights long after the others are asleep.'

In this early stage of the final push for the pole, Scott seems to have entered a state bordering on euphoria. The going was very tough, but so long as it wasn't impossible, that always appealed to Scott's taste for the heroic struggle. 'I think that after the Last Return Party left him there is a load off his mind,' wrote Cherry-Garrard. 'The thing had worked so far, it was up to *them* now: that great mass of figures and weights and averages, those years of preparation, those months of anxiety – not one of them had been in vain. They were up to date in distance, and there was a very good amount of food, and probably more than was necessary to see them to the Pole, and off the plateau on full rations ... Here with him was a fine party, tested and strong, and only 148 miles from the Pole.'

That first day they made 12.5 miles for their nine-hour slog. Their daily mileages continued to improve on the plateau, despite wading through a surface of sandy snow crystals. But the sun came out, warming their backs and casting shadows that helped in the now precarious business of steering straight. During the rests they could dry their equipment. 'It is wonderful to see how neatly everything stows on a little sledge, thanks to Evans,' wrote Scott. 'I was anxious to see how we could pull it, and glad to find we went easy enough.' And then again, 'Tonight it is a flat calm; the sun so warm that in spite of the temperature we can stand about outside in the greatest comfort ... I wonder what is in store for us. At present everything seems to be going with extraordinary smoothness ... We feel the cold very little, the great comfort of our situation is the excellent drying effect of the sun ... Our food continues to amply satisfy. What luck to have hit on such an excellent ration! We really are an excellently found party ... we lie so very comfortably, warmly clothed in comfortable bags, sleeping in our double tent ... the sleeping bags remain in good condition ... it is quite impossible to speak too highly of my companions.'

Comfort, comfortable – mantra-like, he repeats the words as if under the influence of some mood-lifting substance. Perhaps he was. Scott was clearly on one of his highs: his excitement rose to fever pitch as they climbed to the summit of the plateau. He was buoyed above all by the prospect of overtaking Shackleton's record for reaching the point furthest south. It neared every day they plodded on. On 9 January, five days after they waved farewell to the second supporting party, they reached 88 degrees 25 minutes. 'RECORD,' wrote Scott in his journal. He was not one for the demon-strativeness of upper case, but this was a moment to savour, just as it was for Amundsen when he too passed into unvisited latitudes. It was, perhaps not coincidentally, exactly three years since Shackleton had stood on almost the same spot. Scott had kept track of his and Wilson's old sledging partner the whole way, and now they had overtaken him. With 95 miles to the pole, Shackleton had chosen his fate: ' ... better a live donkey,' as he explained to his wife, 'than a dead lion'.

Scott was proud of his fellow lions. 'It is amusing to stand thus and remember the constant horrors of our situation as they were painted for us by S.' This was perhaps an unwarranted dig at Shackleton, though not necessarily as malicious as Scott's debunkers would claim. He had won a race, if not the main one, and he was in the mood for celebration as the next day they made a depot to lighten their load. They were less than 100 miles from the South Pole.

'Then something happened,' wrote Cherry-Garrard.

* * * * * * * * * * *

As the four-strong modern British team leaves to make the final push for its own pole, the men seem to grow more acutely conscious that they are marching against history. Scott's journal now makes for regular reading in the tent. Their new goal is to match their predecessor's distances – to make 10 nautical miles a day on the way to the pole, and 15 on the way back.

They immediately fall behind. The first day is, in Mark's estimation, 'physically not the hardest, but psychologically far and away the hardest: we haven't got anywhere.' For the first week, they manage parsimonious average distances of 5 nautical miles. On Day 69 they march for 7.4. In mitigation, they are still getting used to man-hauling a heavier sledge, and the more they eat, the less they will have to pull. As they watch themselves come up short of Scott's distances, Bruce makes two decisions in this phase of the journey. To save time they will follow Scott's model of building only two cairns a day – one at the lunch stop, another when they camp. And every three days they will depot more food and fuel to lighten the sledge. It's not what Scott did at the equivalent moment, but they justify it to themselves as spiritually if not historically accurate. 'We've taken a chance on how fast we're going to get to the pole,' explains Bruce. 'If we get it wrong, we're going to suffer ... As we've only got 99 not 150 days, the only way we'll be able to replicate in a small way the problems he had is to give ourselves a few more risks. We're taking risks for the sake of exploring more pain.'

The problem, as it was for Scott, is the snow. One day they wake up to discover the sledges snowed under, and the drift rising high on the side of the tent. It is back-breaking work attempting to lug the sledge into motion at the start of each day, and again every time it stops. They pray for sun, as Scott had at the equivalent stage, to come out and melt the soft top layer of snow and impart some glide to the sledge-runners. They get their wish and start to move faster, only to be impeded by the skis, with their barely upturned tips, sticking into the snow. Chris says that their progress would be even better if the surface would only melt and then refreeze. Mark, who keeps falling over, decides to take off his skis and walk. All, apart from Rory who is navigating, do the same, and even he joins them in the end. They immediately find themselves using muscles they haven't needed for weeks. It occurs to Bruce that one criticism of Scott is unfair. 'What Scott's slagged off for is not practising on skis, whereas actually it's a fallacy. The action you need is a walking technique. We discovered that ourselves. You can have done years of Telemarking and been no better than a novice when it comes to pulling this.' Then the sun goes in, the snow turns to mush and they put their skis on again, only to find it almost impossible to get the sledge going, and then it moves for no more than a few feet. 'This is so inefficient,' says Bruce. 'We've done 10 yards in half an hour.' They decide to stop two hours early. It is a typical day for this part of the journey. 'The hardest pulling we've done,' says Rory. 'No grip or movement. A couple of times we couldn't pull it at all. In half an hour we've gone from good pulling to an absolute nightmare.' 'We simply have to go faster than this,' Bruce concludes, 'or we'll run out of food … Scott would definitely have felt this. Going through the Beardmore Glacier he had really bad snow conditions and they would have struggled just like this, and on other occasions. Unluckily for us, it's come at the wrong time, when our sledge is the heaviest.'

Their interest in the particulars of Scott's journey, as annotated in his journal, seems to increase the closer they match their own experiences. They are struck by how Bowers's lack of skis was mentioned by Scott on this very day. 'Scott spent at least as much time fretting about this surface as we have,' says Bruce. 'He said on his Day 65 that he didn't know how he could have managed without skis, and he didn't know how Bowers was coping.' In these desperate conditions, as they begin to contemplate real suffering for the first time, they are more and more humbled by the ordeal undergone by their Edwardian predecessors. 'I'm awestruck reading of the conditions what they went through,' says Chris. 'What's so inspiring about reading these diaries is what these men must have been thinking as their food ran out and the temperature dropped. If we have a 5-mile day, it'll be boring. If they have a 5-mile day, they might die. It's lovely to have the historical parallel, but I still don't feel we can really compete with them for bravery, courage and hardship.'

Add to this the problems of navigation. Their dead reckoning has been reliable, but the decision to make depots every three days means that they need to find them again. Chris is now the main navigator, and feels the pressure of getting accurate readings off a 90-year-old theodolite in extreme cold on those rare occasions that the sun makes an appearance. 'At the moment I can't navigate accurately enough with the theodolite to guarantee placing us to within 10 miles on the map,' he says. 'But in a white-out you can barely see a cairn 500 yards away, so it's all got to be very precise. We have to weigh up the time costs of building the cairns versus the navigational costs on the way back of not finding them.'

On Day 68 Rory can barely see a 6-foot cairn from 10 feet away. When a white-out descends it is also much harder to move in a straight line. They discuss the possibility of switching their hours of travel to avoid the worst conditions of the day, but can't agree about which part of the day that is. Finally they decide to switch to night travel only if conditions change significantly.

Although their rate of physical decline is levelling out according to the physiological tests done by Rory, they worry about the effects of dehydration, which started to afflict Scott's men at this stage. Rory reports that after a hard day's sweat he is 'chronically dehydrated'. Mark forces himself to drink water in the morning to the point of bloatedness. Then there are the external injuries. Mark's hips are aching badly from the hauling; one of the harnesses has trapped a nerve and given him a dead leg. More seriously, his bruised heels are causing him more problems, it turns out, at times have been 'excruciatingly painful'; but, like Oates, he kept stoically quiet about it when Bruce was making his selection. Chris's extremities are stiffening in the cold. He also suffers from what he calls 'a very minor foot injury'. Only the thought of others hurting far more than him alleviates the pain. 'Can you imagine Oates walking on feet dead to the ankle?' he wonders. 'I count myself among the luckiest of men really to have only a blister on my heel.'

They become experts in all types of snow. One curious phenomenon they note is the snowquake, which they have read about in Cherry-Garrard. Mark describes it as 'the tendency for large areas of snow pack to drop suddenly as we go over. There must be a layer of soft powder beneath the crust which compresses under our weight. The first couple of times gave me a fright – a tremendous crump sound, from all around in stereo. We and the sledge drop several inches. Cherry-Garrard wrote of dropping several feet. I wonder if he was exaggerating.' 'I think he was,' says Bruce. (These quakes, making a noise like thunder or a passing plane, scare the Norwegian team's dogs.)

With such short marching days, they have a lot of time in the tent to write and read out their own diaries, as well as those of Scott's men who kept diaries. Chris is particularly in awe of his fellow doctor, Wilson, especially his diary of the winter journey to fetch penguin's eggs. 'He says on the second day that all their feet get frostbitten on the soles. Can you imagine anything more horrific? He writes about getting a spit of boiling blubber in his eye and says, "It's causing me some trouble this evening." Cherry-Garrard, who writes more prosaically, just says, "Wilson was in agony and could barely stifle his sobs all night." '

'They are nails,' says Bruce, as in 'hard as nails'. It is their favourite word of approval. 'It's only when you copy them a little that you get an inkling.'

No sooner do they make their first depot than they encounter even more hideous conditions. On Day 72 they wake up to a blizzard and cover less than 1.5 miles before Bruce decides to stop, as there is a genuine danger they may not be able to erect the tent. The next two days they fail to make 5 miles, and the two after that they do less than 3 miles; on the second of them, the sledge has to be dug out from an overnight snow drift. It becomes apparent to the four men that they really have volunteered for something horrifically akin to what their five predecessors suffered. 'This is horribly hard work,' says Mark. 'We've only done 2.8 miles all day. It's almost four o'clock. This is the worst going we've had yet. We're really having to fight for every inch. The sledge stops the whole time, and starting it again is knackering and painful. The wind has even half-blown the load off the sledge, despite all the lashings and straps. It's very disappointing. Retrospectively, we're all going to look back and think we're glad we had such foul luck because Scott did. This is just like his last ten days. He had really bad pulling conditions, his food was running out and his fuel was low. Unlike Scott, of course, we're not going to die, but we've depoted too early as it turns out. At this rate we're going to struggle to make the pole', let alone get back to pick up the food. Each day we think our luck can't keep on this bad, but each day it gets worse.'

By the time they get to within 100 miles of the pole, they are a week behind and time is dragging. 'I can see why Scott focuses all the time on weather, distance and wind,' says Rory. 'That's all we're thinking about now. For Scott it must have been at the foremost of his mind all day long.' It's not quite all they talk about. In the tent one night they also wonder how the Norwegian team is doing with the dogs. They have crossed their tracks again, and think they must be at least ten days old. Mark insists they will still be on the ice cap. Bruce thinks they will be long off it. They admit that they wouldn't like to have the dogs back, but think that Scott would have been desperate for them up on the plateau.

Food looms large in the conversation. Even on their full ration – all qualms about eating pemmican have disappeared – they are now hungry all the time, to the extent that food is even becoming a political issue. There is a daily routine, admits Bruce, in which 'we all watch the thickness of the spreading on biscuits. We watch how many people have out, we watch who hoards and all that. It's nice to air it as there's nothing worse than harbouring resentment. If you have it out and make a little joke, you can resolve an issue that might become big and you stay friends.' Chris, for example, is a hoarder: he saves his daily ration of biscuits for bedtime, preferring to haul on an empty stomach and sleep on a full one. 'It's hard to exaggerate the misery of this really,' he says. 'About an hour after breakfast I start feeling hungry and all you can think about is the hunger. The thought of doing this on half rations is very discouraging.'

But the prospect looms. 'It's march or fail,' says Bruce on Day 76. 'We've got nine days to do 90 miles. It's not looking good, to be honest. We depoted a load of food this morning to try and make a lightweight sprint to the pole. Desperate measures. I hope it works, but this weather has to change or we won't make it.' Then the mileage goes back down to 5.2. 'Not my favourite day at all,' adds the normally buoyant Rory. 'I would rather be anywhere else rather than here right now.'

* * * * * * * * * * * *

The snow conditions that afflict the modern team now also dogged Scott. 'The marching is growing terribly monotonous,' he wrote on the plateau. After they made their last depot on 9 January, and surpassed Shackleton's record, an air of deflation permeated the atmosphere of the tent. 'Time after time,' observed Cherry-Garrard as he collated their accounts of the journey, 'in their diaries you find crystals – crystals: crystals falling through the air, crystals bearding the sastrugi, crystals lying loose upon the snow. Sandy crystals, upon which the sun shines and which made pulling a terrible effort.' Wilson complained of 'the worst wind-cut sastrugi I have seen ... covered with a growth of bunches of crystals exactly like gorse ... Ice blink all round ... hairy faces and mouths dreadfully iced up on the march ... and often one's hands very cold indeed holding ski sticks.'

The surface was so bad that Scott took the extraordinary decision to depot his skis, only to turn back when the sastrugi disappeared and the going became flat and powdery. 'I never had such pulling,' Scott wrote. 'All the time the sledge rasps and creaks ... can we keep this up for seven days? ... None of us has ever had such hard work before.'

The wind started to whip through their clothing. 'At camping tonight everyone was chilled and we guessed a cold snap,' noted Scott on 12 January, 'but to our surprise the actual temperature was higher than last night, when we could dawdle in the sun.' It was the same two days later. 'Again we noticed the cold ... ' Their physical depletion was beginning to take its toll, though they didn't yet know it: Scott insisted that they were still 'all very fit'. The temperatures plummeted, as they do on the plateau in January. 'A low temperature when it is calm,' wrote Cherry-Garrard, 'is paradise compared to a higher temperature with a wind, and it is this constant pitiless wind, combined with the altitude and low temperatures, which has made travelling on the Antarctic plateau so difficult.' They walked into a headwind for their entire trip across the plateau. No wonder Bowers 'could not tell if I had a frostbite on my face now as it is all scales. So are my lips and nose.' 'Oh! For a few fine days!' pleaded Scott. 'So close it seems and only the weather to baulk us.'

It was not just Scott succumbing to one of his debilitating bouts of pessimism. All the men's diaries at this point are a crescendoing chorus of misery. The one who felt it worst was Oates, who got out of the wrong side of his reindeer sleeping bag on 15 January. He had told no one about his festering war wound, and his heels must have been hurting by now, but, as ever, his private thoughts were committed to paper. 'My pemmican must have disagreed with me at breakfast, for coming along I felt very depressed and homesick.' It was the only cross word that any of them had for their food. They may have eaten heartily, but their daily expenditure of energy was not replenished by a diet of pemmican and biscuits. Also there was the mounting problem of dehydration.

But they were bearing down on the pole. At this moment of what they hoped was their imminent triumph, Bowers took two photographs of his companions in the act of hauling the sledge, which suggests the pictures were posed. The only evidence of discomfort is the accumulation of ice on their beards. By the time Bowers took more photographs at the pole, they had shaved. 'It is wonderful to think that two long marches would land us at the pole,' Scott wrote on the night Oates's pemmican disagreed with him. 'It ought to be a certain thing now, and the only appalling possibility the sight of the Norwegian flag forestalling ours.'

* * * * * * * * * * * *

The mileages of the modern British team slowly improve as the thought of starvation drives them on. 'It's now getting to the point where if you drop a raisin, you will rip the tent apart to get it,' says Mark. In conditions that might have kept them tent-bound earlier in the journey, they press on and start to break the 7-mile barrier. The next day they do the same distance by lunchtime, despite problems with Chris's foot. After nine hours they have done nearly 11 miles. Their cairn-building is now more pragmatic: in order to stay on the move, they build smaller snow beacons and spend less time on them. On Day 78 they break the 12-mile barrier. It is the day Scott reached the pole. They have just under a degree of latitude to go. 'In many ways I'm disappointed,' says Bruce. 'I'd always hoped we would be equalling Scott's mileages. Up till recently we were. The last two weeks with that slow weather just put us out of kilter. In real terms we're a degree behind. Every expedition is different. Although Scott had worse temperatures than us, our pulling conditions have been as bad or as worse than his.'

These distances are not won without a price. Mark's heels are in terrible shape after the 12 hours and 12 miles of Day 78. 'Last night I couldn't sleep on my back because of my heels. Any contact with the floor felt like hell. It's going to be a long day.' Oates, who was in the same cavalry regiment, is constantly on his mind now: 'I think of Oates soldiering on with his blackened feet and I feel a bit of a wimp.' The fear grows that if and when they make the pole, the return journey is going to be purgatory. In better snow conditions, but lower temperatures, they start to walk for longer hours. Two more days of 9.1 and then 9.9 miles, and then on Days 81 and 82, with the pole just over the horizon, they put in two record-breaking marches of over 16 miles each.

By now Bruce, like Scott as he bore down on Shackleton's record, has become irrepressibly cheery. He is plainly disinclined to trumpet his achievement, but he has led his men through 80 days and nearly 700 nautical miles. The pole is almost upon them and there have been no arguments to speak of. In the end it is his leadership that has got them this far.

Knowing their polar history, they start scanning the horizon for a Norwegian flag.

Bruce Parry's Diary

DAY 62

Sad farewells to Arthur and Rupert. Great, great guys and a real shame to lose them both. I felt really quite bad saying goodbye to Rupert as, of course, I did have the power to take five people forwards, but it was not to be and he was leaving. I wish I had spent more time in his company.

So with two guys gone, it suddenly felt quite lonely. A complete sense of isolation crept over us all and no longer were there dogs or another sledge to think about, but just the four of us. Weird.

The sail was looking awesome. I've expeditioned with Mark before and always known his skills at handyman stuff, but I'd never fully appreciated his true genius at craftsmanship and manufacture. The square rig was solid and looked like it would really work, and to top it all, and for probably only the second or third day in the whole expedition, we had a following wind. Awesome. So finishing touches and then the packing of what looked like the biggest sledge ever pulled (half a ton and as big as a car). It really was massive, and all of Chris's personal stuff and nav gear, etc. made it almost impossible to load. A good 6 inches of sticky powder snow ominously covered everything from the night before, so when we were finally ready to go, it took a good couple of minutes to get the f**ker unstuck. A slow series of pulls and we could barely move.

DAY 63

What a f**king day. Slow, slow, slow. By far and away our slowest and hardest pulling day to date. Eight hours in the end and only 4 nautical miles. Half a mile an hour. Not good.

DAY 64

Could hear the wind and snow all night against the tent. I thought it was spindrift, so was hoping for a day with the snow blown away, but on exiting the tent realized that it was a whole new half-foot snowfall. Bugger. So here we were facing another shitty day of pulling half a ton through porridge.

Mark did a good job of navigating in white-out nearly all day. No one spoke all day, and we only stopped about three or four times, so time went reasonably quickly. Just hoping that the conditions improve soon else we won't even reach the pole (5 miles today).

Day 65

Disaster struck when the sun went in and the slightly wet powder turned to wallpaper paste. We simply could not pull it at all. Really quite frustrating to say the least, and we soon tried no skis, then no outer ski boots, but still no joy. By the end we'd covered 100 yards in half an hour, so I called for a stop at 4 p.m. which everyone readily agreed to, with the condition for a 4 a.m. start tomorrow. The right decision I'm sure. Tent routine was slick tonight until Mark spilt the whole pan of water. No issue at all in the tent, though, which was nice because of course it could have been any one of us (and may well be me tomorrow). To my mind, this is a great sign of the tent dynamic, as I hate nothing more than getting irate and pissed off over spilt milk as there is nothing that can be done about it except help mop up and make the poor fellow who did it (and feels bad enough) feel a little better.

DAY 66

Got up at 4 a.m., lit stove and promptly fell asleep again. Boring, shitty, normal day. Pole still at least two weeks away. No sign of the snow conditions improving and none of us wants to be here for the full 99 days.

DAY 67

The going was really good today, so after days of pissing around, it was nice to do some miles. Over eight in the end, and I'm happy with that.

DAY 68

Completely surreal white-out conditions. Not much fun.

DAY 69

Great day. It seemed there was a slight air of negativity while we packed the sledge first thing. I therefore decided to break the silence and got Chris chatting and soon we put the whole world to rights. DNA, genes, religion, superstition, diet, health, fitness, people and lots more. Great day and went so fast.

DAY 70

Woke to a white-out again and high northerly winds. The surface seemed better but on starting to haul, we realized that it was as bad as ever. Soon we had ground to a crawl and the wind was increasing dramatically in force. Not cold, but very strong. Come midday, I decided to call a halt and luckily had a five-minute lull in the wind ferocity while we erected the tent. All inside soon after having storm-proofed our luxurious emerald palace. What ensued was one of the most interesting and funny afternoons of the trip to date, with Mark telling many a war story about Bosnia. As Rory would say, 'I love this tent'.

DAY 71

Total white-out all day long and a headwind to boot, which got colder and colder. My goggles were misted and frozen most of the day, and I was only navigating, wasn't I? Not a single word of conversation from anyone all day long. In the end I only stopped three times in the whole day. Three three-hour stints is my preferred day routine, and the others seemed to like it. In fact, for them the day went rather quickly in their respective daydream states.

This weather is beginning to get a bit tiresome. Of course I expect shitty weather, and we've been rather lucky to date if the truth be known, but to have so much fresh, sticky snow under foot at this late stage is really rather unfortunate and will quite probably cause us real food and fuel issues on our return from the pole. I remain ever optimistic, but reading Scott's diary again, it reminds me that their swift progress on returning from the pole was due in no small way to their sail and the visibility of their outward tracks neither of which is very likely for us. Oh well.

DAY 72

We talk now more often of our potential problems and the real possibility that we won't achieve all our aims. Like Scott, we have been cursed by the weather, and although we've had nothing like the extreme temperatures he experienced, it surely is no less taxing to pull a sledge through.

I've decided to make the pole our principal aim, and if we go hungry on our return trip, then so be it. Our spirits are high and we are a tight group in all respects. We all have our specific roles, which I have delegated according to ability and temperament. Rory is king of organization. He is first in the tent and organizes the space and gets our personal items out for our arrival. He sorts the food and starts to cook, while the rest of us are still outside unpacking the sledge and storm-proofing the tent. I also recently asked if he would take control of packing the sledge in the morning too. Each morning there were the four of us all giving advice. It was getting really quite frustrating, and good old Chris could never hold his tongue, always offering suggestions on how to pack the sledge in a new and improved manner until we were running the risk of never going anywhere. Chris is now lead navigator and cairn builder. Then there's my old buddy Mark. He truly is a genius at fixing, maintaining and making things, and he has been instrumental – no absolutely essential – at keeping this trip on the go. Much of our antiquated or period equipment and clothing has simply not lasted the duration, and were it not for Mark and his toolbox, twine, sewing kit, strapping and know-how, we'd be many many miles short of our present location. My only concern with Mark is his sense of humour, which is somehow not fitting in with the present group we have, and

I'm surprised at him for perpetuating it when it clearly isn't helping the dynamic. There have been too many occasions now when he has joked about the rest of the team, or even individuals in a way that can only leave a bad taste or resentment.

He called the rest of us wimps because he never wore insoles and we did. This was, in my view, a case of people in glasshouses throwing stones, and I believe he was on thin ice to be playing with our sensitivities so. First, he had just spent that entire hauling stop fixing his own insoles and not doing any communal tasks; second, he is the only guy permanently on painkillers; and third, he's the only person in the team who has ever asked to stop the sledge (on numerous occasions) because of his cold hands. Not really in a position to call the other team members wimps at all. Anyway, it secured a short negative retort from me about painkillers to shut him up, which it did, but it also left me feeling really bad about doing that and left me thinking of nothing else for the next three hours.

There's 100 miles to go and it's all to play for.

DAY 73
What a day. What a f**king day. Almost 3 miles done all day. Not good at all. Almost definitely the windiest day outside the *piteraq*. We started bravely and gave it a good shot, but it really was ridiculous. Hardly any movement at all and just me shouting ready – go, ready – go (which, as an order, didn't last long), then back to the old 3, 2, 1, go as we just got stuck every few minutes. The tent was half-hanging down the side of the sledge at our first stop, then we had a complete blizzard for a short while (otherwise the day was quite clear for the most part), and the final blow at about 4 p.m. was when we just couldn't get the bloody thing going again. Mark asked if I would try calling the countdown slower, but when that didn't work either, someone noticed that the sledge was on its side. F**king blown over. Well, that was it and I called it a day. Just as well, 'cos it's now 8 p.m. and the wind hasn't stopped at all. The one bonus is an early night and a good kip.

DAY 74
Still bloody windy, so decided to have a lie-in. How wonderful. Totally uncalled for but lovely. No sooner had we started than we realized that despite the surface looking better, it was definitely (and I mean it this time) the hardest pulling of the exped so far. Just like the proverbial bathtub and sandpaper.

We stopped literally every minute and took ages to get going again at a real cost to our shoulders, knees and hips. I started counting up rather than the usual 3, 2, 1, go, and we got into the twenties on a few occasions trying to get the bloody thing going. Not sticky this time, nor feeling particularly heavy – just real nasty friction and not the slightest glide either. In fact, quite the reverse, and it often felt like an elephant was pulling against us in the opposite direction. Well, sort of anyway.

So gave up, absolutely knackered, at 6 p.m. and we all agreed that it was the worst day yet.

DAY 75
Another shit day in hell.

DAY 76
These days all just sound exactly the same, but this one, according to the others, was actually really different and in fact constituted their *actual* worse day yet. Honestly. Just been told by Chris that that didn't include him, but no matter – it was obviously a toughie. The irony is, however, that I actually enjoyed today, so it's never simple round here.

The wind really was quite extraordinary and very beautiful. It picked up all the sandy snow grains into a very visible weaving spindrift, which flowed along the surface of the ice cap while there was still a strong sun and a clear blue sky. We all had sharp shadows, yet it seemed like we were in a huge snowstorm. Looking at anything at a distance on ground level only gave you a hazy hundred yards or so of vision, while looking skyward was totally clear. Looking towards the wind was surreal and quite beautiful. The shifting sands were quite something else (shit description but I'm really tired and want to go to bed).

DAY 77
Pole 72 nautical miles. I woke in the night and it was totally still. No wind at all, but of course by the time it came to wake up, the wind was back up and gusting. To all our amazement and delight, we found ourselves going at what was a half-decent pace. Amusingly, no one said a word for the first ten minutes because we just didn't want to tempt providence. But sure enough, on our first stop after a couple of hours, we had managed an average of over a mile an hour. Magnificent.

Chris admitted that yesterday in the wind he had suffered some cold injury from snow getting into his boot and freezing his heel. Not great but he was uncomplaining and soldiering on. I think the coming weeks will be quite telling on all our bodies and I'm definitely feeling the hunger more during the day as well.

Big talk about whether or not we'll make the pole.

DAY 78

Pole - 60.5 nautical miles. Covered about 12.5 nautical miles. Today was the day that Scott reached the pole.

Bored

    Bored

        Bored

DAY 79

Pole 50 nautical miles. We did 9.5 miles in about nine hours for a quite difficult day's pulling. Never mind.

The big issue is Mark and Chris's feet. Both guys are tough and fit, but now is the stage of the trip when they are both in very real pain, and of course there is no respite at all. In fact, from here on in, the distances and speed must be the largest of the trip so far to necessitate our survival. We have absolutely no contingency at all for any tent-bound days or slow progress, so the pressure is on. Ten miles a day until the pole and 15 miles a day on the return. That means that for every day back we're doing half as much again, and I just know we're going to feel it quite badly. Our depots en route to the pole are at every half a degree (i.e. 30 nautical miles) which we're now doing in roughly three days. The depots themselves, however, only contain two days' food for our return because of our estimated higher speed. When we leave the pole, therefore, we will only have two days' food on the sledge and no extra time to make the next depot. Any losing of the way, slow pace or anything else can only lead to abject hunger.

DAY 80

Pole 40 nautical miles. Mark is very brave and uncomplaining, but there is no doubt that his feet are getting worse. Today he was on painkillers as usual, but as the day drew to a close it was very evident that he was in a great deal of pain and, for the first time, he had a small outburst.

DAY 81.

Pole 23 nautical miles. Great, great, great. Finally we've had a fantastic day for pulling. Just a dream at last and we were all happy all day. There was no question that we were going to do 12 hours, and later we agreed to do more as well. Poor Mark needed a full dose of analgesia, which helped, but the rest of us were in fine fettle and for the first half of the day we just raced along. It was almost like the early days when we could hardly feel the sledge behind us at all.

17 miles done. Not bad. Now trying to shift to a night routine.

DAY 82

Pole 6 nautical miles. Been going since midday and finished at 1.30 this morning. So we've done our usual night routine and then prepared for bed. Unfortunately, I've got the runs, so had to go out into a very cold night to have a dump. Really not pleasant, but an unfortunate necessity. After that I prepared for an early night while the others were still busy. It has been a good day's journey today (or tonight really, as most of our journey was evening and night, despite of course the sun being up the whole time). The pulling conditions were absolutely fantastic and we were all on a real high. We are managing 2 miles an hour first thing, then down to about 1.5 mph for the rest of the day. It reminded us of how it used to be during the early days, and it is very different work from that of the past few weeks. The sky was fantastic this evening. Bright streaks of white and grey in the distance that, had you painted them, nobody would have taken seriously. In fact, it looked much more like paintbrush strokes than clouds at all.

Chris and I have had some tricky moments today, and in fact the last couple of days. Difficult for me because I really admire him, but I have been very annoyed and frustrated with him of late, and of course I'm sure he has been with me too. We've both been quite short with each other recently and it's got to be sorted out. My issue comes with his endless arguing about all decisions. I'm sure he would make a fantastic leader, and he's certainly extremely bright and intelligent, but sometimes when you're not leading you just need to shut up. Good ideas are always welcome, but incessant input at every juncture just slows things down and puts my back up. Quality rather than quantity is what I need, and I've hinted at this to him for some weeks, but he still has something to say about every single idea or decision I've made of late. An example was the packing of the sledge. Chris would often add advice over where items should go, all decent suggestions, but often not much different from the way it was already being done. I'd give the suggestion due consideration and then discuss the relative merits when I didn't really want to. In the end it got to me so much that I just delegated Rory as sledge packer. It worked perfectly, and now we all just work as a fantastic team again with no discussion or disagreement. I know full well that in this issue I am as much to blame as Chris is, but it is also understandable that we all get somewhat irritable with each other under what are really quite extreme circumstances. The reason I've been irritated of late is because of our approach to the pole and the fact that Chris is again in a position to argue and discuss issues and points that are presently quite clear in my head. In many ways it is a fault of my style of open leadership that I get so frustrated over this. Other leaders just wouldn't take shit and would dictate their decisions. I think Chris would be fine with this too, but I have made it clear that I'm happy to discuss things, so I should accept any comments happily, but reciprocally, I think that he should be a bit more like the others, giving the odd piece of advice or comment when really necessary rather than as a matter of course. Anyway – I'm sure it will pass, and the really important thing is that I don't snap or upset the proceedings. I must bite my lip and stay cool and remind myself of how much I really like him and don't want to upset that. In fact, just writing this is quite cathartic. Airing it puts it back into perspective.

CHAPTER TWELVE

Pole

YES, IF ONLY YOU KNEW MOTHER, AND YOU SAAMUND AND T. AND
SVEIN AND HELGA AND HANS, THAT NOW I'M SITTING HERE AT THE
SOUTH POLE AND WRITING, YOU'D CELEBRATE FOR ME.
Olav Bjaaland

When, in 2002, Pen Hadow, the British Arctic explorer, became the first person to man-haul without outside assistance to the North Pole from the North American continent, at the climactic moment he held in his gloved hand a small piece of equipment that could tell him precisely when he stood at the pole itself. In *Solo – The North Pole: Alone and Unsupported* (2004) he recounts how, for the briefest moment, the device tracked his drift on an ice pan to 90 degrees 00 minutes north, and he stood simultaneously in all 24 time zones.

Scott and Amundsen didn't have global positioning systems in 1911, and in the reconstruction of their journeys they are also unavailable. So Rune Gjeldnes and Bruce Parry have to find their pole by the traditional means used by their predecessors.

As Amundsen, Bjaaland, Hanssen, Hassel and Wisting bore down on the South Pole, one overriding fear obsessed them: the prospect of being forestalled. On 13 December Hassel spotted what he thought was a black flag. It turned out to be a patch of droppings. A dog must have run loose the night before and planted an optical illusion in their path. They woke on the morning of 14 December knowing that this was the day. They ate their breakfast and struck camp more quickly than usual, almost as if shaving a few seconds here or there would make a difference to the result of the race. By noon their dead reckoning told them they were 7 nautical miles from 90 degrees south, but the arrival of cloud cover prevented them from taking a midday reading off the sun. Hanssen, as usual, led, with instructions from his leader to keep a sharp eye not only on his steering compass but also on the horizon. According to Amundsen, Hanssen's neck 'grew twice as long as before in his endeavour to see a few inches farther ... But however keenly he stared, he could not descry anything but the endless flat plain ahead of us.'

They needn't have worried. On 15 December Scott's party of 12 men were still grappling with the Beardmore Glacier nearly 360 miles, or six degrees of latitude, behind. Scott would not stand at this ultimate latitude for another month.

Amundsen makes no mention of it in his book, but Hanssen's final contribution on the journey south was to ask the expedition leader to lead. When Amundsen wondered why the routine that had worked so well through nearly 700 miles needed changing, Hanssen rustled up an excuse about not being able to get the dogs to pull without a front-runner in these conditions. Thus it was that at three in the afternoon, when the dog-drivers, working from dead reckoning supplied by the ticking sledge-meters, called a collective 'Halt!', it was Roald Amundsen who became the first man to set foot on – or at the very least near – the South Pole.

And now they knew it. There were no flags – no black flags, no Union Jacks. Here at the bottom of the world there was literally nothing but snow and ice and wind and sky. There were ten handshakes as each man formally congratulated his colleagues. Out came the Norwegian flag, attached to a ski pole, and at Amundsen's insistence they planted it together in the yielding snow, the five of them each with a frost-nipped fist gripping the bamboo stick.

'This was the only way in which I could show my gratitude to my comrades in this desolate spot. I could see that they understood and accepted in the spirit in which it was offered.' They named the bare expanse of white after their monarch: King Haakon VII's Plateau. It was 'the greatest and most solemn act of the whole journey ... that moment will certainly be remembered by all of us who stood there.'

It was remembered differently by each of them. That night in the tent, his belly groaning with a celebratory helping of seal steak, Bjaaland stolidly inscribed in his diary, 'the great thing is we are here as the first men, no English flag waves, but a three-coloured Norwegian'. The terrain, he added, 'is as flat as the lake at Morgedal and the skiing is good'. From Hanssen, with his own priorities to consider, there was a practical sigh of relief that he would no longer 'have to stare down at the compass in the biting wind that constantly blew against us while we drove southwards, but which we now would have behind us'. Hassel and Wisting did not keep diaries, so their specific reactions went unrecorded. But Amundsen? Amundsen was puzzled at the chain of events that had drawn him here. 'I cannot say – though I know it would sound much more effective – that the object of my life was attained. That would be romancing rather too barefacedly. I had better be honest and admit straight out that I have never known any man to be placed in such a diametrically opposite position to the goal of his desires as I was at that moment. The regions around the North Pole – well, yes, the North Pole itself – had attracted me from childhood, and here I was at the South Pole. Can anything more topsy-turvy be imagined?'

Amundsen was not, of course, one for romancing. Both he and Bjaaland took pictures, but they kept the official business to a minimum. It was too cold for standing around, and they had work to do. They killed Hanssen's favourite dog, by now completely worn out, and fed him to the other 16, pitched the tent, cooked, ate and talked. An hour before midnight they were up again in time to make an observation of the sun at its lowest point in the sky. From their readings they calculated they were at 89 degrees 56 minutes south. They were 4 miles from the pole. To snuff out the faintest possibility of the sort of wrangling that met Cook and Peary when they returned from the North Pole, Amundsen grasped the importance of finding it as accurately as possible.

It was now early in the morning on 15 December and Amundsen's strategy was to box the coordinate by sending three skiers out in separate directions. Two would go right and left at 90 degrees to their southerly course, and one would plough on straight ahead. After 10 nautical miles they were to stop, plant a dark brown flag erected on spare runners from Bjaaland's sledge, which they no longer needed, and turn round. Despite their lack of a full night's sleep, Bjaaland suggested that he, Wisting and Hassel set off at once. 'We have lots of time to sleep when we get back,' he told Amundsen. Armed with 30 biscuits each, they skied away at 2.30 a.m. 'amid laughter and chaff' despite the precariousness of their mission. It wasn't so much the journey out but trying to find their way back to a tent that Amundsen compared to 'a needle in a haystack'. They could not carry the heavy sledge-compasses, so they had to steer by the sun or, if that went in, by their tracks. 'But to trust to tracks in these regions is a dangerous thing. Before you know where you are, the whole plain may be one mass of driving snow, obliterating all tracks as soon as they are made.'

It is utterly typical of Amundsen's fortunes on the polar journey that the weather held. The three men glided off to a point just over the horizon and returned almost simultaneously in less than eight hours to the news that the pole certainly stood inside the square their quartet of flags described. They brought back equally cheering news that there were still no other flags to be found fluttering in this desolate vicinity.

At the South Pole (and the North) there is no such thing as longitude, so their primary task was to establish their latitude to within a mile. The problem is that the height of the sun in the sky varies little throughout the day, so Amundsen proposed to take readings every hour from 6 a.m. to 7 p.m. After four hours he and Hanssen had worked out that they were 5.5 nautical miles from the pole. All they had to do now was find the pole directly down the meridian to the south. The next morning, 16 December, they packed up the camp, organized the remaining dogs into two teams and stood Bjaaland's sledge upright in the snow. From this they would take a bearing when they came to a halt at what they thought was their destination. With the champion skier now charged with steering due south from the front, and Amundsen checking his direction from the rear, the party of five Norwegian explorers prepared to complete the final furlongs of this greatest of races. They were heading for a place they now named even before they had reached it: Polheim.

Happily released from his sledge ('thank God I am quit the fuss and bother of my dogs'), Bjaaland went first and ploughed a straight course. After the required distance, they immediately erected the tent and divided into two groups of two. For the next 24 hours Amundsen and Hanssen took turns with Wisting and Hassel to sleep and make hourly observations. In his understated way, the leader marvelled at the sight of the sun making its stately progress round the dial of the horizon with no perceptible variation in altitude. 'Very strange,' he noted.

By midday on 17 December the vigil was over, and the four navigators signed their collective findings. They now judged that they were still 1.5 miles away from the pole, so Bjaaland and Hanssen boxed it again, skiing off in three directions to plant yet more flags. That night in the tent Bjaaland made a formal speech and, with the words, 'Keep this to remind you of the Pole', produced a box of cigars for his leader. Amundsen was amazed and moved. 'Speeches had not hitherto been a feature of this journey.' He handed round the cigars, though Bjaaland was not a smoker.

The next morning their three-day sojourn at 90 degrees south came to a ceremonial end. They put up a small spare tent, the original purpose of which was to provide shelter for a returning party if they had travelled, as originally planned, as a group of eight. An extra pole was attached to the tent pole with two pennants: the Norwegian flag and a white pennant with the word 'Fram' inscribed on it. It stood 13 feet above the flat, featureless plain. The tent was the creation of the *Fram*'s sail-maker, who had stitched two notes written on strips of leather inside the tent. One said, 'Good luck';

the other, 'Welcome to 90 degrees'. They found them when they each went inside to sign their names on a tablet. It must have cheered them immensely to chance upon even the faintest whiff of old friends here. Inside they left some unwanted equipment – a hypsometer case, a sextant, 'some reindeer-skin foot bags, kamiks and mitts'. Amundsen had also composed two short letters. One was for King Haakon.

'Your Majesty. We have determined the Southernmost extremity of the great "Ross Ice Barrier", together with the junctions of Victoria Land and King Edward VII Land at the same place. We have discovered a mighty mountain range with peaks up to 22,000 ft a.s.l [above sea level], which I have taken the liberty of calling – with permission, I hope – "Queen Maud's Range". We found that the great inland plateau ... began to slope gently downwards from 89° ... We have called this gently sloping plain on which we have succeeded in establishing the position of the Geographic South Pole – with I hope Your Majesty's permission – "King Haakon VII's Plateau."

The other letter was for Captain Scott 'who, I assumed, would be the first one to find the tent'.

* * * * * * * * * * * *

The two modern expeditions are not looking for the South Pole. They are looking for their own designated pole, which is in fact a point on the Greenland ice cap selected specifically because it is 690 nautical miles from the starting point. This was the distance Amundsen and his men travelled from Framheim to Polheim. Its actual coordinates are 75 degrees 25 minutes north, 29 degrees 29 minutes west. It may not be 90 degrees south, but it has a great deal in common with it. It stands at roughly the same altitude, and there is absolutely nothing there. Or is there? As the Norwegian team's caravan approaches, Inge Solheim, who as usual is trail-breaking on skis in front, spots an unnatural feature from a distance. When they get close it resembles a small cairn. 'Maybe it's the British team that have come here,' he wonders.

It isn't. It is Day 44 of their expedition. The British team is

314 miles behind them, and still getting used to man-hauling after losing their dogs five days earlier.

The Norwegian team haven't beaten just their modern rivals. The conditions have been different – the terrain, the weather, the snow, the temperatures – but in broadly similar circumstances they have shaved nearly two weeks off Amundsen's journey. And for all the advantages they took into the contest, they have also had to work with some disadvantages: unfamiliarity with the equipment, a very short period to prepare and get to know one another, and intolerance of the food.

This final morning begins cold. Inge has what he calls 'sub-optimal conditions'. His skis sink through the top layer of snow by up to 8 inches. 'But today proves it is all in the head. Even if the conditions are harder, I don't get as tired as usual, so either I've suddenly become fit or I've proven that motivation is everything.' They are not sure how far they are from the pole, but they think it is up to 15 nautical miles, the same distance as Amundsen had to cover on the final day. With a two-hour stop for Harald Kippenes to make observations, they think they will be at their pole by mid-afternoon. Harald's dogs have other ideas. They are giving him trouble and he falls behind. Frustration with the huskies is not a good way to prepare for two hours of crucial arithmetic.

Although he is nearly a thousand miles from an actual pole, Harald has something of the same problem Amundsen encountered: the flatness of the sun's curve through the sky makes it difficult to know which reading to take on the sextant for the meridian passage – the precise second when the sun reaches its highest point. Meanwhile, Rune becomes thoughtful. 'I have been thinking quite a lot about Amundsen and his team travelling to the South Pole,' he says. 'The big difference is that he actually went to the South Pole, while we are just walking to a fixed position, so in some ways maybe they had a much stronger motivation – they knew they wanted to be the first ones ever to be there. I'm sure we are the first people at this position as well. The motivation to reach this position has been very good on the team.'

After his two hours of maths Harald announces that the pole

is 6.6 miles due north. 'I'm quite confident that's right because out of the eight observations I did before and the eight I did after the meridian, six appear to give more or less the same results divided by a few seconds, and the meridian observation was very good, so that gives us a good, accurate position ... we'll probably be there in two hours.' He is not alone in sparing a thought for the British team. 'I find it hard to believe that they have managed to come ahead of us. It would be very disappointing. I have a feeling we are way ahead of them because we have been travelling very efficiently, doing big distances and they have fewer dogs. With man-hauling the sledges, they must have had a much harder time than we have.'

Shortly before 5 p.m. Harald checks his sledge-meter for the final time and hollers to the others in front, to be answered by a chorus of whooping. Rune congratulates his navigator. They have reached their pole. As in 1911, there is no sign of any Englishmen. 'What a surprise,' says Ketil Reitan mordantly. Paying all due homage to an identical scene that took place 96 years earlier, the Norwegian flag is retrieved from one of the sledges and planted by five fists in the snow. 'We hereby name this place Polheim,' intones Rune. And then they hug.

The ceremonies are not allowed to get too solemn.

'Shall we hold hands and sing the national song now?' says Harald. Then adds, 'I'm kidding, I'm kidding.'

'Are you getting all emotional on us?' asks Inge.

Rune proposes that they set up their tent.

'Later we can start crying,' says Harald.

'We made it,' says Ketil, who already has itchy feet. 'I can't believe it. It is almost unreal. We have been travelling so many days and now we are here. A good rest day tomorrow and then we'll turn around. A long way back. I can't wait to see all the snow cairns we have built and it's going to be great. The dogs are perfect, fit, getting better every day. It's great to be here.'

In the tent their celebrations deviate somewhat from precedent. The aroma of cigar, smoked by Harald, fills the tent, much as Amundsen's did at the South Pole. They also eat seal meat. But Rune breaks with the alcohol-free tradition by producing a hip flask, and they all don party hats and blow up balloons, which they release to fly around the tent.

Inge spares a thought for their defeated rivals. 'I really admire their courage,' he says, 'because I think they're having a harder time physically than we have. I think they're also having harder challenges mentally. So I really wish them good luck on the rest of their journey.'

The Norwegians' job now is to find the pole as accurately as possible. Harald devotes the next morning to taking more readings and refining his navigation, while Rune writes a letter for Bruce and his team. In the afternoon the five of them head off on skis in a westerly direction for 2 miles to where Harald thinks the pole is. Just as Amundsen did, three men ski off in three different directions – east, north and south – to box the pole, although they don't go anything like as far as Amundsen's men. After a mile or so, Ketil, Inge and John Huston each plant a flag and ski back. Meanwhile, Rune and Harald build an 8-foot snow cairn. When they have finished, Harald climbs on his leader's back and places a Norwegian flag on top of the cairn. Rune also puts a chocolate tin in a pigeon-hole in the cairn's wall. 'This is a gift to the British team when they come in this area,' he explains. 'There's a letter from us, the Norwegian team, and we offer them 100 grams of chocolate, and Harald has offered them some candy. It's not much,' he adds, 'because we don't have much.' They all shake hands and cheer, then they ski back to their tent and make ready for the return journey.

Harald's calculations turn out to be incredibly accurate. The cairn stands on a spot only a quarter of a mile from the stipulated coordinate. He is the hero of the hour, minute and second.

* * * * * * * * * * * *

The modern British team, who are almost forty days behind the Norwegians, wonder what Rune will have left them at the pole. Bruce believes they will observe historical accuracy: he is expecting to find two letters in a tent, one for him, the other for the Norwegian monarch. Unlike Scott, they are convinced the rival team will get there first. 'We all think they'll be at the pole before us,' says Bruce. 'We won't be disappointed to see a Norwegian tent at the pole. It won't bother me.' They are even able to admit that they never expected to reach the pole first. 'No one thinks there's still a chance we might win,' says Mark Anstice. 'From the moment we slept in on the start line ... '

By the time they move into the vicinity of the pole, they have their lightest sledge yet. Almost everything has been depoted. 'If we can't pull this,' warns Rory O'Connor, 'we can't pull anything.' In 12 hours they do nearly 17 miles. According to their dead reckoning, the pole is just 5.5 miles away. There are no signs of any cairns. Chris van Tulleken, who is as cold as he has ever been on the journey, gets out the theodolite. 'Imagine poor little Bowers doing this every day,' he says. 'Bowers did have it easier than me in one respect. They were going to the pole, so he never had to worry about longtitude; they just had to keep going south. Once there was no more south to go, they were there. The number of ways in which I can go wrong is enormous.' Bruce is worried that, thanks to a defective compass, they have veered to the west. The calculations, he hopes, will tell them how far. They don't have food to look for the pole for more than a day before they have to turn for home or go hungry. 'I have absolute faith in Chris,' he says. 'This is the climax in many ways. He's going to tell us how close. I haven't had any idea how close in a hundred-odd miles. It's really quite tense.'

In the tent Chris calculates, while Mark is as usual repairing items of kit: he may have been in the same regiment as Oates, but his role is more akin to that of Taff Evans. 'According to Scott's diary it was Evans who did most of the repairs,' he says. 'Once the horses had gone, Oates was just a plodder. Pull the sledge – that's it. I'm getting very bored of having cold hands the whole time. Even bending a split pin becomes a major task.' (At least his hands were only cold. Evans's hand, injured modifying the sledges at the top of the Beardmore, was showing no sign of healing.) Rory O'Connor chooses this evening to start discoursing on Epicurean philosophy. 'Epicurus emphasized that the pleasureable results of action must be weighed against any possible side-effects,' he explains to the rest of the tent. 'He also believed that the pleasure of the short term must be weighed against the more lasting pleasure of the long term. He emphasised that pleasure does not always mean sensual pleasure: desire must be curbed and serenity will help us to endure pain.' In his tolerance for the conditions, Rory is certainly the most epicurean of the British team. Bruce and Mark are now fixating on the endlessly deferred pleasure of escape from the ice. 'As soon as we get to the pole, we can turn around and get the hell out of here,' says Mark. 'With the last couple of weeks being such hard work, it's become more of a personal goal than I ever thought it would.' Bruce wants to get to the pole because 'I want to get home. There's no other reason at all really. That is it.'

As tomorrow's climactic moment beckons, Bruce mentions something that has only just occurred to him: 'When I was looking at the photograph of them at the pole which we have to emulate, they'd shaved. I hadn't ever noticed that before.' There is no mention of it in the diaries, but perhaps Scott ordered his men to spruce themselves up for posterity. (Amundsen's men clipped their beards every Saturday night in the tent – 'not so much from motives of vanity as from considerations of utility and comfort'.) 'That photo is quite awful,' says Rory. 'You can see the despair, the suffering.' 'Oates's hunched posture is the most telling,' adds Chris. 'He can't stand up for the photo. They look physically and mentally wrecked. We have some sense of what they went through, but I am still completely in awe of them. For them it mattered much more to get there first. For us the achievement will be the journey. It doesn't matter if the Norwegians are there first. Our suffering so far has been nothing compared to Scott's team, which is interesting. We're in much better health than them. I don't know why that is.'

They have three days' food to get to the pole and back, but Bruce admits they are becoming 'tenser and tenser about everything. It's all in good humour but underlying it we have to share all the calories. "Yours is a thicker spread than mine" – it's getting like that.' For all the worries about going hungry, they wake up the next morning in a euphoric frame of mind. It could be Christmas. Rory is 'much more excited than I thought'. Bruce 'can't wait to see what's there – if the Norwegians have got a tent up or anything at all. It's really a culmination of a lot of days and a lot of pain and fun in many ways. A great feeling to be here.'

After much deliberation, they decide that the pole is 4.5 miles away. Every one of those miles is unforgiving: the snow is difficult and the sun is in their eyes, as is a fierce wind. The sledge-meter ticks away until the miles have slipped by under their skis. After 690 nautical miles, they have reached their destination. 'The pole, gentlemen,' says Rory. The air is thick with a sense of mild anticlimax. 'Great God! This is a shit-hole,' intones Bruce, misquoting his predecessor. 'I suppose we should shake hands or hug or something.'

'No, we're British,' says Mark. 'We don't hug.' Like all of them, he can see no evidence of human visitors. 'It seems the Norwegians are behind us, or they've got it right or wrong.' But at the final hurdle, the navigation has failed the Brits. The Norwegians have gone to a different point on this vast plane of snow, and Bruce's team doesn't have time to look for evidence of their visit. Chris is circumspect. 'I would be surprised if we're more than 20 miles away, I'd be disappointed to be much more than ten, and I'd be astonished if we were closer than five.'

'I don't care how far we are from the real pole or where the Norwegians are,' says Bruce. 'I just want to say I think we've done fantastically. This is our pole. It doesn't look like much round here, but I am delighted to be in this spot with you guys. I hereby name this the South Pole.' All four of them plant a black flag. In the event they do hug. Bruce produces a bottle of rum and proposes two toasts: to the four men who started the expedition with them, and to the five men of the *Terra Nova* who reached the South Pole on 17 January 1912.

The cold puts a dampener on any feelings of joy they may harbour inside, and stills the impulse to celebrate demonstratively. 'I was going to have a snowball fight,' says Bruce, 'but I didn't want to because it was f**king cold.'

They don't know it, but until the last day their navigation by dead reckoning has been perfect. Only on this day of days are they are suddenly a few miles out. So here, at what they think is the pole, they see no tracks, no flags, no evidence of dogs in the snow, no tent. They don't see the Norwegian cairn erected there 39 days earlier. And Bruce never reads the note left for him in the chocolate tin. Rune built his final cairn in vain.

****

In all Amundsen and his men raised ten flags at the pole: one bearing the word 'Fram', two of them the Norwegian national emblem, and the rest fashioned out of brown or black scrags of material. It was the last of them that Bowers saw when he looked up from his weary trudge. Amundsen had planted it on or near the meridian that runs down through the Beardmore. Scott was beaten.

The tracks, they noted, were old: at least a fortnight, perhaps more than three weeks. Wilson could discern only two ski tracks, but evidence of 'many dogs', wrote Scott. 'This told us the whole story.' They stopped to discuss things. The Norwegians, they concluded from the diagonal intersection of the tracks, had obviously found another way up on to the plateau – 'an easy way up', remarked Scott ungenerously. They ploughed on to where they thought the pole was, and the next morning joined Amundsen's tracks for three hours until they petered out under the fresh coating of snow. The diaries don't reveal their thoughts in this remotest of places, as they found themselves following a track laid by other men, so they can only be imagined. They also saw that many dogs had been this way and concluded – perhaps a little loftily from the evidence of the dog droppings – that Amundsen had not been feeding his many draught animals well.

It was an exhausting day. Oates, Evans and Bowers were badly frostbitten that afternoon of 17 January. It was, said Wilson, 'the coldest march I ever remember. It was difficult to keep one's hands from freezing in double woollen and fur mitts.' The wind blew ice crystals in their faces. They did their observations at lunch, then four more times up until 2 a.m. In the tent that night, as they pulled themselves into frozen sleeping bags, they had a double helping of pemmican hoosh and a few last bits of chocolate. The snow, Bowers noted in his meteorological record, was so powdery it 'makes very little water for its bulk when melted'. Wilson produced cigarettes kept in reserve for the pole. Apart from Bowers, they all smoked them gratefully. 'We are not a very happy party tonight,' remarked Oates. 'Scott is taking his defeat much better than I expected.'

Not in the privacy of his diary, he wasn't. 'The worst has happened, or nearly the worst ... The Norwegians have forestalled us and are first at the pole. It is a terrible disappointment, and I am very sorry for my loyal companions.' And then, 'The pole. Yes, but under very different circumstances from those expected ... companions labouring on with cold feet and hands ... there is that curious damp, cold feeling in the air which chills one to the bone in no time.... Great God! This is an awful place, and terrible enough for us to have laboured to it without the reward of priority. Well, it is something to have got here.'

That epic ejaculation of despair looms large in the pantheon of Scott's famous phrases. But his men all responded to the triumph of Amundsen in their own way. Oates, who had told the Norwegian Gran back at Cape Evans that 'he hated all foreigners from the bottom of his heart', chose this moment to forget his principles: 'I must say that man must have his head screwed on right ... The Norskies ... seem to have had a comfortable trip with their dog teams, very different to our wretched man-hauling.' Putting a brave face on it in his diary, Wilson perhaps felt he spoke for them all. They were 'all agreed that he can claim prior right to the Pole itself. He has beaten us in so far as he made a race of it. We have done what we came for all the same and as our programme was made out.' Trust plucky Bowers to look on the bright side in the face of such monumental cause for depression. He was merely sad to have finished second, 'but I am glad that we have done it by good British man-haulage. That is the traditional British sledging method and this is the greatest journey done by man since we left our transport at the foot of the Glacier.' Not keeping a diary, unlike his fellow petty officer Lashly, Evans's thoughts went unrecorded. Possibly that Swansea pub of his dimmed a little on the horizon of his imagination.

They were in the area of the pole for much less time than Amundsen. It being past mid-January, they could hardly afford to stay, and there was no need. They were out of their tent at 5 a.m.

and marching 3.75 miles to where they judged the pole to be. On the way it was Bowers once more who looked up and spotted Polheim 2 miles away. They made for Amundsen's tent and found inside the list of men who had been here, with a date but 'no news as to what they had done', wrote Wilson. In fact, there was news, but it was in Norwegian: the letter to the king, which Scott discovered that he was to deliver when he read his own letter:

Dear Captain Scott,
As you probably are the first to reach this area after us,
I will ask you kindly to forward this letter to King Haakon
VII. If you can use any of the articles left in the tent please
do not hesitate to do so. With kind regards I wish you a
safe return.
Yours truly,
Roald Amundsen

Scott noted the request with an exclamation mark, and no wonder. Polheim was the remotest letter-box on the planet.

Wilson made an inventory of the discarded items in his diary, and fell upon the broken hypsometer. 'I took away the spirit lamp of it, which I have wanted for sterilizing and making disinfectant lotions of snow.' Scott concluded from the deposit of socks, trousers and sleeping bags that Amundsen had planned for worse weather than he had encountered. Bowers accepted the offer of reindeer mitts. He also took the semi-posed photograph of the four others standing rather aimlessly around the neat little pyramid of the Polheim tent. The tent was held firm by a spider's web of guy ropes secured, Wilson noted, by 'tent-pegs of yellow wood'. These were the ones carefully fashioned by Johansen at Framheim over the winter. In Amundsen's approving description, they 'were the opposite of what such pegs usually are; in other words, they were flat instead of being high ... besides being so much lighter, they were many times stronger ... Most of them were brought home undamaged.' Johansen may have been banned from the polar journey, but his pegs were part of the victory. Remarkably, Wilson did some sketching here, perhaps because there was actually something to record apart from sky and snow.

Scott left his own note in the tent 'to say I had visited the tent with companions', knowing that no one would ever read it. They headed off for their own pole. Here they put up their own tent and lunched, built a cairn, hoisted 'our poor slighted Union Jack'. Bringing out four of their own flags, they took more photographs. Bowers is behind the camera for two of them; in the others he activates it by an all but indiscernable string. The five of them posed, in three different formations. In one photograph they stood in a row in front of the tent. Scott and Wilson both gripped flag poles in their left hands. They also did two shots of three standing and two sitting in front. In the first of these Bowers sits; in the second he stands. In one picture Wilson had his hands on his hips, as if impatient to get on with it. Oates and Evans both look horribly burnt, and the tip of Evans's frostbitten nose is white. The shadows are cast behind them: the five of them are looking more or less directly into the sun. This cannot be the only reason Scott's gaze is downcast. 'Mighty cold work all of it,' he wrote. In another, he is looking off to his left, perhaps in the direction of Polheim.

They took another reading off the sun and then went a further half-mile to the southeast to plant a second Union Jack. Nearby they spotted yet another of Amundsen's flags. Wilson was sent to retrieve it, along with the sledge-runner to which it was attached: it would make a useful part of a sail with the wind behind them. Wilson found a note signed by Amundsen, this time in English, with the polar coordinates and a date. 'There is no doubt that our predecessors have made thoroughly sure of their mark and fully carried out their program.'

And with that, they pointed their skis north. How unwittingly did Scott's diary toll the bell? 'We have turned our back now on the goal of our ambitions with sore feelings and must face our 800 miles of solid dragging – and good-bye to most of the day dreams!'

Rune Gjeldnes's Diary

DAY 43

New day and it's very windy outside, but the sun's out, which will keep us going. Have missed two meridian readings the last couple of days, but we know that it's 10–15 nautical miles left to our destination. We'll keep going until 10.45 and then put up the tent and do the necessary readings to get it as exact as possible, and keep a very steady course for the last few miles. It's going to be a good day. Important that we keep a steady course on the last leg and keep check of the distances. Then we'll mount the flag together. It's going to be an exciting day, this, even if we're not on a real pole. Would have been much more excited if we were. Have planned to let Inge make the mark furthest north as he's been going at the head of the team. Let's see what the day brings. The wind might make it somewhat bitter, but we'll manage.

We reached the pole after a few hours. Arrival 16.50. Had a three-hour 15-minute break to find our position. Harald discovered we were too far east, so we changed the course and then we were there. Not too solemn, but we planted the flag and named the place the Heath of King Harald. Solemn enough. No tears, but I think everyone is happy to get here. I am. A bit of rest, and so we go southwards. That'll be great. Harald will have a busy day finding the exact positions tomorrow, and the rest of us will be marking the compass points by going out to the sides, checking the sledges, food etc. And we'll have a nice time.

Have to work out the distance from here to 82 depot, so we have a better overview of the way back. Should write a letter to the British team as well. Leave it in a milk bottle on a beacon. Hopefully, they'll get here too one day.

And now we're celebrating in the tent. Whisky and good atmosphere. It's good on the pole, knowing that the next time we're on our skis we'll be heading southwards and home. We have to go out and mark the pole first.

DAY 44

08.00 and the others are still asleep. We're basically where we should be, and people deserve a lie-in. Everyone has done a tremendous job. We ought to be a bit proud. Good to be here. Let the experience sink in. A lot has happened between the first few days and now. Progress is the right word. Big things are not done on impulse, but through many small actions taken together. That's what we've done. Time has been short, but we've used it to the full. You have to hand it to Amundsen on his South Pole expedition. He made the most out of the time he had and did the job before he started. The rest is history.

A success story. We still have half the way to go, and a lot can happen. Halfway and we can rejoice a bit.

We've been out marking our South Pole. Harald and John were outside for three hours taking observations. Good work. They built wind-protectors and stayed out there. Harald sat for two hours doing calculations afterwards. We went out around 3 p.m. Harald had estimated that the pole was 1500 yards from our camp. We went there and built a huge beacon. Ketil, Inge and John went out and marked north, east and south with flags. The west is marked already. We marked our pole point. Left a box with a letter for the British team, a chocolate bar and four sweets. Now we're back in the tent and enjoying ourselves. Harald has done a great job.

Bruce Parry's Diary

DAY 82

Same day although we've been to bed and it feels like the next day. And what a change. Firstly, Chris is being an absolute star and we're back to being best buddies again. The real thing is that we are in the middle of our ongoing theodolite recordings and the pole is looking tantalizingly close. Last night's 17–18 miles put us at a position about 6 nautical miles from the pole as far as my dead reckoning was concerned. Of course, I know that, with over a hundred miles covered since our last theodolite reading, we are going to have deviated somewhat from our planned course. Hopefully, this won't be in terms of distance, but more in bearing, but either way we need to ascertain our true position accurately in order to determine the actual pole position.
It was tempting yesterday to track the extra distance to our actual dead reckoning pole, but we decided to stop early, partly because of Mark's feet, and partly because if we stopped early and ascertained our position in advance, we could cut any corners in our advance to the real pole if we are wildly off course. So now we are in the middle of doing our sun sights and making the proverbial cocked hat triangles on the map to ascertain our true position. Very exhilarating and somewhat nerve-racking as we guess whether or not we are within striking distance of the pole.

We have counted our food supplies and decided that we can stay here making more and more sun sights until perhaps midday tomorrow, when we can dash to the pole. From midday tomorrow Rory and I have calculated that we have three whole days' food to make the dash there and back to this location. The question, of course, is whether it is close enough to ski there at speed, or whether we should take all our gear (tent and sledge), which is much slower. Mark has ascertained that he can make a manual sledge-meter (milometer) to be dragged if we go solo on ski. The good news is that it seems we are not too far from the pole in latitude at least. We reckon so far that it is about 6 nautical miles: it's just a question of on which bearing. It is worth staying where we are for as long as possible to gain as much accuracy as we can for our dash because we will not have time to do any more readings when we get there. So far we have seen no signs of the Norwegians, but I expect to do so when we make our final approach. They may not have had longer at the pole than us to more accurately pinpoint the actual position, so if we see their tent or poles, we will obviously go to that as well, but as far as planting a flag is concerned, we will do so at our own estimated position. It will, of course, be interesting to see where they are in relation to us.

So today then is a pretty relaxing day. Poor Chris is constantly in and out of the tent into what has turned out to be a pretty shitty, cold windy day to do sun sights and shout the time and angles to us scribbling the results in the comfort of the tent. The readings so far have been good, but our 'coded lat', as it's called (i.e. the triangle on the map in which we estimate that we are), is still quite large to say the least, and we really need as many more readings as we can get to draw more lines and reduce its size so as to get a better estimate of our true position. From here we will make our final journey on a distance and bearing and decide how lightweight to make the journey. I may also decide to stay here a bit longer to improve the accuracy, but of course at the cost of food and the contingency that may give us on our return journey. Tense, tense, tense moments, and as I write this, Chris is adding another line to the map.

New line done and it's good news, but still not accurate enough, so more are required. Our newest estimations are about 6.8 miles to the pole, so we would probably take the tent and sledge with us for at least some of that distance, especially as we hope and expect to see the Norwegian flag (and maybe tent) in the vicinity.

I'm so glad that I never brought my Chris worries at silly niggles to a head because, having bitten my lip (as he did too), we are now best chums again. It's amazing how quickly irritations come and go, and by maintaining in your head that we are all mates really, despite petty issues, almost anything can be overcome. My irritation earlier was genuine and to a degree rational, but not worth upsetting what is quite a fine and potentially great balance. It would have been wrong of me (or him) and unnecessary and foolish, and now look at us – we're on great form. I must admit that knowing how to overcome such potential misunderstandings and irritations within the group has allowed us all to avoid such problems before, and I spoke of it right from the start (in fact, I mentioned it to Chris in my interview of him). I've often started a conversation with someone, even though I didn't want to because I was in a bad mood with that person, just to break the negative spell, and sure enough, it always has. Thank God for that understanding, else this trip would be a totally different affair. Enough.

DAY 83

Woke at 9 a.m. then promptly decreed a lie-in. So we lay in bed till 11 a.m. (bliss) and then rolled back the bags for making tea. To our horror, though, there was a massive pool of water under both Mark and Rory's sleeping bags. Chris and I eagerly checked ours and they were fine(ish) but poor M and R's bags were literally dripping wet from the substantial puddle in the old stove depression. There really is *nothing at all* worse than getting wet in these conditions. We can all cope with cold snow and wind if it's dry, but the minute something is wet, our problems become manifold. If the temperature were to drop now, any of their clothes would fully freeze and that of course would be very dangerous. Even in a bright sun, their bags will take some time to dry fully, and once it has soaked through fully, it will only mean endless uncomfortable nights. Not good at all.

Now we've just done one more sun sight and we're waiting for the calculations to try and pinpoint our position more accurately yet. So far we have a number of arbitrary lines on a map all crossing one another like the game pick up sticks (or like a box of matches thrown to the floor). From this we've got to try and find the mean central position, but on the map we get distracted by where we want it to be (i.e. near the pole at our dead reckoning position) and we keep making centres of the 'cocked hat' only to add another line and use that to finely adjust our previous point, rather than look at the whole thing afresh. With this in mind then, I've asked Chris to continue doing his lines on my map so that I can estimate our rough distance from the pole and use this to plan our next movements in broad terms, but also that he too (or maybe Rory) plot all the lines on a clean sheet of paper so that we can all use our various methods to estimate the central point. This is vitally important to our whole mission because only when we have an actual point can we then determine an accurate bearing and distance to walk on to get to our pole.

So – we f**king did it. The pole is ours. We finally did our last line plot on our map and blank sheet and decided that there was not much point in doing any other lines. (If we stayed for days and did many more lines, that might be of use, but the arbitrary slope of the lines at present meant that just one more addition really wasn't going to do much at all.) So, on plotting the line, we all got around the makeshift box-lid table and, using various methods with drawing compass, circles and estimations, we all came up with our estimated position for where we were. We all added our crosses on the map, which all looked quite close to each other (but were in fact all miles apart), and then I asked Chris to choose an average location. He did so, which happened to be Mark's chosen point, then he and I measured the distance and bearing from that point to the pole. It really was quite an exciting time and we all waited eagerly for the results. As ever, there were some discrepancies (it was all so inaccurate really that it didn't cause any concern), and Chris and I took an average of our results and then that was it. We had our pole. Amazingly, it turned out to only be 4.5 nautical miles from our current assumed new position. The start of the journey there was quite amazing. We loaded the sledge with our day bags and bag with white jackets, flask and chocolate and it looked skeletal. We harnessed up (it was my turn to navigate) and set off. Instantly, the pace was so fast that the compass in my belt didn't have enough tension to stay horizontal and I couldn't see it properly. Mark and Rory were pulling and getting tangled in Chris and my trace lines as we were all going so fast and not used to it. Mayhem. After a few hundred yards we decided that Chris and I should go ahead to navigate alone, while the others pulled behind. This worked fine and we were off again.

Interestingly, there was not much excitement on our approach to the pole, but I did remark on a number of occasions how weird it was to be doing something different after so long of just pulling a sledge. Skiing alone without being tied to anything was really quite odd.

The ski was really quite quick and we were getting some way ahead of the others, so we waited for them and decided to ski to the pole together.

The countdown finally came to a stop at typically a patch of snowy land exactly the same as every other stretch of ground we'd seen for the last 80-odd days, but that FINALLY was it. We were at the pole.

Weirdly, no one was in a particularly jubilant mood. Mark and Rory had been talking about camper vans, for f**k's sake, and Chris and I were just thinking about it. Anyway, it soon became congratulations all round and a few funny words about how shit it all looked, and was this it? I then took a black flag and we donned our fantastic fur mitts and planted it with a few words in some sastrugi. I then revealed the final, final bottle of whisky and toasted absent friends and Scott's *Terra Nova* expedition. Everyone in turn took a swig, and all said a few words of their own, which generally revolved around Dave, Art and Rupert. All very nice but bloody cold, so the photographs we'd planned were taken as quickly as possible before we decided to get on our way. (NB the photos were copies of the same sorry poses that Scott and his team took in 1912.)

Chris and I took the now-empty sledge back, while the others flew off to prep dinner. It had all been quite a surreal experience, and although something of a visual and verbal anticlimax, we were all very aware of its true worth and enormity and both Chris and I talked of how odd but nice it was to be following tracks for the first time and actually, of course, going home (as we passed our first flag).

CHAPTER THIRTEEN

Return

I REMEMBER WHEN I WAS YOUNG AND READ ABOUT SCOTT I THOUGHT, ONLY 11 MILES FROM SAFETY, WHY COULDN'T THEY JUST HAVE GOT ON AND DONE IT? I DIDN'T UNDERSTAND WHAT IT WAS LIKE. NOW THAT I'VE BEEN HERE, I CAN EMPATHIZE IN A SMALL WAY. WHEN I WALKED OUT OF THE TENT IN THE *PITERAQ* I COULDN'T SEE IT FROM 5 YARDS AWAY. THEY WOULDN'T HAVE BEEN ABLE TO FIND ONE TON CAMP. WE TRIED WALKING A MILE AND A HALF IN THE *PITERAQ* AND MISSED A FLAG BY HUNDREDS OF YARDS. MY UNDERSTANDING OF THE STORY HAS GROWN GREATLY AND I'M EMBITTERED BY THE MALIGNING THAT SCOTT'S HAD. HE DID A FANTASTIC JOB. AND HE WAS UNLUCKY.
Bruce Parry

So began the trek home. From this distance it has taken on the shape and hue of a journey into myth. But as Scott and his men pointed their sledges north, they cannot have been thinking of immortality. Their mortality was rather more of a preoccupation. There were those crevasse fields to negotiate, the treacherous path through the mountains. Somewhere in all that ice and, if they were unlucky, those blizzards, they had to find their depots of food and fuel. All the while it wasn't getting any warmer: no sooner had the Antarctic summer opened its curtains than it began to close them again.

If Scott, in particular, had harboured any dreams of seeing his own image up on a plinth, that would have been instantly wiped by the sight of Amundsen's black flag. He also had the deadening knowledge that the world would have to wait more than a year for news of the polar party. The *Terra Nova* would enter the Ross Sea some time in the new year, but could remain only while the waters were navigable. There was no guarantee that the sea ice would let her in at all. Back in May the previous winter, Scott had told his men that the polar party would be out for 144 days, and would return to Hut Point by the end of March. 'Therefore the Pole party will almost certainly be too late for the ship.' Scott had already resigned himself to the prospect of keeping the British public waiting another year for news.

Amundsen had an eye on the more immediate future. As he turned around, he thought only of the sprint back to Framheim, where he hoped that the *Fram* would be waiting for him in the Bay of Whales. To be finally certain of a Norwegian victory, he needed the world to hear of it.

* * * * * * * * * * * *

It was 'with much relief', wrote Bowers, that Scott's party 'left all traces of the Norwegians behind us' as they hauled away from the South Pole on 19 January. Initially, their prospects looked good. Having marched into the teeth of a gale to reach the pole, they now had a following wind that allowed them to erect a sail. The wind picked up sufficiently that Bowers, whose skis were lying uselessly 200 miles to the north, had to go round the back of the sledge to control it. 'She ran like a bird,' he enthused as he resumed his station there three days later. With a light sledge, their distances in these days were prodigious: 16, 16.1, 5.5, 19.5, 16.5, 5.2. It was bad weather that held them up. On 24 January they came up short of their One and a Half Degree Depot, made on the day they reached Shackleton's furthest south record. A blizzard, which had made pitching the tent nearly impossible the day before, confined them to it until 10 p.m. They made the few miles to the depot and took stock.

Despite the mileages, there was cause for concern. The snow conditions were unhelpful. On the first day out from the pole the generally phlegmatic Wilson wrote of 'an absolutely awful surface with no glide at all for ski and sledge, and just like fine sand'. When the wind really got up, the sledge grew unruly. More than once it took two men to control it from the back and stop it from over-running. It was a much colder job than pulling. They had already camped early once because Evans's nose, gleaming white in Bowers's polar snapshots, was 'rather seriously congested with frequent frost-bites', noted his leader. 'He is very much annoyed with himself, which is not a good sign.' Evans's fingers were also a worry, and now at the start of the fourth act in this great drama, Oates's feet made their entry.

'Our hands are never warm enough in camp to do any neat work now,' wrote Wilson. Wilson, who scoured the snow in front of them for cairns and their old tracks, also had an attack of snow-blindness so debilitating that he couldn't proceed on skis: he lent his pair to Bowers. A second blizzard in six days had Scott worrying. 'I don't like the look of it. Is the weather breaking up? If so, God help us, with the tremendous summit journey and scant food. Wilson and Bowers are my stand-by. I don't like the easy way in which Oates and Evans get frost-bitten.' They were eating well, but the tremendous daily distances were eating into their bodily reserves. Bowers for the first time entertained food fantasies, though typically he sounded guilty about it: 'I sometimes spend much thought on the march with plans for making a pig of myself on the first opportunity. As that will be after a further march of 700 miles they are a bit premature.'

Only a few hours after Bowers wrote those words, Amundsen and his four companions returned to Framheim.

※ ※ ※ ※ ※ ※ ※ ※ ※ ※ ※ ※

Strong winds had mostly blown over their tracks, but Amundsen's men picked their way back over the plateau thanks to the efficacy of the beacons. They were only 3 feet in height, but 'when the sun was on them,' Amundsen beamed, 'they shone like electric lighthouses; and when the sun was on the other side, they looked so dark in the shadow that one would have taken them for black rocks'.

They decided to switch to night travel so that the sun would be behind them. The wind was also at their backs, and they hared through their daily distances so swiftly that they had to camp for up to 16 hours a day. It was possible to do far more than the 15 nautical miles they covered, but Amundsen was neurotic about preserving the strength of the remaining dogs, one of whom they killed on 19 December and fed to his 15 comrades. It was Amundsen's favourite. The next day was the turn of one of Wisting's, who was so weak that he had had to be put on the sledge. 'On arrival at the camping-ground he had his reward. A little blow of the back of the axe was enough for him; without making a sound the worn-out animal collapsed.' The diaries put a brave face on it, but these executions must have been demoralizing. Not every dog earned the same gratitude. A third was killed on 23 December. Amundsen described him as a reprobate. 'Bad character. If a man, he would have ended in penal servitude.' In the end, only one husky out of the original shipment of 110 would make it all the way back to Norway.

They romped up the hill towards their first depot. It wasn't all easy going. At midday in the tent they roasted and got hugely bored, while the three skiers in particular were increasingly troubled by shortness of breath and pangs of hunger. 'There were days – only a few days, be it said – when I believe any of us three – Bjaaland, Hassel, and myself – would have swallowed pebbles without winking.' It was easier for Hanssen and Wisting, who clung on to the sledges (though Wisting had to rig up a sail to keep up with the lead dog team). Amundsen and Hassel found it difficult to match the pace of the dogs. Amundsen gave thanks that he could not see the mess of his technique as he struggled to keep up: 'If I had been able to, I am sure I should have been in fits of laughter'. Toiling to break the trail ahead of them, the champion skier Bjaaland hankered for the lower altitude that awaited them on the other side of the glacier. 'I wish to God we were down on the Barrier,' he grumbled, 'here it is hard to breathe, and the nights are as long as the Devil.' But the depots along their route were groaning with supplies, and Amundsen could afford to distribute extra rations of pemmican. The men were grateful.

They chose to stop taking breaks, during which their muscles would seize up, and instead do their distance in one stretch. At Christmas they feasted on a porridge made of dried milk and biscuit crumbs harvested by Wisting, and they smoked the cigars presented by Bjaaland to his leader at the pole. They also fell gratefully on the extra rations of chocolate waiting for them at the first depot. Four days later they crested the plateau and headed for the mountains now creeping up over the horizon to the north a good degree of latitude earlier than they were expecting. 'That we were astonished is a mild expression,' observed Amundsen of the tricks of light played by the atmosphere this far south.

Perhaps it was the sight of land, but by now Amundsen and his men were exulting in their success. He was amazed to note that the dogs were actually putting on weight, and their speed endured not only over the flat ice, but also, in good visibility, the intermittent sastrugi. By Amundsen's own admission, they were fortunate. Under clear skies they spotted the Devil's Ballroom and the Devil's Glacier, and contrived to evade both of them. There was one night when they camped nervously on top of a filled-in crevasse, but that was the worst of their trials. 'With incredible luck we had slipped past all those ugly and dangerous places.' In bad weather they missed their depot, but had enough food for this not to be critical. Nonetheless, when they spotted it, Hanssen and Bjaaland volunteered to return the 15 miles to retrieve it. Taking an empty sledge, they did it in ten hours, but the hunt for the depot was not without its drama thanks to fog wafting across their path. When they found it, wrote Bjaaland, 'Our pleasure was vast, you can be sure.' So was Amundsen's when they hoved into view in his telescope. He prepared food and drink while the others slept, and when Hanssen and Bjaaland got there he took care of their dogs for them. Although it involved backtracking, Hanssen and Bjaaland's journey of 42 miles uninterrupted by sleep was the longest any of them would do on the polar journey.

* * * * * * * * * * * *

For the two modern expeditions, the return veers away from essential elements of the original race. The British team are particularly conscious of it. They have made their pole without suffering the huge psychological blow of defeat. 'No way we can replicate Scott's mindset,' says Mark Anstice. 'We're not running for our lives. The utter desolation of putting all that effort in just to be beaten – no way we can replicate that. All we can do is have two more weeks of misery, then check into a nice hotel.' Although it wouldn't be historically accurate, Chris van Tulleken says he would 'almost be pleased if we go a bit on half rations. Although I don't want to do it, I will be pleased to have done it.'

Bruce Parry sums it up as they pick up two and a half days' food at their first depot. 'Right now we're in a better mood than Scott.'

The Norwegian team turn on Day 45, and begin the long journey back to their starting point. The British team reach the pole on Day 83. With so little time left, they have no viable destination to head for. One Ton, the depot Scott failed to make it back to, is out of the question. However, they need to eat, and there are depots strewn across their path where they will find food.

Despite discrepancies with the original journey, there are still telling contrasts between the teams. The Norwegians have learnt from Amundsen's mistake on the plateau. Where he eked out safe, conservative distances as he made his way towards the mountains, and condemned himself and his men to hours of tent-bound tedium, Rune Gjeldnes decides to step on it. 'The pole is not the goal,' he says before the start of the expedition. 'The goal is a safe return.' They are down to two sledges now, with John Huston joining Rune and Inge Solheim as ski-runners. Everything about their teamwork is now so precision-tooled that it seems nothing can go wrong. Even the remaining dogs have more or less given up fighting. Day after day they get up, cook, eat, pack up the camp, harness the two husky teams and proceed to do a marathon and a half. Their daily distances as they race away from the pole are, on average, double the amount covered by their predecessors. On Day 52, a week into their return, they set a record of 35.8 nautical miles. This is despite the fact that they frequently travel in white-out conditions, meaning poor visibility for locating cairns.

Their sustained speed over the endless flat is breathtaking, a proper tribute to the genius of Amundsen and the Norwegian method. The measure of their success is that they are so fast they have more food than they need: just like Amundsen. John speaks for his team members when he explains the point of their achievement. 'We did our very best to show how Amundsen's model of travel was way ahead of its time. It is great to go out and show that there was a lot of intelligent thought behind it and that it really is what brought us to the pole so quickly. His equipment, planning and mental approach were unparalleled. He was extremely detailed and thought of so many little things. I think we really benefited from that, and are still benefiting in our daily comforts from his design.'

They have white-outs on Days 50 and 59 in which they cannot move. On Day 60 they fight their way through very bad weather to a depot because they are running low on dog pemmican. But the white-out refuses to lift. Having completed 375 nautical miles from the pole, there is nothing more to prove. They rest and talk and await the Twin Otter from Tassilaq, which arrives through a clearing sky on Day 69. The journey of the Norwegian team is over.

* * * * * * * * * * * *

It was now 1912, though Amundsen says they were thoroughly confused about dates and times. On a clear 3 January, with the plateau behind them, they decided to lengthen their daily distances. That first day they did 25 miles, in the course of which they found an old beacon. It had crumpled under the heat of the sun that forced Amundsen's men to travel in 'somewhat unseemly' attire. The next day, despite the mystifying appearance of mountains they had somehow missed on the way south, they located Wisting's broken ski sticking out of the all but molten beacon of the Butcher's Shop depot. Mountains of dog meat awaited. The slope now grew so sharp that they had to fit ropes on the sledge-runners as brakes. They camped and woke at 1 a.m. to a spectacular view of sun and shadow performing a slow dance on the flanks of vast peaks. They sped down to the next night's camp. As on the day before, they were lucky: the snow was powdery, reducing the speed of the sledges over the surface. The skiers enjoyed themselves. 'A wonderful sport,' said Amundsen. Bjaaland 'had many good runs and raced with the captain'. The dogs and their drivers had less fun edging their way through crevasse fields, but they made it. On their final day in the mountains, the Axel Heiberg Glacier beckoned. Instead of circum-navigating it as they had in the opposite direction, they proceeded straight down it and on 6 January found themselves on the Barrier 'after a stay of 51 days on land', noted Amundsen.

On the Barrier they located their first depot, but found the sun had burnt through the mound of snow and turned the pemmican rancid. For all that, the sledges so groaned with rations that Amundsen claimed they were now 'living among the fleshpots of Egypt'. They also made a strange gesture as two of them skied over to Mount Betty to collect geological specimens. They built a rock cairn and beside it left 4.5 gallons of paraffin, 20 boxes of matches and an account of their journey. 'Possibly,' noted Amundsen, 'someone may find a use for these things in the future.' (If only he had been passing this way, Scott would have found a use: he was to have problems with evaporating fuel at the depots. A full can of Amundsen's fuel was found on Mount Betty in 1960.)

Having lost a dog in the mountains, they now made their last killing, leaving 11 huskies to pull the sledges back to Framheim.

Across the Barrier Amundsen and his men profited from a routine they had begun on the glacier. They travelled for 15 miles, then rested for six hours. Bad weather closed in and they put on their sealskin clothing, collected from the depot, and pressed on. Bjaaland, roped to Hassel, nearly plunged into a crevasse. The days melted into one another as they now chewed up whole degrees of latitude in two or three days, as opposed to the four days projected in their original, conservative plan. On 11 January they saw the last of the mountains just as two skuas materialized overhead and parked themselves on a beacon the Norwegians had built two months earlier. Here was confirmation that Amundsen's men had left the land behind, and that the sea beckoned. They all cheered, and Bjaaland fired shots into the air – to celebrate, rather than to introduce variety into their diet. 'Can anyone who reads these lines form an idea of the effect this had upon us?' wrote Amundsen. 'It is hardly likely. They brought a message from the living world into this realm of death – a message of all that was dear to us ... They did allow themselves a long rest ... they sat still a while, no doubt wondering who we were, then rose aloft and flew on to the south. Mysterious creatures! They were now exactly half-way between Framheim and the Pole, and yet they were going farther inland. Were they going over to the other side?'

The more practical side of Amundsen soon piped up: he worried that whole flocks of skuas would be feasting on their depots further to the north. But for the moment they had more food than they could possibly eat, including fresh seal meat picked up at each of the depots, and started to feed their rations to the dogs, who were even introduced to the taste of chocolate. As they raced towards each new depot, they left box upon box of food piled in their wake. There was no need to take it. Depots were reduced to signposts in the snow. Skiing from the front, Bjaaland led them towards each beacon, though Hanssen on the lead sledge kept a beady eye on his tendency to veer to the right. If not, observed Amundsen, 'in the course of an hour or so [Bjaaland] would probably have described a beautiful circle and brought himself back to the spot from which he had started'. At least it meant that when they couldn't find their markers, they knew which direction to look in. 'We gradually became so familiar with Bjaaland's right-handed tendencies that we actually counted on them.'

On 13 January they went a whole day without seeing a single beacon as they searched for the depot at 83 degrees south. As they were putting up the tent to wait for clearer visibility, the fog briefly lifted and there, more or less under their noses, was the depot. Scott never had this sort of luck. Here they found baffling evidence that some of the dogs who ran off on the way south had been at the depot until perhaps two days ago, but had not eaten any of the food. Three days later they reached the depot at 82 degrees south, the most southerly point they reached on the series of autumn journeys, and found that the runaway dogs had broken into the ration boxes, and also eaten two carcasses of slaughtered huskies, but not those of eight puppies. Amundsen was not worried. He had more food than he knew what to do with.

They were now at the start of the home stretch. To celebrate Wisting concocted a chocolate pudding out of biscuit crumbs, dried milk, chocolate and water. 'We all agreed that it came nearer perfection than anything it had hitherto fallen to our lot to taste.' As they raced on, they picked up a trail of splinters made from packing-case and left in the snow ten months earlier. Pressure ridges and crevasse fields lay in their path as they made their way to the depot at 81 degrees south, where the first dog they had slaughtered awaited the remaining huskies. On the way to the depot at 80 degrees south they left their last snow beacon behind. 'I cannot deny it was with a certain feeling of melancholy that we saw it vanish,' wrote Amundsen. 'We had grown so fond of our beacons, and whenever we met them we greeted them as old friends.' The beacons were not only their lifeline. They were symbols of the existence that was now coming to an end: the camaraderie, the simplicity. They must have already intuited that they would look back on these days as the best of their lives.

No sooner did they reach the depot than they had their first human contact in the form of a message from Prestrud, who had passed here with Stubberud and Johansen in November. The dogs attacked the seal meat, but they couldn't make much of a dent in the huge supply of food so laboriously dragged out here nearly a year earlier. On 25 January the snow conditions were unfavourable, but they ploughed on to within 18 miles of their destination, made camp and slept to gather strength for the final stretch. It was snowing heavily when they set out, and visibility was down to zero. They got lost, and when the weather cleared, were lucky enough to see an object in the snow 2 miles off, which turned out to be a sledge they had left here in October. The sun appeared and picked out Framheim, its chimney piping smoke out into the ether. It was the most remote hut on the entire planet, and after 99 days and 1400 nautical miles they had found it.

'We stood and waited for each other outside the door in the early morning,' wrote Amundsen; 'our appearance must be made all together. It was so still and quiet – they must be all asleep. We came in. Stubberud started up in his bunk and glared at us; no doubt he took us for ghosts.'

The return journey, brilliantly executed, miraculously smooth, accounted for only 39 of those 99 days. Within just a few more days, Amundsen was on the *Fram* and sailing north with news of his astounding triumph.

* * * * * * * * * * * *

By the time they arrive on Day 83, they are reasonably fit but nevertheless hungry, tired, cold, thin and desperate to go home. Under the terms of the re-enactment, they must carry on.

They start for home on Day 85 and, like Scott accelerating away from the South Pole with the wind behind him, they start to put in some impressive distances. These distances are partly the result of a sort of trick they play on themselves. On Day 86, having picked up their first depot away from the pole, they man-haul their biggest distance of the entire expedition. At 19.4 nautical miles, it's nearly 2 miles more than their best distance with the dogs, way back on Day 31. During one of the breaks, Bruce suggests a radical alteration of their daily cycle, in which they switch to 30-hour days. This would allow them to march through 12 hours, as they have been doing, but to get an eight-hour sleep on top of it. Despite Rory O'Connor's mumbles about jetlag, the proposal is passed unanimously.

As ever, there are still problems. Chris's knee is giving him trouble – he fell over several times the previous day. On Day 86, within spitting distance of Scott's record march, Bruce pulls up short because of it, though Chris is as keen as him to press on and claim equality with their predecessors. 'It is more important we stay as a team,' says Bruce, 'and that nobody gets annoyed because I'm pushing for an arbitrary silly thing when Scott had a force ten gale behind him pushing a sail. We are close, but it doesn't matter. It means nothing.' And then there are Mark's inflamed heels, which are now causing him enough agony to afford the merest glimpse of what his fellow officer of the 6th Inniskilling Dragoons must have endured. On top of these things, Chris and Mark are suffering from the cold owing to extreme weight loss. By now they have shed between a quarter and a third of their starting body weight as they put themselves through an extraordinarily gruelling schedule of physical labour. 'There is no fat left on me at all,' says Mark. 'I'm getting near the stage where I'm going to atrophy – metabolize my own muscle because I'm not getting enough food. There is no fat on me so there is no way to keep warm.'

On Day 87 Chris is navigating and has a bad day at the office. They travel two-thirds of a mile away from their correct bearing and spend the latter part of the day looking for a flag in a white-out. If they don't find their flag, they won't find their depot. The anxiety it induces opens the merest window into the worry that attended Scott and his men as they hunted for their depots across 700 miles of ice.

Food fantasies are now with them the whole time. Just as they are afforded a harrowing insight into the sufferings that, at a later stage of the *Terra Nova* expedition, began to sap the energy and morale of Scott and his men, they end the march with a heart-warming success when they find a depot marked by a huge cairn. It is groaning with food. The euphoria is short-lived. Day 89 dawns. 'What a miserable day,' says Mark. 'I really, really hate this day. It's just grim. This place is death, it really is. Things come out here to die. All we see here is dead birds. I wouldn't let this place kill me, but I can see it'd be very easy to die here. Man's not supposed to be up here.'

Bruce and Rory are more buoyant: perhaps it is the prospect of going home, but they now say that, given the chance, they would happily have gone the full distance. 'We're here to replicate Scott's conditions and equipment,' says Rory. 'If, like him, we had to do 149 days, I would do it. And I'd be happy to do it.' This sparks a debate about whether they would actually meet the same fate. The doctors would like to think that they'd pull through. 'We are fitter and stronger than Scott,' says Chris, 'and mentally we're fitter than Scott because our dreams and hopes haven't been destroyed. If we had 50 days to go, I would be very concerned, and I think it's possible we would all get serious injuries from frostbite, hypothermia, weight loss and nutritional problems. But I would at this point be surprised if we died.' Mark, however, confesses that he'd 'have doubts about getting out unscathed. The season is closing in on us. It will start getting colder, I've got no fat left to lose, my feet are getting worse and worse, and we've had minor back problems. The kit is on its last legs. The sledge is not going to get any lighter. If a storm came in and we didn't make our depot, we haven't got enough contingency; we'd have to go on half-rations. Pulling on half-rations we haven't tried, but I think the speed with which our bodies are deteriorating would double. We are unlikely to get the same temperatures as them, but we'd be in just as much trouble.'

'One thing that is potentially crippling is the diet,' says Bruce. 'We don't know enough about micronutrients in the diet and whether we're going to get run down from lack of vitamins. Although we all feel strong now, I wouldn't be surprised if we reached a peak and came off the other side. It's very likely that we would all start to deteriorate quickly. And the longer you're out here, the more susceptible you are to injury. If you're running for your life and the weather turns bad and someone is holding you back ... we're just as susceptible to that as Scott. We're all on a high now, but we also know deep down that we're in a dangerous position and anything that goes wrong could be lethal. The expedition has finished at a good time.'

On Day 90 they are duly told they are going home. On Day 91, their last full day in harness, the Greenland ice cap grants them a parting gift, a spectacular perihelion, which has all of them in rhapsody. On the equivalent day, Scott had a gloomier cast of mind: 'We shall be lucky if we escape without injury,' he wrote in his diary.

Rune Gjeldnes's Diary

DAY 48

Evening is here, and we've done a good day and set a new record in distance. That's good. Good, good, and I've had a good thinking, dreaming and planning day. Good, good. It'll be sad to send off the last dogs, but that's the way it is. The beacons are standing in a nice line one after another, it looks nicer and nicer. Possibly a bit colder up here and they are built better. The dogs have been good today, except for two fights. I'm lucky not to have to decide which to send home. My whole team is going. Happy but a bit wary if it's the right decision. John's sledge is going out. Mine and his are quite similar. And quite a bit of rubbish with it. Need to get rid of some weight. Have thought about many things.

DAY 50

White-out, but it seems to have cleared. All clear. And we've had a discussion about changing from day to night, and came to a solution everyone is happy with. We're starting at 02.00 and finishing at 10.00. Agreed that must be the best time to be moving. The snow is at its coldest then, and hopefully the air's OK. We've had temperatures under minus 15 degrees Celsius the last six days. Summer must be here. The going is always best in the morning.

Looking forward to being further south again. We're going home to success. Heading towards our goal and success is more than enough motivation for me.

I'm wondering if we should really go for it. Do 12-hour days as long as we're able. With the conditions we had yesterday we can do 40 miles. We've got more than enough food for the dogs. It depends if the conditions hold for long enough for us to do it. Just SPEED and take a resting day halfway. Surprise everybody: 40 days less than estimated. As long as it doesn't get too hot, it should work. We'll manage fine. The dogs are the big question mark. Have to discuss it with the others first, especially Ketil.

Consequence: tired dogs and men more exhausted.

DAY 51

Weird, but I'm starting by saying: 'The day is over'. We've done 11 hours and more than 36 miles. Well pleased with the day. Was keen to see what the others would say about the plan to really push it now. When they'd had time to think about it, the smiles came on their faces. Think it's motivating for everyone to set new and higher targets. Tried 11 hours tonight and hoping to try 12 tomorrow. We have to speed up.

A lot of change in the routines now. Incredibly beautiful from midnight on. The beacons lighting up like candles on a dusky ice plateau. Wonderful and a bit cold. The dogs liked it.

Still Saturday and everyone has been sleeping like logs. Big change in routines, but it'll just get better. We've had a rest now, which helps. Wondering how the dogs will get on tonight. Ketil's lead dog was very skittish yesterday and delayed us for an hour at least. Very annoying for him and for us too, plus Inge who had to stand waiting and freezing. Put wax on the skis, which glued us to the snow for the first few hours, but then we did the first 12 miles in three hours. Bloody good and the first 29 in seven and a half hours. Then the air went out of the dogs. We reached Butcher's, and after that there were no tracks, and few beacons to go by: three a day and the flags. Think we did it the same way as Amundsen. More and more towards the pole. We should have had small beacons all the way plus the big ones! Trying to do 12 hours today, and if it works, that's good. Have a few choices: 11-hour days with no resting day before we reach our goal; 12 hours with one resting day; or basically just pushing on as long as the weather and the going allows it. Exciting and I think most of us like it. Always a special feeling when you start pushing it. Good and bad. We're going to KICK SOME ASS!

DAY 58
New day over and a good 12 hours. We have one beacon left before the journey is over. Tomorrow we'll take off towards south-southwest, and we're being picked up there on Wednesday. Long way yet, but only four legs left. A great day, but cold with a good deal of wind. First day when we feel as though we're going downwards. Tomorrow we'll get to the last depot before the end. Weird. A lot of thoughts about what to do when I get home. And special memories from being on the ice. Otherwise all is routine. We're just going to kill time and distance.

DAY 63
We're at journey's end. Tears of joy. A happy team, a good team, with very different personalities, who didn't know each other very well before we came to Greenland. Strong personalities. How would it go? I was filled with anticipation, but it's gone far better than expected. Not that I was sceptical, but anyway, it was a challenge. Strong opinions, great experiences. Being diplomatic has been extremely important. Have been lucky that everyone has been very loyal to me, and that everyone has been loyal to our 'democracy',

so to speak, loyal to our common goal. Pride has been a great motivator. Do your best all the time and everybody has understood that's it's about cooperating as a team.

The experience of the team has made most of my job easy. We did the preparations as well as possible considering the time we had available. Everyone should get credit for that. And the preparations were reflected in the performance, through enthusiasm and focus on making this project a real success. It wasn't given to us on a plate! In January I didn't believe it would be possible to carry out this project. I knew before we started that I wouldn't be an authoritarian leader. I never have been. In our case I think that worked well. I've led the group without it being noticeable. Showed respect for everyone's capacities and experiences when it counted. I've gotten or had respect from the others all along. I've had tons of patience. Everybody took responsibility for their own things, and that gives people something to be proud of. The tasks have been carried out in the best possible way. Not all problems have been solved the way I thought best, but as long as it doesn't affect our progress and the result, it's unnecessary to hassle people or take away from their happiness. Routines have gradually evolved, not by themselves, but with a few basic guidelines before we started. Everyone has found their place. Good routines are absolutely essential on an expedition. If they're not good, you give up.

The discussions we had before starting were very important. I think people have kept them in the back of their minds. It would have been good to have had more chats, but overall it doesn't seem like it would have made much difference now.

Inclusive leadership has been key for me all along. I don't know if that is a real term, but it's been my aim. This expedition included a lot of fields that I didn't know much about. A new type of expedition for me. Then it's important that everyone contributes their own knowledge and experiences. As long as I've had the last word or felt that the decision taken was the right one, that's been fine. Listening has been very important. Listening to what people knew about other fields. Everyone appreciates if you listen to them, and it creates a feeling of being valued. It is important, and makes everyone do a better job.

I think everyone should be proud of the job they've done as individuals in the team. Everyone has had important roles and everyone has carried out their tasks with pride and in the best way possible.

The attitude towards the project and every task it involved has determined our success. A positive attitude and a focus on what's in everybody's best interest. This team scores high. Very high. There are, of course, a lot of things we could have done better, but if there weren't, then what would have motivated us to improve? A team with its feet firmly planted on the ground. The target was 70 days. Not to break any records, but as a team it was a target to aim for. It has been very motivating, and I think we should be pleased. A big thank you for the hard work!

Bruce Parry's Diary

Day 85
So – what an odd feeling, but fantastic to be going home at last. We set off with a sledge that was so low to the ground and so light that we could hardly feel it. Our tracks were very usable, flags in sight, it was a beautiful day and everyone was in a great mood. The first couple of hours we did at about 2 miles an hour, then the surface became quite grainy and sandy, but we still pulled at a good rate (had the sledge been its usual weight, we all agreed we'd hardly have moved at all). Great to be going past flags all day long.

My Achilles heel has started to play up, which is really quite annoying. It's not rasping and is totally manageable, but will not of course get any rest, and I don't want it to be an issue when I get home.

DAY 86
Best day yet by far. 20.8 on the meter, so a 20-mile day. Fantastic. We also came across our first cairn and our first depot too. So as I sit in the tent tonight, we have 24 or so miles to the next depot and over three days' food to do it. Easy!

I put it to the team today that we dispense with the 24-hour day in favour of a more flexible arrangement. The point being to allow us to go for more than 12 hours at a time if we so desire without eating into our sleep time. The idea seemed to be ok so everyone agreed to give it a go. In essence, the previous method of trekking 12 hours, three hours' wake up and pack sledge, three hours' put up tent and cook left us only six hours' sleep. If, however, the going was slower, say 1 mile an hour, and we needed to do 15 hours in order to do our 15 miles, then we would only get three hours' sleep. Likewise, if we were having a good day, like today, and felt strong enough to go on, we should not feel limited in any way. By dispensing with the 24-hour day, it also means that the 5000 calories we have for a 24-hour period could be stretched to cover the new time, thereby giving us more miles for our calories. A very real benefit, and better than going on to half rations. Of course, the downside is a calorie defect over time, but not substantial, I believe, and the new routine would seem to me to be far more efficient. Other problems could be the playing with the body clock and subsequent morning shit routines (who cares) and trekking through the coldest part of the day because we will cycle through the 24-hour period at different rates. Other benefits include a less stressful, structured day and much more sleep, which is really required for these long marches. Anyway – we shall see and revert if it doesn't work out.

The evening routine was quite relaxed suddenly, and there was a calm air in the tent tonight.

The reason we stopped at 20 miles today and didn't give Scott's record distance of 25 miles a go was because Chris had mentioned that he had twisted his knee a bit, so despite his insistence that he was ok to go on, I decided that we'd call it a day rather than push any potential injury. This was definitely the right decision and he was quite grateful, I believe. Mark's feet seem to be a sustained plateau of pain, but manageable, and he is cool with the new routine, provided the painkillers last.

DAY 87
Woke late after a glorious lie-in. It's now 1.30 p.m. and we haven't looked outside yet, but all seems ok so far with the new routine. Very mellow start to the day. In fact, a few of us are writing our diaries and just quite relaxed about getting started. A nice change. I am very hungry, though, so we'll see if it is worth it later in the day.

The day went well at first, with a good glide and a subsequent rate of 2 mph, which was fantastic. After some hours, however, the mist came in a bit and the light became very flat, which meant that Chris, who was navigating, started having quite a bad time. Our bearing seemed off as he had to resort to compass and distance as the tracks became less obvious and eventually invisible.

After some time and an erratic rate, we crossed an open expanse and we missed our flag. I was a bit concerned, but the group concern was that it had probably fallen over, so we ignored it and went on to the next, with the weather looking quite ominous in most directions and a cold wind picking up to boot.

As we approached the prescribed distance, it was obvious that there was no flag, so I instigated our lost procedure for the first time, which entailed us getting warm gear on and doing a search. I was convinced the flag was over to our right, so we set off together and left people at various points as the visibility of the last person reduced until we were all straddled out in a long line away from the sledge, hoping that the furthest person would have a view of the flag (and cairn). As it turned out, we'd only left Chris behind before all of us (except me) spotted the cairn during a break in the clouds, so we were safe again.

We drew an arrow in the snow then returned for the sledge and set off to retrieve our track. I sent Chris ahead so that he could do his navigating on his own (to enable him to stop and start while trekking without holding us up) and while in principle I still like this idea, of course the remaining three of us instantly had an uphill grainy sand grind for our first mile. Typical.

Anyway, all was happy again back at the cairn and we set off for the next flag back on our old tracks.

Chris today, however, was in an odd mood. He was obviously a bit depressed about his errors in tracking and that upset him, despite my endlessly repeating that he shouldn't worry and it was a tough job. Nevertheless, he was still down in the mouth most of the day. Thoughtful, quiet and not willing to enter into conversation. While I sympathize with his feelings, it is never good when any one of us is feeling like that as it affects the whole group, so I was happy to see that during the evening, back in the tent, he slowly returned to his old self.

Now it's 5 a.m. (ish) on Monday and we're about to have another mammoth sleep. I intend to start at 10 p.m. tonight. Great new system and we're all very happy.

DAY 88
Woke at 4 p.m. today and now still in bed at 5.45. Everyone has slept well and we're enjoying the new routine, even though we are eating less often than before.

I've said we'll start at 10 p.m. with the sail erected, so in essence we've lost a day (or in our case, because we're so keen to get home, we've gained a day). Seems all a bit lax, but out here the only thing that matters is our food and distance to the next food.

DAY 89
Another good day today. Sometimes it was bright and the shadows of the tracks were obvious, other times I could hardly make out my own tracks which made seeing the old ones virtually impossible. The sky was fantastic today – big and bold and awesome. Purple, mauve, grey and blue over a white expanse with patches of mist. At one time I left the track because Mark was tripping over my line while I tried to navigate, so was able to see the guys from afar. What a sight for the first time in ages. I got a reminder of what we look like. They just looked so remarkable and surreal against the stormy purple sky with the sea of spindrift under their sledge. They looked like they were

flying. That, coupled with the sighting of a distant cairn half-glowing from the sun's reflection, dodging in and out of the mist, was quite a lovely moment for me while I skied alone.

The going was quite good, but there was a large hill to climb today and the flags and cairns were about 3 miles apart, so the breaks were few and some way between. We are all quite quiet on the march these days, and most of our thoughts are fixed on our impending departure.

CHAPTER FOURTEEN

End

'I'M JUST GOING OUTSIDE AND MAY BE SOME TIME.'
Oates, as quoted by Captain Scott

On 29 January Scott's polar party broke its record: 19.5 nautical miles, nearly a third of a degree of latitude. During the course of it, they met the tracks of Teddy Evans's second returning party. Bowers, at the back of the sledge to control it in the breeze, spent the morning without his dog-skin mitts and his hands were 'perished', which is perhaps why he made his last proper diary entry on this day. 'We picked up the memorable camp where I transferred to the advance party. How glad I was to change over.'

Two days later they picked up Bowers's skis, as well as a week's rations. Wilson was travelling with a strained tendon in his left leg which swelled painfully, but their productive mileages continued unabated. Scott fell on a slippery surface and injured his shoulder on 2 February. His audit for the day was not hopeful: 'We shall be lucky if we get through without serious injury ... The extra food is certainly helping us, but we are getting pretty hungry ... It is time we were off the summit – pray God another four days will see us pretty well clear of it. Our bags are getting very wet and we ought to have more sleep.'

At least it was (fleetingly) warmer. The mountains appeared in front of them, but the price for getting off the plateau was the broken surfaces through which they were now forced to negotiate a path. 'February 5,' wrote Wilson. '18.2 miles. We had a difficult day, getting in amongst a frightful chaos of broad chasm-like crevasses … February 6. Got in amongst great chasms running E. and W. and had to come out again … Very cold March: many crevasses; I walking by the sledge on foot found a good many; the others all on ski.' The next day they found the Upper Glacier Depot and bade farewell to the plateau. It came not a moment too soon for one of their number, with cuts on his hands refusing to heal and a nose more or less destroyed by frostbite. 'Another week might have had a very bad effect on P.O. Evans, who is going steadily down-hill,' wrote Scott, who elsewhere described him as 'dull and incapable' and observed that 'altogether he shows considerable signs of being played out'.

Their awareness grew that there was only one fate in store for a man in such a predicament. 'A man on a sledge is a very serious weight,' wrote Cherry-Garrard in hindsight. 'Practically any man who undertakes big polar journeys must face the possibility of having to commit suicide to save his companions.' He had some knowledge of the terrain after undertaking the winter journey to fetch penguin eggs, when he, Wilson and Bowers sometimes fantasized about death as a release from the unimaginable cold. Despite his firm Christian convictions, Bowers had had 'a scheme of doing himself in with a pick-axe if necessity arose, though how he could have accomplished it I don't know'.

The Beardmore brought relief, in the form of warmer temperatures and stimulation: 'Camped right by the moraine under the great sandstone cliffs of Mt Buckley, out of the wind and quite warm again; it was a wonderful change,' wrote Wilson on 8 February. 'After lunch we all geologized on till supper, and I was very late turning in, examining the moraine after supper.' Even if it allowed Evans to rest in the tent, an entire afternoon given over to science seems an extravagant use of time for hungry men, but Scott no doubt felt that here was their chance to have something to show for this quixotic trek: if not the pole, then a gain in human knowledge. Thirty-five pounds' worth of samples were loaded on to a sledge Cherry-Garrard described as 'featherweight'. The next day Wilson was given half an hour among the rocks 'and again got some good things written up in the sketch-book'. He continued studying rocks all the way down the glacier.

On 11 February their progress was suddenly, dramatically impeded. Like the other two returning parties, they found it much harder to see ice falls and crevasses on the way down than on the way up, and 'got into the worst ice mess I have ever been in', admitted Scott. 'For three hours we plunged on on ski, first thing we were too much to the right, then too much to the left; meanwhile the disturbance got worse and my spirits received a very rude shock. There were times when it seemed almost impossible to find a way out of the awful turmoil in which we found ourselves.' They had similar problems the following day. Their labours as they fought through this interminable, demoralizing maze can only be guessed at. Scott's diary makes reference to 'divided councils'. There must have been cross words as they struggled to find a path. By the end of it, Oates tersely noted, 'we were absolutely done'.

It was now vital that they find the Mid-Barrier Depot. They had built no cairns to help them through, on the assumption that they could navigate by landmark alone. 'It's a tight place,' admitted Scott, and the next day, which they had begun with a solitary biscuit apiece, he observed, 'We mustn't get into a hole like this again.' Luckily for Scott, the flag lifted out of the fog and they could breathe again. But it was a temporary let-off. Quite apart from the snow-blindness now afflicting Wilson and Bowers, and a blistered foot that Evans suddenly revealed, they were now permanently hungry. Scott admitted that as camp cook he was 'serving something under the full allowance'. Wilson's diary refers to 'thin meals' and 'thin hoosh'. As they tried to replenish themselves on a diet of what must have been flavoured molten snow, they were coming to understand the terrible equation between food, strength and distances.

'Tomorrow,' wrote Wilson two days later as they chased down the Lower Barrier Depot, 'we have to make one day's food which remains last over the two.' By now Oates's toes were black from frostbite, but they heard no complaint from him. Evans, on the other hand, had twice fallen into crevasses and seemed to have injured his head. Scott noted that he was now in a 'stupor' and constantly 'stupid'. It must have been the Welshman's moaning that goaded Oates into an unsparing assessment: 'It is an extraordinary thing about Evans, he's lost his guts and behaves like an old woman or worse. He's quite worn out with the work, and how he's going to do the 400-odd miles we've still got to do, I don't know.' Oates didn't have to wait long for the answer. On the first of those half-ration days, Evans collapsed and, agonizingly, despite the desperate need to press on, they were forced to camp early. On the second, his ski shoes kept coming off, and he was eventually told to unharness and come on at his own speed. He fell behind and when they stopped for lunch he had still not caught up. They went back to look for him. 'I was the first to reach him, the poor man, and shocked at his appearance,' wrote Scott; 'he was on his knees with clothing disarranged, hands uncovered and frostbitten, and a wild look in his eyes. Asked what was the matter, he replied with a slow speech that he didn't know.' Oates stayed with him while the others went to get the sledge and they all dragged him back to where they made camp. According to Wilson, he was in a coma by the time he was placed in the tent. He stopped breathing at 10 p.m. They were too hungry to observe the appropriate obsequies. After a short rest and a short prayer they struck camp and raced to the depot, leaving Evans's huge husk of a body in the snow.

'A very terrible day,' wrote Scott of the trusted sledging partner he had doggedly brought all this way. The team's conclusion was that he had started to weaken before the pole. 'It is a terrible thing to lose a companion in this way, but calm reflection shows that there could not have been a better ending to the terrible anxieties of the past week.' Later he wrote, 'the safety of the remainder seemed to demand his abandonment, but Providence mercifully removed him at the critical moment'.

They were back down to four in the tent, with rations for five men awaiting them on the journey home. After five hours' sleep, they headed for Shambles Camp, and still found time to make a last visit to a rock moraine. They feasted gratefully on pony meat and exchanged their short sledge for a longer one depoted on the journey south. Respite was temporary. One Ton Depot was 240 miles to the north, and as well as a week's worth of pony meat, they had four weeks of food depoted on the Barrier. They didn't need to match their progress on the plateau to make a safe return, but they were nonetheless alarmed to see their daily mileages shorten as they picked up the next two depots: in one they found the pony meat had gone rancid; in the next – not for the last time – the cooking fuel had evaporated from some of the cans. Scott's diary started to strike an ominous chord. 'Pray God we get better travelling, as we are not so fit as we were, and the season is advancing ... Heavy toiling all day inspiring gloomiest thoughts at times... we can't go on like this.'

For several days they did around 12 miles, but it suddenly grew very cold: never having gone below minus 28 degrees Celsius, it now plunged to minus 40, turning the surface into sandy crystals that made it much harder to pull the sledge. It has subsequently been established that these were hugely abnormal temperatures for the Barrier at this time of year. Scott had fatally travelled into freak weather, and now it stayed with him to the end. Meanwhile, the winds they had hoped for to push them along the Barrier failed to appear at their backs. On 2 March, during his lunch break, Scott stopped beating about the bush. 'We are in *very* Queer Street, since there is no doubt we cannot do the extra marches and feel the cold horribly.' They had discovered another shortfall of fuel at the Middle Barrier Depot, and Oates chose this moment to reveal the full horror show of his frostbitten toes. It was so cold that they had to give 90 minutes to the task of putting on their frozen foot-gear.

More than anything it was the cold, and its effect on the conditions under foot, that would kill them. Perhaps Scott intuited as much when the next day he gave in to more dark thoughts. 'God help us, we can't keep up this pulling, that is certain. Amongst ourselves we are unendingly cheerful, but what each man feels in his heart I can only guess.' Posterity cannot tell us either because

Wilson had now followed Bowers into silence: he had lost the will to keep up his diary. But at least they kept up appearances. 'I don't know what I should do if Wilson and Bowers weren't so determinedly cheerful over things,' Scott wrote the next day. There was very little to be cheerful over. The paucity of fuel meant they couldn't heat enough snow to rehydrate themselves, and Oates's feet were 'in a wretched condition'. 'The poor Soldier nearly done,' he wrote on 5 March. 'It is pathetic enough because we can do nothing for him; more hot food might do a little, but only a little, I fear.' A day later he had become 'a terrible hindrance'. And the next day, 'Poor Titus is the greatest handicap'.

Unbeknown to them, Cherry-Garrard and the dog-driver Gerof had spent the last six days at One Ton Camp. Despite his short sight and his inability to navigate, it had fallen to Cherry-Garrard to fulfil Scott's orders of coming to meet the returning party. Meares had left on the ship. Atkinson was too busy treating the stricken Teddy Evans, and Wright had important scientific work to do. He and Gerof sat at One Ton and considered heading further south, but there was no more dog food, and the dogs could not feed on dog because Scott, looking beyond the coming winter, had left specific instructions that they were needed for another season of sledging. Anyway, there was a blizzard for four of their six days' waiting, it was intolerably cold and Gerof suffered temporary (and possibly imaginary) paralysis in his right side. Cherry-Garrard left a note in a film canister, with a minimum amount of food and fuel. 'Dear Sir, We leave this morning with the dogs for Hut Point. We have made no depots on the way in being off course all the way, and so I have not been able to leave you a note before. Yours sincerely, Apsley Cherry-Garrard.'

As they entered the final straight, with Oates all but finished and the end coming into view for them all, their profound suffering lifted Scott's prose on to a higher plane. With Wilson and Bowers silent (Bowers had also given up his meteorological record), the leader was now the only witness to their appalling plight. It was as if he was aware of the responsibility as the diary made a gradual gear change. He was no longer writing about the prospect of survival. He was now staring death in the face, and describing what he saw. 'We mean to see the game through with a proper spirit, but it's tough work to be pulling harder than we ever pulled in our lives for long hours, and to feel that the progress is so slow. One can only say "God help us!" and plod on our weary way, cold and very miserable, though outwardly cheerful. We talk of all sorts of subjects in the tent, not much of food now.' They even went through the extraordinary charade of talking 'of what we will do together at home'.

Oates could no longer pull. 'One feels for Oates the crisis is near,' Scott wrote in the same diary entry. Their next depot, the vast snow cairn erected by Teddy Evans's motor party and named Mount Hooper after the steward, provided further grounds for disappointment. They made the depot to find not only a shortage of fuel, but also food. The vague hope that Meares might bring some rations out with the dogs was dashed. 'It's a miserable jumble,' wrote Scott in a black moment of self-loathing. They camped in a blizzard. At camp the following night Oates asked Wilson if he had a chance of survival. 'Of course Bill had to say he didn't know. In point of fact he has none. Apart from him, if he went under now, I doubt whether *we* could get through. With great care we might have a dog's chance, but no more.'

On 11 March, all they could do was encourage the dying man to soldier on. Back at Cape Evans Oates had argued for the stowing of a firearm on the polar sledge: 'If anyone breaks down he should have the privilege of using it.' There was no pistol, but Scott told Wilson to distribute the means for each man to end his own life. 'Wilson had no choice between doing so and our ransacking the medicine case. We have 30 opium tabloids apiece and he is left with a tube of morphine.' This may have been his version of a *coup de grâce* for Oates, but there is no evidence for it.

Scott calculated the daily distances needed to make it to One Ton Camp, and noted grimly that in the bitter temperatures, travelling over terrible surfaces in a weakened condition, they would probably not make it. 'No idea there could be temperatures like this at this time of year with such winds. Truly awful outside the tent. Must fight it out to the last biscuit; but can't reduce rations.' It's a mark of their deterioration that Scott now became confused over dates. On either 16 or 17 March he wrote, 'At lunch, the day before yesterday, poor Titus Oates said he couldn't go on; he proposed we should leave him in his sleeping-bag. That we could not do, and we induced him to come on … at night he was worse and we knew the end had come.' It still took an intervention from Oates himself to bring the curtain down on his own tragedy. Spurning the opium, Oates woke the following morning and chose to take his own life. With frostbitten fingers, he must have needed help untying the lashings as he opened the tent and crawled out into the blizzard.

His famous last words, as reported by Scott, have inscribed themselves in the British imagination: 'I'm just going outside and may be some time.'

'We have not seen him since,' noted Scott somewhat superfluously, though they did make an effort to look for him. 'We knew that poor Oates was walking to his death, but though we tried to dissuade him, we knew it was the act of a brave man and an English gentleman. We all hope to meet the end with a similar spirit, and assuredly the end is not far.'

Now it remained only for Scott, Wilson and Bowers to stagger through to One Ton Camp, in the almost certain knowledge that the effort would be fruitless. They were 'on the verge of serious frostbites'. At the next camp they lightened the sledge by depositing the theodolite, camera and Oates's sleeping bag, but also started to think practically of their legacy. 'Diaries, etc., and geological specimens carried at Wilson's special request, will be found with us or on our sledge.' The next day Scott admitted that his right foot had gone rapidly downhill: 'Amputation is the least I can hope for now, but will the trouble spread?' They still managed better distances. On 21 March they covered ten miles, which brought them to what would be the final camp. They were 11 miles short of One Ton, and had run out of fuel. Scott's diary at this point more or less petered out. Bowers wrote to his mother, Wilson to his wife, parents and Oates's mother, while Scott hammered out a dozen letters – to his wife (in the letters he called her his widow), friends, benefactors and, stirringly, to the general public. Most of them touched on the theme of English valour. But one letter, to J.M. Barrie, the author of *Peter Pan*, painted a rosy picture of these harrowing days in the tent. 'We have done the greatest march ever made and come very near to great success … we are in a desperate state, feet frozen, etc. No fuel and a long way from food, but it would do your heart good to be in our tent, to hear our songs and the cheery conversation as to what we will do when we get to Hut Point. Later – We are very near the end, but have not and will not lose our good cheer.'

And as he wrote, they lay in their tent hoping for the blizzard to clear so that they could strike out for the depot. On 29 March Scott made his final diary entry:

> 'Since the 21st we have had a continuous gale from W.S.W, and S.W. We had fuel to make two cups of tea apiece and bare food for two days on the 20th. Every day we have been ready to start for our depot *11 miles* away, but outside the door of the tent it remains a scene of whirling drift. I do not think we can hope for any better things now. We shall stick it out to the end, but we are getting weaker, of course, and the end cannot be far.
>
> It seems a pity, but I do not think I can write more.
>
> *R. Scott*
>
> [Last entry]
> For God's sake, look after our people.'

Two days earlier Atkinson and Keohane ventured out on to the Barrier without the dogs. After three days they turned back, by which time all three men in the tent were probably dead – from starvation and extreme cold. When their bodies were found seven months later, Cherry-Garrard – who had come so close to this place back in March – chose not to record in his diary what he saw in the tent beyond the barest essentials: 'Scott lay in the centre, Bill on his left, with his head towards the door, and Birdie on his right, lying with his feet towards the door. Bill especially had died very quietly with his hands folded over his chest. Birdie also quietly.' Scott's arm was flung over Wilson's body, and his sleeping bag open.

It took a Norwegian not to flinch in the face of Scott's final torment: 'It was clear,' Gran wrote, 'that he had had a few very hard last minutes.'

His more famous compatriot was informed of Scott's death while in Wisconsin on a lecture tour of the United States. They had never met – Amundsen had made sure of it – but he found the appropriate words. 'I am grieved beyond measure at the report.'

Acknowledgements

This book would not have happened without the support and indeed the invitation of KEO Films: my thanks to Zam Baring, Tom Beard, Wayne Derrick, Claire Hamilton, Helen Hawken, Andrew Palmer and Sean Smith.

Thanks also to Kirsti Boger, the translator of the Norwegian edition of this book, for her tireless contribution.

I would also like to pay tribute to the two teams – not only for supplying the meat of the narrative, but also for generously giving of their time in Tassilaq when they were busy with preparation: Mark Anstice, Rupert Elderkin, Nick Akers, Rune Gjeldnes, John Huston, Arthur Jeffes, Harald Kippenes, Rory O'Connor, Bruce Parry, Dave Pearce, Ketil Reitan, Inge Solheim and Chris van Tulleken.

Every book about the Heroic Age of polar exploration is an anthology. Of no work is this truer than Apsley Cherry-Garrard's *The Worst Journey in the World* which, as well as being one of the more remarkable books of the twentieth century in any genre, is a goldmine of the key primary sources – the diaries and journals kept on the march by himself and others. The following books have also been helpful:

ROALD AMUNDSEN, *The South Pole: An Account of the Norwegian Antarctic Expedition in the 'Fram', 1910–12* (Birlinn)
HERBERT PONTING, *With Scott to the Pole: The Terra Nova*

Expedition 1910–1913 – The Photographs of Herbert Ponting (Bloomsbury)

ROLAND HUNTFORD, *Scott and Amundsen: The Last Place on Earth* (Abacus)

RANULPH FIENNES, *Captain Scott* (Hodder & Stoughton)

SARA WHEELER, *Cherry: A Life of Apsley Cherry-Garrard* (Jonathan Cape)

BEAU RIFFENBURGH, *Nimrod: Ernest Shackleton and the Extraordinary Story of the 1907-09 British Antarctic Expedition* (Bloomsbury)

MICHAEL SMITH, *I'm Just Going Outside: Captain Oates – Antarctic Tragedy* (Spellmount)

FRANCIS SPUFFORD, *I May Be Some Time: Ice and the English Imagination* (Faber & Faber)

MAX JONES, *The Last Great Quest: Captain Scott's Antarctic Sacrifice* (Oxford University Press)

Picture Credits

Index